THE

FULLY RAW

DIET

Cassandra!
Many many hugs!

THE
FULLY RAW
DIET

21 DAYS TO BETTER HEALTH, WITH MEAL AND EXERCISE PLANS, TIPS, AND 75 RECIPES

Kristina Carrillo-Bucaram

Founder of

HOUGHTON MIFFLIN HARCOURT

BOSTON NEW YORK

To all of you: my family, my friends, my fans,
my followers, my volunteers, my co-operators,
to each and every one of you who has touched my
heart. You have kept me motivated and inspired.

This book presents the research and ideas of its author. It is not intended
to be a substitute for consultation with a professional healthcare provider.
Consult with your healthcare provider before starting any exercise routine
or diet. The publisher and the author disclaim responsibility for any adverse
effects resulting directly or indirectly from information contained in this book.

Library of Congress Cataloging-in-Publication Data
Names: Carrillo-Bucaram, Kristina, author.
Title: The fully raw diet : 21 days to better health with meal and exercise
    plans, tips, and 130 recipes / Kristina Carrillo-Bucaram.
Description: New York, New York : Houghton Mifflin Harcourt, [2016]
Identifiers: LCCN 2015037776| ISBN 9780544559110 (paperback) | ISBN
    9780544562363 (ebook)
Subjects: LCSH: Raw food diet. | Vegetarianism. | Cooking (Vegetables) | Raw
    foods--Therapeutic use. | BISAC: COOKING / Vegetarian & Vegan. | COOKING /
    Health & Healing / Weight Control. | LCGFT: Cookbooks.
Classification: LCC RM236 .C29 2016 | DDC 641.5/636--dc23
LC record available at http://lccn.loc.gov/2015037776

Printed in the United States of America
DOC 10 9 8 7 6 5 4 3 2
4500583055

CONTENTS

ACKNOWLEDGMENTS

My heart is filled with so many THANKS. To everyone. To YOU, who have helped me create this masterpiece, even if I don't know you personally. Each and every person I have met and every experience I have had have shaped me into the woman I am today and have spilled into the creation of this book. To my lovers, I boomerang this magic right back to you. To my haters, whew! You taught me how to take my pain and use it to fuel greatness. For all of you, I am thankful.

Thank you, God, for the opportunity to share my voice and my passion with the world. That freedom is what keeps me driven, motivated, and alive. I am doing what I am meant to be doing: sharing the message of health and just being me, allowing my journey to inspire others. Thank you for allowing me to share this gift of life.

Thank you to my family: my father, my mother, my sister, my brother, Birdie, and my closest friends, who have walked with me through what has sometimes felt like fire. You have held me accountable, pushed me when I needed to make strides, and held my hand when I felt like I was in a dark corner. You have all taught me to be strong. You have brought color into my life and shown me LOVE, not only by standing by my side, but also by giving this lifestyle a try and supporting it, even if you didn't understand it at first. You encouraged me to find my voice and to stand by it no matter what. You have supported me in my endeavor to spread the message of health to everyone I know. To my family, to my friends, I love you.

Special thanks to John Rose for introducing me to this lifestyle. You showed me that rebirth is possible. What a gift! Thank you to Dr. Douglas Graham for your support, guidance, and mentorship. To my mentors and teachers, thank you for never letting me get away with anything less than my best.

Thank you to HMH for the opportunity to write my first book and to put the past ten years into this beautiful compilation. Thank you to Sally Ekus, Stephanie Fletcher, Linda Ingroia, Andy Schloss, Laurie Masters, Melissa Skorpil, Kristina Wolter, the photography team, the film team, nutritionist Dana McDonald, and fitness expert Hanna Davis for their part in shaping this work, and to Mr. and Mrs. Nigel Bell for sharing their beautiful kitchen for the photo shoot. It would not have been possible without each of you. To my sister Bianca Bucaram, who has helped me throughout the entire process, I do not know how I could have done this without you.

To my community in Texas, the Rawfully Organic Co-op "ROC" stars, you are family to me. To everyone who has offered a hand to volunteer, thrown watermelons in a line, dripped sweat in the Texas heat, or opened up your arms to give the best hugs, you have helped a beautiful dream become a powerful reality. We are continuing to change the world together. Thank you to this community for supporting me through the rough times to help keep the co-op going. Your belief in this cooperative has given it life and continues to shape it as it evolves into the force that it is.

My thank-yous will never end, only grow. I hope that you all enjoy this book. You helped me write it, and you were a major piece of this FullyRaw pie. I love you.

PART ONE

THE 21-DAY DIET

Meals, Tips, and Workouts

HOW TO START EATING FULLY RAW

I am excited to be with you as you start this 21-day diet. It takes time to turn good intentions into healthy habits, and we will use the following 21 days to build you a new life. As I teach you how to live and eat Fully Raw, you will learn about eating more fruits and vegetables: uncooked, unprocessed, ripe, and pure. As opposed to other diets that promise quick weight loss and a lifetime of calorie restriction, relying on completely unprocessed raw fruits and vegetables that are naturally high in phytonutrients, moderate in calories, and low in fat allows you to eat all you want, every meal of every day. Not only will you be feasting on vibrant fresh produce, but I will be with you as you progress, showing you creative ways to combine that bounty into colorful salads, rich satisfying smoothies, fortifying juices, elegant main dishes, and tantalizing desserts. I will give you all the tips, tricks, recipes, and strategies you need to succeed!

If eating Fully Raw is new to you, the switch to eating 100 percent fresh raw produce may feel strange at first, but once you get the hang of it and start to embrace its benefits, you will find it to be a lifestyle that is easily adapted to your needs and one that you will come to love. I've been eating Fully Raw for ten years, and I have come to *love* the way that I eat and live. I have helped many others get off the diet treadmill and I will do the same for you.

Even if you're not sure about consuming a 100 percent raw food diet, eating one Fully Raw meal a day can be a great start. The switch from eating cooked to raw foods is just a matter of increasing the percentage of raw fruits and vegetables that you consume. The more fruits and vegetables you eat, the less room you'll have for cooked and processed foods and animal products. Many people find it easiest to start by having a fruit smoothie or a large fresh fruit juice and some perfectly ripe seasonal fruit for breakfast, while leaving everything else they eat the same. Or you might want to eat Fully Raw for several days and then eat other foods for a meal or for a day. It has been my experience that once you take that first baby step, you will find it easier and easier to eat more Fully Raw meals and may eventually take the leap. Even including just one Fully Raw meal a day reaps tons of benefits. And once you do that, within a week you will feel your energy increase, your skin clear, your digestion improve, and your spirit soar. Start slowly and be mindful of your body. You aren't just starting a diet; you are building a new life!

There are several established methods to incorporate raw food into your eating. I cover them in detail in The Benefits of Eating Raw—Comparison of Raw Diets (page 21), but before you get started, I think it would be helpful to go over the basic principles of what distinguishes Fully Raw from the rest. Fully Raw follows the outline of the 80/10/10 diet, which was created by Dr. Douglas Graham—80 percent of calories from carbohydrates (minimum), 10 percent from protein (maximum), and 10 percent from fat (maxium). I have found that I can tweak these levels depending on my activity and what is available, but over time the 80/10/10 rule plays out. This is a high-carbohydrate diet designed to give you a lot of energy. Carbohydrates are plentiful in fruit, starches, and grains, but of these three main sources, the carbs in fruit are the most digestible and quickest to metabolize. In addition, the carbohydrates in grains and grain-based foods, like bread and pasta, and starchy vegetables, like potatoes, need to be processed (cooked) in order to be made digestible for humans. Fortunately, fresh raw fruit is readily available and requires no cooking. It gives you all of the calories and most of the nutrients you need to thrive. Green leafy vegetables, along with a small amount of fat-rich nuts and seeds or a serving of avocado, fill in the additional protein and nutrients that are not plentiful in most fruits.

Once you get up to speed, you'll want to aim for at least 6 pounds of fruit each day, about 1 to 1½ ounces of nuts and seeds or ½ to 1 ounce of avocado, and as many greens and veggies as possible (1 to 2 pounds).

While this new lifestyle begins with the food, it doesn't end with food. It improves your mind and spirit, as well as your body. Take it one step at a time, one day at time. Be patient with yourself: It's about the journey *and* the destination. When you eat life-giving food, you transform yourself from the inside out. You will be amazed by the changes you will accomplish!

10 STEPS TO STARTING A RAW FOOD DIET

1. STOCK UP ON FRUITS & VEGETABLES.

The key to success in eating Fully Raw is to have an abundance of fruits and vegetables in your home. If you run out of food or do not have enough produce to eat, you will most likely get hungry and grab something else that is not as healthy. Fruit is your main source of calories. Fruit will satisfy your hunger. But remember that fruits and vegetables are lower in calories than starches and animal proteins, so you must eat more of them to get the necessary amount of fuel that you need to function. If you don't get enough calories, your energy is going to lag. Severe calorie deprivation is one of the main reasons that most diets fail. If weight loss is your goal, going Fully Raw will modify your weight naturally, but in my experience it will also improve your overall health, make your skin radiant, and give you unbounded energy. Fruit is the key ingredient to achieving all of these goals. Stock your kitchen with enough fruits and greens to last you about a week. Dispose of or donate all the "junk" food in your refrigerator to give you more room to store fresh produce. Junk includes processed foods, packaged goods, canned goods, boxed foods, concentrated sugars, and anything with ingredients you cannot pronounce. If it does

BUYING PRODUCE BY THE CASE

Typical case sizes of popular fruits and vegetables

PRODUCE	CASE SIZE	
FRUIT	POUND	COUNT
Apple, 3" diameter	30	100
Apricot, jumbo	6	40
Banana	40	115
Blackberries, half pint	n/a	12
Blueberries, pint	n/a	12
Cantaloupe	50	15
Cherries	9-12	n/a
Figs, pint	5	6
Grapefruit	40	40
Grapes, bunch	12	24
Guava	10	30
Honeydew	26	7
Mango	10	14
Orange	40	44-80
Papaya	10	7-10
Peach	20	30-50
Pear	45	100
Pineapple	20	6
Plum	28	50
Raspberries, half pint	n/a	12
Strawberries, pint	n/a	12
Tangerine	12	30-60
Watermelon	80	4

PRODUCE	CASE SIZE	
VEGETABLE	POUND	COUNT
Beets, bunch	40	24
Bell pepper	10	25
Carrots, bunch	25	24
Chard, bunch	30	24
Cucumber	26	24
Jerusalem artichoke	12	16-24
Kale, bunch	18	24
Mushroom	5	n/a
Romaine	40	24
Spinach, bag	20	26

Notes: 1) Case counts are subject to change based upon the way they are packaged and distributed.
2) Botanically, bell peppers and cucumbers are fruits, but in the culinary world we most often use them in vegetable dishes.

not have an expiration date, it's most likely not real food. Out with the old . . . in with the new!

If you are planning to eat Fully Raw for a whole week, that first big shopping trip to stock your kitchen can be daunting, but don't let the abundance of produce in your cart throw you. Granted, fresh produce can be more expensive than grains and dried legumes, but it does not cost more than many of the high-fat, high-protein animal products and meat substitutes you likely have been buying. I share many strategies for purchasing large quantities of high-quality produce in Money Matters (page 56), but one of the most important is to make friends with the produce manager at your local market. Let him or her know that you will be upping your purchases from single items to cases, and you will immediately become one of the store's best customers. That manager will reward your patronage with case discounts and the best selection that can be offered. I know buying fruit by the case feels excessive, but it really isn't. For example, a case of grapes weighs 12 pounds. That's enough for three mono-meals, four smoothies, and three juices. All of those grapes will be consumed in just eight or ten meals over three to four days, and you will have spent less than $2 a meal on ingredients.

2. MAKE YOUR FIRST MEAL OF THE DAY A LARGE JUICE OR SMOOTHIE. When I first wake up in the morning, I typically drink two large glasses of freshly squeezed lemon water (or about a quart of fruit-infused water, see page 96). Approximately a half an hour later, I follow this with a large juice or smoothie. And when I say large, I mean *large!* It is not unusual when going Fully Raw to consume 32 to 64 ounces (1 to 2 quarts) of juice or smoothie in the morning. This meal jump-starts your energy for the day. After a night of rest and fasting, your body is fully charged with energy, but it needs an influx of fuel to turn that energy into activity, both mental and physical (see Fuel vs. Energy, page 254). Breakfast "breaks" your nightlong fast, and by pureeing or juicing whole fresh fruits and vegetables, you streamline digestion and make all of their nutrients readily available to your body. Some of my favorite juices and smoothies in the morning include Lemon Ginger Blast (page 111), Sunburst Juice (page 108), the Holy Grale (page 118), The Invincible Hulk (page 100), Carrot Apple Ginger Juice (page 107), Fully Raw Veggilicious Juice (page 113), and the Sour Punch Smoothies (page 126).

Many people worry that consuming a large amount of fluid first thing after waking will keep them tied to a bathroom for the rest of the morning. Understandable. However, when you first start eating more Fully Raw foods and drinking more juices and smoothies, your body will detox at a much faster rate. Eventually, it becomes accustomed to eating this amount of fiber and liquid. You will cleanse your system, and you will not feel as tied to the restroom as you fear. But you must also understand that switching from cooked to raw food is going to increase the amount of water in your diet substantially. Cooking by its nature dehydrates food. When you eat whole raw food you are getting all of the goodness your ingredients hold, including all of their moisture. Whether you puree your fruits and vegetables into smoothies, crush them into juice, or eat them whole, you are taking in the same amount of fluid in all cases. That added water is great for your physiology, keeping everything moving and helping all of your organs and muscles burn calories at peak efficiency. Unlike cooked-food diets that require you to drink lots of water by the glass to ensure that you are getting enough hydration, eating Fully Raw supplies most of your water in the form of whole food.

SAVING TIME ON MEAL PREP

By choosing to eat Fully Raw you have already saved yourself hours of cooking time in the kitchen. Most raw meals require no more food prep than a quick rinse before you sit down to eat, and if you do pull out a tool or two, they are never more complicated than a sharp knife and a blender or juicer. Except for entertaining or constructing an elaborate main course for a special meal, I don't think I have spent more than 20 minutes preparing a meal in the ten years I have been eating Fully Raw.

Time-Saving Tips

- When you are on the go, choose fruit! Bring fruit with you! It's nature's "fast food." It's literally as easy as bringing an apple with you and as convenient as peeling a banana. No cooking or prepped involved—just eating! Best examples of fast food are bananas, apples, peaches, nectarines, grapes, cherries, pears, and berries. None of these involve food prep.
- Trim and chunk the fruit for your morning smoothie the night before to save time in the morning when you are probably rushed.
- Freeze leftover berries and bananas for blending into instant "Nice" Cream (page 210) or creamy, thick smoothies.
- Make salad dressings when you have extra tomatoes, citrus, or peppers and store them in the refrigerator.
- I break all complex recipes into short, easily accomplished sections. These can each be prepared ahead when you have time, and assembled just before serving.
- Plan your meals for the week. Go shopping and fill up your fridge. Take the guessing game out of wondering what you will eat that week by planning ahead. You will save yourself so much time!

3. MAKE YOUR SECOND MEAL OF THE DAY A HUGE PLATTER OF FRUIT OR A LARGE SMOOTHIE. Eat until you are completely satiated. Gravitate towards sweet fruits, because these tend to have higher calorie content than vegetables for the same volume. This means that you will feel more satisfied after eating a meal of fruit than you would eating a meal of greens or vegetables. By emphasizing fruits over vegetables, you will consume more fuel (calories). Don't freak out; calories are not your enemy. Our society has taught us to eat less when "dieting," but eating Fully Raw is all about eating sufficiently and eating abundantly. If you want to be able to thrive in your day, and thereby stick to your diet, then you must eat enough. It's not about deprivation; it's about consistency and enjoyment. Try to consume 500 to 800 calories at each meal (for a total daily calorie intake of 1,500 to 2,400), more if you are large or particularly active. This amount will ensure that you stay alert and energetic.

I know it may feel counterintuitive to eat a massive amount of fruit when you're on a diet. It takes time to train your mind and body to eat the volume of food you need from a raw food perspective (see Training Your Stomach Muscle, page 27), and that volume will vary depending on your sex, your size, and your appetite. As an example, a small woman just starting to eat Fully Raw may consume three bananas in a meal and feel full, while a seasoned raw food athlete may need seven or more to be satisfied (that's only about 700 calories—just an average-size meal). A great way to eat enough fruit to meet your nutritional needs is by eating "mono-meals." Mono-mealing means eating a meal of one fruit at a time, and it is not uncommon once you get started to consume a hefty volume of fruit in a mono-meal. Mono-meals are beneficial for three reasons:

1) I have found it easier for my digestive system to process a meal of fruit as opposed to a similarly sized meal of diverse fruits and vegetables. In addition, I have found eating one fruit streamlines digestion and helps to prevent and eliminate many common digestive complaints including constipation, gas, heartburn, acid reflux, and burping.

2) In my experience, mono-mealing improves the speed and quality of elimination, cleansing my intestinal tract more efficiently. Believe it or not, my poop actually doesn't smell bad!

3) Mono-mealing is natural. The variety we find at grocery stores nowadays is a beautiful and abundant blessing, but it is unnatural to have so much variety, out-of-season fruits and veggies, and even imported fruits available. If you were out on a farm or in an orchard and hungry after having worked a long day, you would find one fruit growing on a tree or a bush at a time. You might come across a fig tree, and if they were ripe, you would eat figs until you were satiated. If you were very hungry, the first bite of that fig would taste incredible, sweet, and succulent. After twenty figs, your body would start to tell you that it was full, and the last fig would taste different to you because you would be satiated. Mono-meals help us to identify when we are truly full, since we are

eating one fruit at a time until we are satiated rather than exciting our taste buds with dozens of flavors all at once. Most animals in the wild mono-eat. They consume what they find, which by and large is a single food in a single location. Variety is accomplished over time, allowing the animal to eat diverse vegetation as the seasons change. In nature, provided that sufficient food is found, an animal will tend to eat a single food until it is full.

Mono-meals are also convenient. They are an effortless way to have a raw food lunch when you are away from home at work, at school, or on the road. Simply pack a bunch of bananas, a half-dozen apples or pears, or a big bag of grapes, and you will have all you need for a beautiful fresh food meal. Although the shelf life of most fruit is lengthened by storage in a refrigerator, unrefrigerated storage for fruit is not a food safety concern. It is perfectly safe to keep fruit at room temperature for a day or more and eat it whenever you want.

Examples of fruit mono-meals include 6 or 7 bananas (eaten individually or in a smoothie), 8 to 10 oranges, 1¾ to 2½ pounds grapes, 6 to 8 apples, or 5 to 7 persimmons. Aim for approximately 500 to 800 calories, and if you are not sure how much to eat, visit an online nutrition analysis site or download a calorie counter app for your computer or mobile device. Those will tell you how many calories you are consuming in one sitting.

I use CRON-O-Meter and Tap & Track, but many other apps are now easily available and free to use. If you are worried about not being able to eat as much as you need, remember that your stomach is a muscle that can expand and contract to accommodate a large amount of food and shrink back to its original size upon elimination.

EXAMPLES OF FRUIT MONO-MEALS

3 to 4 mangoes = 604 to 806 calories

5 to 7 persimmons = 585 to 819 calories

1 ¾ to 2 ½ pounds grapes = 548 to
    782 calories

2 to 2 ¾ pounds cherries = 571 to 785
    calories

6 to 8 apples = 568 to 757 calories

6 to 7 bananas = 630 to 735 calories

6 to 7 pears = 609 to 710 calories

8 to 10 navel oranges = 549 to 686 calories

4. FOR DINNER, START WITH A SMALL PLATE OF FRUIT AND MOVE ON TO A LARGE SALAD. For dinner, I always start with a small plate of fruit to help satisfy my calorie needs. Even though I will be eating mostly low-calorie vegetables, I still want to consume at least 600 calories in this meal. Like most people, I am not as active in the evening as I am during the day, but I still want to get enough calories to supply my resting body's fuel needs for the next 12 hours. My level of pre-dinner activity determines how much fruit I consume. If I go for a run before dinner, I may eat a large platter of 2 pounds figs, 6 to 10 peaches, 6 to 10 plums, 5 to 7 oranges, or 2 to 3 mangoes before I eat my salad; if I am less active I will probably eat half that amount. Next, the second part of my dinner is almost always a giant colorful rainbow salad. I try to eat approximately 2 heads or bunches of leafy greens in my salad, and I love to top it with chopped bell peppers, cherry tomatoes, chives, avocado, beets,

purple cabbage, or more fruit. The colorful pigments in fruits and vegetables are indications of the powerful nutrition inside. These brightly colored antioxidants—orange carotenes, red/purple anthocyanins, and green chlorophyll—help your body fight disease. The simplest way to make sure that you are getting a full array of these nutrients is to make sure that every salad you prepare *pops* with color!

The key to making any salad truly memorable is a delicious dressing. Store-bought salad dressings are typically loaded with oils, salts, and preservatives. You can easily make your own fat-free or nearly fat-free dressings by blending up a few fresh ingredients that will leave your salad bursting with extra flavor and nutrition! Try the Orange Ginger Sesame Dressing (page 162) or the Red Pepper–Hemp Seed Orange Dressing (page 168), or try using my Epic Marinara Sauce (see Fully Raw Lasagna, page 188) as a dressing. Keep it colorful and filled with life!

5. EAT ENOUGH. One of the main mistakes that people make when they first start eating Fully Raw is that they do not eat enough. More often than not, I hear about people who try eating Fully Raw for one to two weeks, and they feel amazing. They lose weight, have more energy, clearer skin, and feel alive! Then after a few weeks, they begin to feel tired, lethargic, and spacey. When I sit down with these people, what we discover is that they are calorie deficient. They lack energy because they are not consuming enough fuel. Most people need to eat in the vicinity of 2,000 calories each day (the range runs from about 1,500 if you are small and if your activity is limited to 3,000 or more if you are very active). Depending on how active I am during the day, I will consume approximately 2,200 to 2,500 (or more) calories a day. (Note that I eat significantly more calories than most women my age, because I do a lot of regular exercise.)

COMPARING THE CALORIE CONTENT OF FRUITS AND VEGETABLES

VEGETABLE	CALORIES PER POUND
Romaine	77
Cherry tomatoes	82
Spinach	104
Red bell pepper	140
Kale	222
Avocado	758

FRUIT	CALORIES PER POUND
Peach	177
Pineapple	227
Apple	236
Mango	273
Grapes	313
Figs	336

The majority of these calories come from fruit. Fruit is fuel, and it is much easier to get your necessary daily caloric intake consuming fruit than vegetables.

If you are feeling tired, lethargic, frustrated, or restless, this could be because you need to eat more fruit. Calorie *awareness* is so important, but calorie deprivation is disastrous. Most people have been taught to diet with calorie restriction. I'm here to tell you that calorie awareness has nothing to do with restriction. It is knowing in your head and your body how many calories you need to have an active, vibrant life, and getting those calories in the most nutritious, delicious, and life-affirming way possible. Eating Fully Raw is an abundant lifestyle, not a restrictive one. In combination with getting enough sleep and exercise, be sure to eat enough to ensure that you have enough fuel to feel and perform at your best!

I recommend trying to stick to three large meals a day—breakfast, lunch, and dinner—and eating enough at those times so that you do not feel the need to snack in between. If you are currently used to eating five or six small meals per day, it is possible to continue with that meal plan when eating Fully Raw, but this increases the possibility that you will take in more calories. The beauty of the Fully Raw meal plan is that you can always eat to satiety; you never leave the table feeling less than completely satisfied! Doing that three times a day allows you to eat abundantly without eating too much; increasing the number of meals to five or six means that you will have to be more conscious of "counting calories" if your weight is a concern.

6. EXERCISE. Eating is just one component of your overall health. Regular exercise is crucial to helping

you get the healthy body that you desire. Exercise is about moving your body. It's about having play time. All movement exercises the muscles and joints and nerves in your body. It doesn't have to be playing soccer or climbing a stair machine for 45 minutes. The purpose of moving your body is to get your heart pumping, your heart rate increasing, your breath flowing, your muscles working and stretching, and your endorphins flowing. Exercise also alleviates stress and makes you happier. The U.S. Surgeon General recommends at least 20 minutes of exercise each day. I recommend at least 30 minutes to 1 hour of dedicated movement. Play outside and enjoy nature! Go for a walk, take a yoga class, hula hoop, run, ride a bike, or follow YouTube exercise videos. Of course, if you are unused to vigorous exercise, you should consult your doctor to make sure your body is ready for this new positive challenge. Every day of this 21-day diet includes 30 to 45 minutes of fun exercise routines that get you moving. Go at your own pace, but try to move every day or exercise every day.

7. REST. Sleep time is recovery time. Deep, undisturbed sleep also assists in faster weight loss. Although the recommended eight hours is very common, I recommend trying to get as much sleep as your body needs. When I had hyperglycemia before I ate Fully Raw, I could easily sleep for twelve hours a day and still not feel refreshed. My body was sick and lifeless. It was trying to recover, but I was not giving it the proper nutrition (fuel) it needed to heal. When I started eating Fully Raw, I started sleeping eight hours a night and had plenty of energy the next day. Not eating heavy, processed foods has helped me to sleep more deeply and sometimes even less. Many mornings now I wake up after just five to six hours of sleep feeling energetic, excited, and ready to start the day! Allow your body to heal, regenerate, and

restore. Rest and sleep are essential for good health and proper weight maintenance.

8. JOIN A COMMUNITY. When you're in the midst of building a new lifestyle, your success is directly related to the amount of support that surrounds you. Our society revolves around eating. I discuss how to eat Fully Raw in social settings later in this book, but I first want to address the importance of finding and joining a food community of like-minded people with similar interests and values. If you have support, then all the information, work, and know-how aren't just on your shoulders. You build off the knowledge and experiences of the like-minded people around you, as opposed to continuously being surrounded by a non-supportive energy. Everyone's journey is different, and this book contains lots of tips to help you to customize your Fully Raw experience to meet your individual needs, but remember, you are not on this journey alone.

Thousands of people are living the benefits of eating raw foods. Connect with them. They want to support you and they want your support. Search FullyRaw.com, Facebook, Instagram, and Twitter and see who pops up in your area. Search for online raw food forums. Search for raw food YouTube videos. Communicate with the other users and connect. Find a community with which you can share this blessing! Join a co-op or find a potluck near you via web sites like meetup.com. If you hang out at your local farmers' markets long enough, you will meet someone who is connected with a healthy, vegan, or raw community. Someone once told me that the best place to meet people is in the grocery store in the produce section—they were right. You find people who are interested in healthy eating. You can also post to find others on my FullyRaw Facebook page at facebook.com/fullyrawkristina. When you have community, you have a support team around you all the time.

9. EDUCATE YOURSELF. Educate yourself about the benefits of eating a raw, plant-based vegan diet that eliminates animal products. Educate yourself about animal cruelty and environmental neglect. Educate yourself about the benefits of eating more fruits and vegetables. And educate yourself about yourself: My recommendation is to see your doctor and get blood work done to evaluate your overall state of health and to see what nutrients your body may be lacking before you start any new diet. All of these issues interrelate. Feeding yourself is about more than just food. Educating yourself can not only inspire you, but also motivate you as you make changes in what you eat and how you relate to the world. Knowledge makes us strong! Before you start any diet, it is always best to research and make sure that you not only are comfortable with what you choose to dedicate yourself to do, but also that you know how to prepare and succeed. And once you start, don't stop. Keep reading, keep studying, and keep informed! Never stop learning! Understanding the principles that underscore the choices you make is the foundation of living an integrated life. Your health is a journey, and learning about your body (its feelings, its wisdom, its growth, and its changes) is part of the adventure.

The goal of Fully Raw is to get you eating more fruits and vegetables, not to become dependent on pill-form supplements. After you find out from your doctor what nutrients you need, look into the nutritional contents of the fruits and vegetables you like, and when you make your meal selections concentrate on produce that is rich in the nutrients you're after. Getting your nutrition from whole foods is generally preferable to taking pills. The one exception to this practice is vitamin B12 supplements. Vitamin B12, which is essential for making DNA in your cells and building red blood cells, is present only in animal foods. If you are eating a fully vegan diet, you will need to take a supplement. Check with your doctor or pharmacist to see what supplements you should be taking and the proper dosage for your sex and age.

For mental health food, I highly recommend reading books such as T. Colin Campbell's *The China Study*, Dr. Douglas Graham's The *80/10/10 Diet,* Eric Schlosser's *Fast Food Nation,* and Michael Pollan's *The Omnivore's Dilemma,* as well as books by Dr. Neal Barnard. There are also documentaries about the benefits of eating plant-based diets. Check out *Forks Over Knives* (the documentary and the book), *Food, Inc., Food Matters,* and *Dirt! The Movie.* Web sites I recommend include FoodnSport.com and vegsource.com.

10. BE GENTLE WITH YOURSELF; LOVE YOURSELF! Take it one day and one meal at a time. Self-discipline takes time to develop. You wouldn't be here if you didn't have hope that you can change your life. Too often, we put pressure on ourselves to be perfect. Strive for excellence, not perfection. Perfection is an ideal, not a reality. When you look too far ahead, it may be too scary. Don't think about tomorrow or one year from now; think about today. Live in the present, and be present with your food. Be a conscious consumer. Acknowledge that you are the one in control of your life. You have power over your choices and your reactions. No one can take those steps except for you. You can do this!

THE BENEFITS OF EATING RAW—COMPARISON OF RAW DIETS

NOT ALL RAW DIETS ARE THE SAME. I like to say that there are three different ways to eat raw. While you may think that eating raw is just about eating fruits and vegetables, there is a specific way to eat them for the greatest success.

High-Fat Raw Food Diet

When people first come across raw food in restaurants and magazines, they are typically introduced to high-fat raw vegan dishes that I like to call transition food. Nut-based raw pizza crust, burgers, and burritos make transitioning from the concentrated calories of a cooked food diet much easier. However, this can't last for long. With too few carbohydrates, your energy will begin to lag. You may feel great at first, but then after two weeks you will feel a dip in your energy and you will wonder why you feel so tired. While I do recommend a certain amount of raw fat in one's diet, I do not endorse the typical raw food lifestyle centered around fatty nuts and seeds. Fruits and vegetables are rich in vitamins and minerals, so your diet should abound in those foods, complemented by nuts and seeds. A successful raw food lifestyle should provide fruits and vegetables in abundance.

Supplement-Based Raw Food Diet

The second way to eat a raw food diet is by eating meals consisting primarily of supplements. Many people call this a liquid diet; however, it is filled with powdered supplements and other vitamins or pills. While these dry foods and supplements may be beneficial to your health in rare times of acute deficiency, they lack the bulk of nutrition found in raw fruits and vegetables. You cannot live on supplements alone; you must learn to find nutrition in fresh, whole food. I do recommend a few supplements when eating raw vegan food:

- Vitamin B12, which comes only from animal food sources, and vitamin D, if you are not getting out in the sun.
- Green powders (usually made from seaweed) added into a daily smoothie are okay, but relying on powders for your nutrition is not healthy or sustainable.

People crave a mix of solid foods, juices, smoothies, salads, and so on. Supplements are exactly what they sound like: a supplementation to a diet of whole food.

Low-Fat Raw Vegan Lifestyle: The Fully Raw Diet

I personally have found a low-fat raw vegan diet, which I call the Fully Raw diet, to be the most satisfying and successful way to eat. Fruits and vegetables are the core of this lifestyle. A small amount of nuts, seeds, and avocado are incorporated into certain meals to boost your fat intake to about 10 percent of calories. I have found that I can be creative enough with these resources to whip up almost any dish I wish, and I feel satisfied at the end of every meal. I get to enjoy juices, salads, smoothies, desserts, and a great variety of fully satisfying main dishes. Please always do what works best for you, but my goal is to give you the tools that you need to create delicious meals and to live with vitality.

USING THIS BOOK

FOOD

AS YOU READ YOUR WAY through the diet plan and prepare the recipes in this book, you will see that they vary from supernaturally simple to somewhat complex. Whatever you are making, I can promise you three things:

1) If you purchase fresh, wholesome produce, everything you prepare will be delicious and beautiful, from a simple plate of raw figs to extravagant Fully Raw Strawberry Shortcake (page 215).

2) I am personally invested in your success. Everything in these pages has been repeatedly tested by me, my viewers, and culinary professionals, and everything has passed those tests.

3) When I ask you to make something complicated, like my Fully Raw Lasagna (page 188) or Happy Birthday! Carrot Cake (page 212), I promise the results will be spectacularly worthy of your efforts. I love to prepare food, but if I'm going to put my heart and soul into making a meal, I insist that the results live up to my Herculean labors.

Depending on where you are in the world, and what time of year you start the diet, you may find that a specific ingredient called for in a recipe is not in season. In such a case, you'll need to substitute the most similar item that is best and brightest from your local food sources. When a recipe calls for kale, for example, you will learn that it will also work with almost any other dark leafy green. Any cantaloupe recipe can be made with honeydew, and you will find that whether your salad has raspberries or blueberries or blackberries or strawberries, it is going to taste wonderful and be super-healthy.

Throughout the 21 days of this diet, I try to balance the kitchen work to help you build your skills from the very basic—single juices, simple smoothies, and no-nonsense salads—to dinners that are more impressive and take a little more time and skill to prepare. I have included one company-worthy dinner in the first week that takes a little extra effort, and I have included two such meals in the second week and three in the third week to give you practice at all skill levels of raw recipes. In each week I also give you one or more dessert treats.

EXERCISE

I ALSO HAVE ATTEMPTED to balance the amount and types of exercise I recommend as we move through these first 21 days together. Healthy people live in healthy bodies, and healthy bodies *move!* It's important to move your body every day. If you are unused to vigorous exercise, you should consult your doctor to make sure you're ready for it. I'm going to help you by starting slow, but if you are already active you can push yourself harder. The important part is moving and pushing yourself to move a little bit more and a little bit more vigorously every time you exercise. I divide exercising into three basic types of movement:

1. **STRETCHING** Although studies about the benefits of stretching before and after exercise are mixed, my experience tells me that stretching my calves before running or my shoulders before lifting makes me more comfortable. I feel more flexible, getting a broader range of motion more easily, and many experts believe stretching before and after exercise helps reduce the risk of injury. My favorite forms of stretching are yoga poses. Dynamic stretching (stretching using controlled movement) is preferable for stretching pre-exercise, to prepare your body for exercise and promote mobility and flexibility of your joints and muscles. Static stretching (holding still in a single stretch) is more appropriate after exercising.

2. **CARDIO** Cardiovascular exercise, aka aerobic exercise, includes any activity that raises your heart rate—running, dancing, boxing, cycling, skating—any kind of vigorous movement. Your heart is a muscle. So any activity that makes it work harder strengthens it. A strong cardiovascular system means you have more capillaries delivering more oxygen to your muscles, enabling your cells to burn fat more efficiently. Engaging in some form of cardiovascular activity every day is essential if you want to lose weight. My favorite form of cardio is running.

3. **STRENGTH TRAINING** Also known as resistance exercise or weight training, strength training involves making precise, controlled movements that cause specific muscle groups to work harder.

Just as cardio exercise helps to strengthen your heart, moving your arms, shoulders, legs, or back while holding a weight pushes the targeted muscles to work harder, making them stronger and able to burn fat and calories more efficiently. I do stretching and cardio every day, but I usually do strength training every other day, or about three times a week. Although many people feel they need a lot of expensive equipment, or a gym membership, to strength train effectively, I find that I get great exercise from holding a watermelon while doing squats, or doing bicep curls with two pineapple hand weights. Who said fruits and veggies are just for eating!

Over the next 21 days, I will be recommending 30 to 40 minutes of cardio and stretching each day, and three times a week I will add 15 to 20 minutes of strength training exercise.

· · · · ·

Change can be scary, and going Fully Raw can be a challenging journey for many. The first step is always the hardest because it is such a new world—it's a change of lifestyle. When you begin, it does take time to adapt to eating more fruits and veggies, but once you get accustomed, it becomes like second nature and you really feel the benefits. Something to encourage you: You are not giving up anything. It's not about what you are taking out of your diet, it's about all of the amazing new fruit and vegetable varieties that you get to try, experiment with, and have fun eating. Living raw is not about following a "diet," it's about living a healthy life. It's about thriving, allowing your food to nourish your body and send your soul soaring. Believe in yourself! You can do this, and your success is laid before you!

THE 21-DAY DIET, WEEK BY WEEK

WEEK 1

KITCHEN EQUIPMENT

Sharp chopping knife

Cutting board

High-speed blender, such as Vitamix

Citrus juicer

Supply of large drinking vessels (I use quart-size Mason jars)

Big salad bowl

Vegetable juicer

Strainer

Butcher's cleaver or coconut tool, like Coco Jack (see page 235)

DAY 1

MENU

Lemon Water (page 98)

Fresh orange juice

Banana Berry "Nice" Cream (page 210)

Small fruit platter of mangoes and pineapple

Rainbow Salad with Orange
   Avocado Dressing (page 176)

WAKE UP

I start every day with a quart of flavorful, nutritious fruit-infused water, and I've provided a different recipe for each day of the diet in this book (see page 96). Today, start with 32 ounces of Lemon Water. Squeeze the juice of 1 to 2 lemons (depending on their size and how lemony you like your water) into a quart of water.

ALKALIZE YOUR BODY

Drinking a volume of water when you wake up activates all of your bodily systems. Citrus is cleansing and alkalizing. Lemon juice is unquestionably acidic because it is a citrus juice; however, once it is ingested and completely metabolized into your system, its minerals have a net alkalizing effect on your bodily fluids. This mitigates the cellular damage that can be caused by acidic conditions such as inflammation, acid reflux, arthritis, gout, type 2 diabetes, digestive disorders, and chronic fatigue.

BREAKFAST

Wait at least 20 minutes after finishing your water, then drink 32 ounces of juice of your choice. I recommend something super simple for day one like freshly squeezed orange juice (see Citrus Juicing, page 26), and you can add mint leaves for an infusion.

CITRUS JUICING

To make orange juice, you will need a citrus juicer or a simple handheld tool that will help you press your citrus. There is no exact amount of oranges that you will need here. Use however many juice oranges it takes to make a quart. (Generally, it takes about 16 medium to small fruit.) If you want the juice to be smoother, strain it to remove extra pulp.

LUNCH

Lunch is a big bowl of creamy Banana Berry "Nice" Cream, which tastes like ice cream only it's made with just fruit. Frozen bananas are the main ingredient, providing the ideal creamy consistency to make you feel like you are eating soft-serve ice cream. Bananas, loaded with carbohydrates and naturally low in fat, are a perfect lunch to rev you up in the middle of the day as they satisfy your hunger and curb your sweet tooth in a healthy way.

Bananas are a simple sugar, not a complex carbohydrate, so they are easily digested, processed, and absorbed by your body. This "ice cream" is free of animal products, dairy, chemicals, added sugar, and processed ingredients, and is freshly made. In addition, bananas are extremely affordable, so you can eat more—for less.

DINNER

And for dinner, a fruit platter of 3 mangoes and half a pineapple, followed by a Rainbow Salad with Orange Avocado Dressing.

People often ask me why I choose to eat my salads at night and not during the day. I am typically very active during the day, using lots of energy to manage the co-op, run, play, and more. I am using energy, so that's what I need to stock up on. My

body is fueled by the carbohydrates in fruit. In addition, fruit is higher in water and digests much more quickly than greens. Fruits clear from your stomach remarkably quickly, and greens in just a bit longer. I like to feel light on my feet throughout the day, and fruit doesn't make me feel weighed down. In addition, I like to eat my largest meal of the day during the evening, when I can kick my feet up, let my hair down, and enjoy the rest of my evening and my food. While I am chewing my salad, I practice gratitude, meditate on the day, and spend time with my loved ones. It "slows me down," so to speak.

Throwing together a huge salad is time-efficient and less stressful than constructing a full blown company's-coming entree, thereby allowing you to have more time to rest for the evening or simply appreciate and really taste the flavors. I've started off tonight's dinner with 3 or 4 sliced mangoes and approximately half of a ripe pineapple.

On to the salad: I call all of the large, colorful salads I prepare Rainbow Salads. For this Rainbow

Salad, I have chopped 1 head of romaine and 1 bunch of kale into a bowl and topped it with an assortment of colorful vegetables: 1 red bell pepper, 1 yellow bell pepper, 1 cucumber, 1 cup purple cabbage, and 2 cups cherry tomatoes. If you feel that 2 heads or bunches of greens are more than you can eat, eat as many as you can to keep yourself satisfied. Toss it with a dressing made by combining 2½ cups orange juice, ¼ of an avocado, mashed up, and a small handful of chopped fresh herbs. Massage the dressing into your salad. For added energy and color I might add some fruit, like chopped pineapple, diced avocado, and/or a handful of raspberries, on top. See other Rainbow Salad ideas on page 176.

TRAINING YOUR STOMACH MUSCLE

Through years of eating cooked foods, our stomachs get used to feeling full after eating relatively small volumes of calorie-condensed meals. Even though the stomach has the capacity to expand and contract, our stomach muscles can become stiff from lack of stretching and eventually lose their natural elasticity. If you're new to eating raw foods, poor stomach flexibility can cause you to feel full before you've consumed enough fruit and vegetables to fulfill your calorie needs. You need to work out your stomach muscles and build their natural flexibility.

When I first started eating Fully Raw, I felt *so* full; however, I really wasn't eating that many calories. It took me about two weeks to build up to eating enough calories in each day to maintain my weight. Keep in mind that Fully Raw foods are high in water and fiber, but lower in calories, than cooked food, so you need to adjust to eating more of them in order to get the amount of calories that you need. Create a schedule that works best for you, and stick to it. It will take time to adapt, but your stomach is a muscle just like all of the other muscles in your body. It will adapt to what you give it. For now and the next week or so, try to push yourself to eat a little more after you feel full. I know this may make you temporarily uncomfortable, but remember that you are in training. No pain, no gain!

EXERCISE

Let's start easy. Today do about 5 minutes of stretching (page 247) and a 30-minute walk or run.

DAY 2

MENU

Lemon Cucumber Water (page 98)

My Secret Soulshine Juice (page 110)

Banana Celery Smoothie (page 132)

Fruit platter of choice

Abundant Asian Salad with Orange Ginger Sesame Dressing (page 176)

WAKE UP

Start your day off with 32 ounces of Lemon Cucumber Water. Feel free to add other fruits or herbs. Mint tastes amazing with cucumber!

Squeeze the juice of 1 or 2 lemons into a quart of water. Add 1 thinly sliced medium unwaxed cucumber.

CUCUMBER HEALTH

Cucumbers are full of water, about 96 percent. They are high in potassium and magnesium, which are helpful in relieving high blood pressure and bloating. Provided you keep the skins on, they are also a good source of C and B vitamins.

BREAKFAST

Want the secret to my soul shine? Breakfast today is 32 ounces of My Secret Soulshine Juice. The recipe is written for 1 quart, but if you're in need of a big pick-me-up, go for 64 ounces. You won't regret it. This juice is amazing—it's alkalizing, detoxifying, and energizing . . . And, it will give you that Fully Raw glow!

FULLY RAW IS FULL OF LIFE-GIVING WATER

Water makes up about 60 percent of your body weight, and in order to function properly your body needs to take in about 2 quarts of water per day. Fortunately when your diet consists entirely of raw moisture-rich vegetables and fruit, you are already getting water directly from your food. All cooked-food diets call for drinking several large glasses of water a day, but when you're eating Fully Raw, you are going to get water from food, too. Of course, you should always drink whenever you feel thirsty, and I love my delicious infused fruit waters!

LUNCH

Lunch today is a Banana Celery Smoothie. I know this sounds odd, but believe me it is s-o-o-o-o sweet that it will immediately become one of your go-to hunger busters! It is simple, affordable, quick, and delicious, and it has only two ingredients, which complement one another beautifully. Blend 7 bananas with 3 to 4 stalks of celery. I typically use 1 stalk of celery for every 2 bananas. Peel the bananas, place them into your blender, add in the celery, blend, and enjoy. The carbohydrate-rich smoothie is loaded with dietary fiber, and the celery adds a balance of sodium and potassium.

DINNER

I think I'm going to start dinner tonight with a fruit appetizer of 6 or 7 sliced oranges and about 1 pound of strawberries. Or you can set up a platter of any fruit that you desire, like berries, kiwi, pineapple, mango, or pears. Just make sure you get enough fruit to cover at least half of the calories for the meal. While you're noshing on fruit, prepare my Abundant Asian Salad with Orange Ginger Sesame Dressing, an artful assembly of dark leafy greens (lots of minerals), colorful bell peppers, crisp snap peas, antioxidant-rich purple cabbage, and vitamin-superhero broccoli.

EXERCISE

For today's exercise, set aside 1 hour to do any activity of your choice. Since we did 30 minutes of walking yesterday, try an hour today. Or perhaps take a yoga or Pilates class. Make today more intense than Day 1, but not too intense because we will work up our strength over the next 19 days.

KEEP UP YOUR EATING ROUTINE

Just like you have an exercise routine, you need to develop and practice your eating routine. The more you do it, the more it becomes a part of your life and the easier it gets. Keep in mind that you need to eat more when starting a Fully Raw lifestyle to ensure that you are getting the calories you need. You can eat all you want *and* have the body of your dreams!

DAY 3

MENU

Lime Berry Water (page 98)

My Watermelon Juice Secret (page 102)

Totally Tropical Smoothie (page 136)

Rainbow Salad with Cilantro Tahini Dressing
     (page 176)

WAKE UP

Start the day with 32 ounces of Lime Berry Water. Squeeze the juice of 1 lime (or more, depending on the size and how limey you like your water) into 1 quart of water. Add 1 cup of raspberries or sliced strawberries. Berries and lime are an amazing flavor combo, and not bad nutritionally, either. You're getting 170 percent of your daily value of vitamin C in this infused water. It tastes best to make it the night before and let it sit in the refrigerator overnight.

WATER CONTENT OF FRUITS & VEGETABLES

FRUITS		VEGETABLES	
ITEM	PERCENT WATER (%)	ITEM	PERCENT WATER (%)
Apple	84	Cabbage	91
Banana	74	Carrot	87
Blueberry	85	Celery	95
Cantaloupe	90	Cucumber	96
Cherry	81	Eggplant	92
Grape	81	Kale	85
Grapefruit	91	Lettuce	96
Orange	87	Peas	79
Peach	88	Pepper	92
Pear	84	Radish	95
Pineapple	87	Romaine	97
Plum	85	Spinach	92
Strawberry	92	Tomato	94
Watermelon	92	Zucchini	95

FRESH FRUIT EATEN ON THE GO LUNCH NUTRITIONAL BREAKDOWN

#	ITEM	ENERGY	CARB	PROTEIN	FAT	WATER	FIBER	VITAMIN	MINERAL
5	Oranges	343 cal	88 g	6.4 g	1 g	602 g	15 g	A 1,729 IU C 414 mg	Ca 301 mg Mg 77 mg P 161 mg K 1,162 mg
½	Pineapple	226 cal	59 g	2.4 g	.5 g	389 g	6 g	A 262 IU C 216 mg	Fe 1.3 mg Mg 54 mg Mn 4.2 mg
1	Mango	201 cal	50 g	2.8 g	1.3 g	280 g	6 g	A 3,636 IU C 122 mg K 14 ug	Ca 37 mg K 565 mg
1 cup	Kale	8 cal	1.4 g	.7 g	.2 g	13 g	.6 g	A 1,598 IU K 113 ug	Fe .24 mg
8 sprigs	Cilantro	1 cal	.15 g	.1 g	0 g	4 g	.1 g	A 270 IU K 13 ug	
TOTAL		**779 cal**	**199 g**	**12.3 g**	**3 g**	**1289 g**	**28 g**		
% Daily Value		39%	66%	25%	5%	n/a	112%	A 168% C 1,294% K 231%	Ca 43% Fe 18% Mg 44% Mn 240% P 27% K 68%

My Story
HOW I BECAME A VEGETARIAN

IN 2002, WHEN I WAS 15 YEARS OLD, I lived in the Dominican Republic. I went there because I wanted to do community service and experience the life and culture of people I had never met. While I was there, my eyes were opened to the ways animals were raised and slaughtered for food. In big cities, food comes to us fully cleaned and packaged, ready to be consumed. Because of this, we have little knowledge of what it takes to bring an animal up from birth, feed it, care for it, and then kill it so we can eat.

It was from my experience in the Dominican Republic that I became vegetarian. I lived in a small town of barely 200 people called Bahoruco. The town had been devastated by hurricanes and had no basic services—no electricity and no running water—and had massive problems with widespread sickness. I came there through an organization that sent high school students to work with villagers to put their community back together. As I bonded with the families of the village, I learned how to dance salsa and merengue, and how to grow bananas. I ate a ton of rice and beans, and made friends that have lasted to this day. And it was there that I learned to slaughter a chicken. It changed my life.

There were farm animals all around—goats, pigs, and hundreds of little chickens that ran around all over the place. When I first got there, I met a group of little chicks that I immediately adopted, becoming their mother hen. I played with them and raised them, and although I still ate chicken and other meat at the time I never thought about eating these little animals. I loved them.

Time went by and my little chicks grew into big chickens. Because I was raised in a supermarket culture, the only chicken meat I had ever seen was processed and plastic wrapped. I understood intellectually that if you were going to eat animals you had to kill them, but it hadn't really sunk in that people did that firsthand.

One day it was my turn to make dinner and I was shocked when I was told that I would have to kill the chickens to be cooked with the beans and rice and tomato sauce. I cried hysterically; I just couldn't do it. I remember my friends doing it for me. They slit the throats of some of our chickens. They plucked their feathers. They took out their guts. They separated the chicken parts, and they put them in a pot. I couldn't look at the chickens for weeks and I stopped eating all meat for about a year.

It is a particularly traumatic experience to watch an animal being killed. Chickens really do run around for about 10 minutes after their heads have been severed until all of the nerves in their body calm down and they die. It's not an easy thing to watch. It was this experience that made me switch to only eating beans and plantains and fruit—things that we harvested. And I felt so much better from that point on, both physically and spiritually. I know that if everyone had to kill their own food, far more people would be vegetarians and vegans.

There are many reasons why people take on a vegetarian, vegan, or even Fully Raw lifestyle. But whatever your reason for eating a plant-based diet, it brings you towards living a more compassionate, empathetic, loving, healthy, sustainable life, not only for you but for everyone around you. I am so fortunate to have had this experience because it turned me on to the beauty of life at an early age. You don't have to eat another life to feel your own fully.

WATERMELON IS *AMAZING!*

Watermelon is 92 percent water, so it is almost juice even before it goes through a juicer or blender. It is naturally high in lycopene, vitamin C, and beta-carotene (all potent antioxidants), B vitamins like riboflavin, niacin, pantothenic acid, and choline, and lots of minerals, especially potassium, and it is extremely low in sodium. We think watermelon is high in sugar because it is so sweet, when in reality that sweetness comes across due to the fact that it is so low in salt. Our brains, which naturally note the balance of sweet and salty flavors as we eat, perceive that lack of sodium as an elevation in sugar.

BREAKFAST

Breakfast is 32 ounces of My Watermelon Juice Secret. To make this recipe, cut up a half to a whole watermelon, remove and discard the rind, and blend the melon flesh. Strain this "smoothie" of its coarser pulp until it becomes a silky, sweet juice. Pour it into a jar and add mint and basil. Voila! Enjoy!

LUNCH

For lunch today you can blend up a quart or two of my Totally Tropical Smoothie, or simply feast on 600 to 800 calories of fresh fruit and vegetables, cut into one- or two-bite chunks and eaten on the go. This would entail 5 oranges, half a pineapple, 1 sliced mango, 1 cup stemmed kale leaves, and 8 sprigs of cilantro. I don't want anyone to get hung up on counting nutrients, but just to help you see how easy it is to stay on track without doing a ton of counting, this combo of fruit and veggies will give you 39 percent of the calories you will need for the day, assuming you are aiming for 2,000

calories, with 66 percent of your daily value for carbs, 25 percent for protein, and 5 percent for fat.

DINNER

You will notice that we have been right on target all day with our distribution of calories from carbohydrate and protein, and very sparing with the amount of fat. That gives us lots of room for a truly decadent dressing on tonight's Rainbow Salad, made with luscious ripe tomatoes and a splurge of rich and super-nutritious sesame seeds!

The ingredients for tonight's Rainbow Salad are: 2 heads or bunches of leafy greens like romaine, Swiss chard, or kale, 1 red bell pepper, 1 to 2 sliced ripe mangos, 1 cup cherry tomatoes, and a peeled and sectioned orange, tossed with a generous coating of Cilantro Tahini Dressing.

LIVE IN THE PRESENT

It's easy to get wrapped up thinking about the *shouldas* and *couldas* and the *what-ifs*. In moments of doubt or worry, put away your phone, turn off the television, take a deep breath, and count your blessings. The only things you have are the *here* and the *now*. Honor your body right now by nourishing it properly today. Respect your heart by giving it time to beat to its own rhythm. Make peace with the present . . . because *now* is *beautiful.*

EXERCISE

Start with 20 minutes of stretching. Then, do 3 sets of 25 jumping jacks (page 250), followed by 3 sets of 20 jumps to the sky (if you are comfortable doing so; page 250), and 3 sets of 1-minute planks (page 252). After that, go for a 20-minute walk, jog, or run.

DO YOU REALLY HAVE TIME TO EAT FULLY RAW?

ONE OF THE MOST FREQUENT reasons that people backslide on a Fully Raw program is that they simply don't have time to eat 100 percent raw food all of the time. Over years of coaching and counseling people as they make the move to eating more raw food, I have come to learn that food is not the problem; learning how to feel comfortable in a novel lifestyle takes time to understand and adjust to. Eating lunch can sometimes be the most challenging part of the day because things get busy. We lose track of time, or we are in our cars, or we are unable to access good raw food choices at the right time, etc. Eating raw is actually faster than other options. Nothing is easier than taking a bite of an apple or peeling a banana. I usually take about 15 minutes to eat a fruit mono-meal, about the time most people would spend eating a submarine sandwich. And since there is no prep involved, fruit is the ultimate fast food. If time saving is your goal, eating fruit is the most time efficient way to go! If you have time to sit a while and savor your food, a salad or raw soup may be more satisfying.

DAY 4

MENU

Tangerine Blueberry Water (page 99)

Fresh young coconut water (opposite)

Totally Tropical Smoothie (page 136) *or* Super Sweet Pink Smoothie (page 128)

Tropical Fruit Salad with Lemon Crème Dressing (page 167)

WAKE UP

Start the day with 32 ounces of Tangerine Blueberry Water. Today, slice 1 to 2 tangerines or oranges into a quart of water, peel and all. You'll get additional nutrients from the peel. Add approximately ½ to 1 cup blueberries. Mix and enjoy! If you want to squeeze the juice from one of the tangerines into your water, the results will be a little sweeter. For this particular infusion, I sometimes soak the fruit in the water overnight to allow the flavor to bloom.

Drinking a few glasses of fruit-infused water in the morning is not only hydrating, but also nutritious. It's homemade vitamin water, and better for you because all of the ingredients are *real!* Plus you eat the fruit in the end!

BREAKFAST

Wait 20 minutes after drinking the Tangerine Blueberry Water. This morning's breakfast is a refreshing 32 ounces of fresh coconut water. You will need 3 to 4 young coconuts. Because it is impossible to tell the exact amount of water inside a young coconut, it is always good to have an extra around. You'll get between 1 and 2 cups, usually about 1½ cups, from each coconut. Freeze the flesh that is left and use it in smoothies, or in Fully Raw Banana Coconut Crème Pie (page 234) or Fully Raw Cherry Cobbler (page 240).

FRESH YOUNG COCONUT WATER AND YOUNG COCONUT MEAT

Fresh young coconuts (the white kind with pointed tops) are available at Asian markets and grocers like Whole Foods. (They usually cost far less at Asian markets.) Young coconuts usually come wrapped in plastic in the refrigerated produce section of the market. It is best to buy them refrigerated and store them in the refrigerator, because, unlike mature dried coconut, the soft young flesh is pretty perishable. If you open up a young coconut and it is purple inside, it means that it is no longer good. It's hard to tell from the outside, but in general, look for an unblemished surface without holes or discoloration. If you do get a bad one, just bring it back to the store; most produce managers are very understanding when it comes to these fruits. I always buy young coconuts by the case and split the case with friends if I don't think I'm going to use them all within a week. That way we save some money by buying in bulk.

Fresh young green coconuts are available from florida-coconuts.com. If getting hold of fresh young coconuts is too much trouble, you can substitute frozen coconut water that is organic and totally raw (available at most markets, and at all Whole Foods Markets). All the bottled and canned coconut waters I have seen are heat treated, and therefore are no longer raw. They also don't taste as good as the real stuff.

Another advantage of using fresh young coconuts for your coconut water is that you get the added bonus of delicious young coconut meat. Unlike the meat of mature dried coconuts, young coconut meat is super soft, moist, and sweet, like a bowl of coconut mousse. The only hitch is you have to eat the meat within a few hours. It spoils quickly.

LUNCH

Today lunch is your choice, with two options to spark your imagination. Sometimes, I go through phases where I like to drink the same smoothie or juice every day for a while before I switch to a new combination. This gives me the ability to easily use up cases of fruit that I have bought at a discount, but more often I choose what to make by looking at what fruits or veggies are in season and what I have on hand that is fresh, ripe, and ready to go! The following options should give you a satisfying middle-of-the-day meal regardless of what mood you are in or how hungry you are.

The first lunch option is my Totally Tropical Smoothie. It is amazingly filling, so it's perfect if you have been very active or are particularly hungry. It is mainly a mixture of mango and ripe bananas (a great way to use up speckled bananas), and since both of these fruits are pretty high in fiber and moderate in water, we're going to lighten the smoothie with about a cup of coconut water, fresh or frozen. This is also a great smoothie for adding a few kale leaves without compromising the delicious sweet flavors of super-ripe fruit.

The second choice is my Super Sweet Pink Smoothie, which is not only beautiful, but also cleansing and energizing. For this smoothie, I blend strawberries, pineapple, coconut water, and orange juice. The acid in the fruit balances its sweetness and gives it an invigorating tang. And all of these fruits have an alkalizing effect on your circulatory system.

DINNER

Dinner tonight is Tropical Fruit Salad with Lemon Crème Dressing. Unlike the Rainbow Salads you've been enjoying for the past three nights, which are almost 100 percent vegetables, tonight's salad is more than half fruit. By bulking up a green salad with the flavors and nutrition of fresh fruit, you substantially raise its power to satiate. No need for an extra platter of fruit to prime the appetite. This salad is truly a one-step meal. Simply toss together 1 head or bunch of greens (romaine is my standby, but feel free to substitute kale, chard, spinach—you name it), about half that volume of bite-size fruit (I used mangoes, blackberries, and kiwi), a handful of cilantro leaves, a couple cups of halved cherry tomatoes, and a diced cucumber.

And like all streamlined meals, this one can be adjusted to use whatever is brightest and freshest, or to use what you have on hand. Feel free to substitute cantaloupe, oranges, papaya, or pears for the mango; any berry or diced melon for the blackberries, and grapes instead of kiwi. Sometimes, making dinner is as easy as cutting up everything in your fridge and throwing it in a bowl. You choose how simple or complicated you want it.

Making the lemon dressing is easy: Puree 2 tablespoons raw hemp seeds and 1 cup lemon juice plus a little fresh ginger and some herbs, such as mint, basil, oregano, or thyme. Feel free to experiment. Pick your favorites and have fun! This is how you will figure out what you love and what works for you!

The lemon dressing is an example of one of my oil-free, vinegar-free vinaigrettes. Instead of those processed conventional salad dressing ingredients I simply combine a few seeds or nuts with some citrus juice, and a speck of fresh herbs. The seeds naturally provide a bit of fat, the citrus a complement of tang, and the herb some intoxicating aroma. Tonight I'm using hemp seeds blended with lemon juice, but I could just as well blend a handful of raw almonds with orange juice, water, and dill; or pistachios with pomegranate juice and basil; or pumpkin seeds with lime juice, water, and cilantro; or . . .

CHEW YOUR JUICES

Remember to "chew" your juices and smoothies. Take care to eat slowly and taste each sip, giving it time to mix with your saliva. Most people don't know that digestion starts in your mouth. Your saliva is amazing stuff, loaded with digestive enzymes that start to break down food into its nutritional components even before it enters your stomach.

EXERCISE

Stretch for 20 minutes and then take a 40-minute walk, jog, run, or bike ride. If you cannot do any of those things, perhaps you can swim and do some less-intensive muscle training in the water.

DAY 5

MENU

Lime Water (page 98)

Beetle Juice (page 104)

Watermelon Gazpacho (page 142)

Heavenly Peach Avocado Salad (page 184)

WAKE UP

Start the day with 32 ounces of Lime Water. Squeeze the juice of 1 to 3 limes (depending on the size and how limey you like your water) into a quart of water. I recommend 2 or 3 if you want the water to be super potent. I love drinking this citrus in the morning because it jump-starts my system and "gets things moving."

WATER WORKS AT THE CELLULAR LEVEL

Drinking water in the morning gets your body up and working on the cellular level. Your body is about 60 percent water, and keeping that balance is essential to maintaining digestion, circulation, transportation of nutrients, and body temperature. Cells that don't keep up their balance of fluids and electrolytes shrivel, resulting in muscle fatigue. Your skin contains lots of water and keeping your skin hydrated is an essential part of looking good. But don't expect drinking extra water to get rid of wrinkles. It is true that dehydration can make your skin look more wrinkly, but taking in more water than your skin needs doesn't puff up natural wrinkle lines. Once your body is adequately hydrated, your kidneys eliminate any extra.

BREAKFAST

Breakfast today is a beet and apple juice I call "Beetle Juice." Many people think beets are dirty, partially because they turn your mouth red and also because people interpret the aromatic earthy components of beets as tasting like dirt. Nothing could be further from the truth! Beets are one of the strongest cleansers of your liver, kidneys, and urinary tract. When you combine beets with something sweet and invigorating, like apples, you have the perfect pairing for a rich, delicious, and nutritionally beneficial drink. Plus, the color is spectacular!

RED AND HEALTHY

The pigments in vegetables and fruit—green, yellow, orange, purple, red—are indicative of powerful nutrients inside, but when it comes to brightly hued health, beets are unique. Beets and chard (both varieties of the same plant species) are colored by betaines, which are potent antioxidants that help to fight inflammation throughout your body. Ongoing inflammation leads to overall ill health and plays a role in many maladies, including arthritis, cardio-vascular disease, certain cancers, even Alzheimer's disease. Your body has a limited ability to metabolize betaines, so when you eat a lot of beets some of the pigment passes through your system without being broken down. This can make your urine and feces turn red.

LUNCH

Lunch today is Watermelon Gazpacho. Like all gazpachos, this dish isn't quite a soup, nor is it quite a salad. It is a delicious hybrid—refreshing and crisp like a salad, but as filling and nutritious as any soup. When watermelon is in season you can't have too many recipes to take advantage of the bounty. I eat watermelon mono-meals right out of the rind, drink watermelon juice, use it as a garnish for salads, as a healthy sweetener in smoothies, and as the base for this spectacular Technicolor soup. This gazpacho is light, cleansing, refreshing, sweet, savory, and juicy! It is practically effortless to prepare, but you do have to chop the watermelon by hand. The other veggies can go into a food processor, but if you process the watermelon you will lose all of its crunch, and who wants silky smooth gazpacho? Don't worry about overeating this one; watermelon is so low in calories (and exceptionally low in sodium) that you can't overdo it.

DINNER

Today, we are gonna make a seriously delicious salad that is close to 50 percent fruit: Heavenly Peach Avocado Salad. The fruits in this salad (peach and avocado) give you most of your vitamins and boost the sweetness and calorie content. So you can play with the calories in this dinner by altering the ratio of fruit to vegetables.

The first thing I do when I make any salad is choose my greens. There are so many greens out there, so if you like kale better than chard, that's okay. Pick your favorite! Common options include spinach, romaine, kale, Swiss chard, watercress, arugula, mesclun, endive, frisée, chicory, and collards. Don't be afraid to eat only your favorites, until you feel like branching out more. I like to get all my produce and greens from my produce co-op here in Houston, Rawfully Organic (RawfullyOrganic.com), where I know everyone and I can be sure that I am getting great produce right from the farm. If you are lucky enough to find a source that allows you to buy directly from farmers, of course you get fresher products, but you also get exposed to vegetables that you've never tried before.

After I pick my green, I raid my fridge for what will go with it, and I find as many colors as I possibly can. In my head I'm thinking, "It's Rainbow Salad time, Baby!" The secret is making sure that you always have abundant produce in your house so you have variety to choose from! Think of your home like a grocery store. You want to have it fully stocked at all times for building your at-home salad bar!

Bell peppers, celery, cherry tomatoes, carrots, chard stems, mango, oranges . . . I like to mix fruit in with my salads sometimes because the sweetness makes it more delicious. Feel free to go to town!

EATING MINDFULLY

Sometimes I am in my car on the way to the co-op or coming home from a stressful day and I have to eat on the go or in a place that isn't quite optimal for a peaceful meal. When I am on the go, or stressed, or thinking about something else, I have a much greater tendency to eat emotionally, rather than purposefully, and get carried away by eating too much. I have become much more conscious of this behavior, and now I always try to focus on staying present when I eat my meals. Eating on the go and acknowledging my tendencies to emotionally "stuff myself" has become a blessing in disguise for me, because I have learned how to find calm in the midst of a storm.

Here's how I do it: 1) I chew slowly and taste each bite, taking note of the evolving flavors on my tongue and feeling the food mix with my saliva. After I swallow, I take a few seconds or more to relax and think a bit about what I just ate and feel thankful for it. 2) When I am about halfway through my meal, I start to pay attention about how full I'm getting, and pace myself accordingly. 3) Although I usually drink separately from eating solid food, I am careful to not confuse hunger with thirst. If I find that I am thirsty in the middle of a meal I will drink some water, but generally, because raw food is naturally moist, I do not find that necessary.

EXERCISE

Since yesterday was cardio focused, today is more strength based. Try doing some weights at the gym, doing a barre class, or even 100 squats (page 251) or jumping squats (page 252) at home.

DAY 6

MENU

Berry Water (page 98)

Sunburst Juice (page 108)

Mono-meal of peaches, nectarines, or mangoes

Fully Raw Lasagna (page 188)

WAKE UP

Start the day with 32 ounces of Berry Water. It's best to put this together the night before. Unlike lemons and limes, you can't squeeze the juice out of a berry, so it takes some time for the flavor and nutrients from berries to infuse into the water. Just drop a handful of sliced strawberries and whole blueberries into water and refrigerate overnight. It is super refreshing and tastes like candy water. It's also an antioxidant blast, and you get to eat the fruit in the end.

Feel free to substitute raspberries or blackberries if those are available to you. Keep in mind that you can always take fruit water with you wherever you go, whether that be to work, to school, on errands, etc. It looks beautiful in a glass jar and carrying it around is always a good conversation starter.

ANTIOXIDANTS

The purple and red pigments in berries are potent nutrients—antioxidants that help repair stress that occurs during normal cell metabolism. A small percentage of your cells are constantly being damaged, releasing uncharged molecules called free radicals that can start a chain reaction, harming more cells. Antioxidants keep free radicals from forming. Unchecked, free radicals have been linked to cancers, heart disease, and Alzheimer's and Parkinson's diseases.

BREAKFAST

Today's breakfast is 32 ounces of Sunburst Juice. This powerhouse, a blend of pineapple, apple, orange, lemon, and kale, is multidimensional in color (sunburst yellow with flecks of green), flavor (the sweet spark of pineapple, mellowed by floral apple, and the refreshing tang of orange and lemon), and nutrition. It is high in bromelain, vitamin C, vitamin K, and vitamin A, which helps with inflammation, arthritis, acne, digestion, and migraines. It is packed with simple carbohydrates to keep you energized throughout the morning, and I find it gives me a special glow that makes me feel beautiful!

LUNCH

I'm ready for something simple, how about you? For lunch today, let's take it easy with a mono-meal consisting either of 10 peaches or nectarines, or 4 to 5 mangoes! If bringing this much fruit with you to lunch is too difficult, you can always blend it into a smoothie beforehand with some greens or berries and take it with you in a jar. Another option is to pre-cut your fruit and bring it with you in a resealable container. Remember that fruit is natural fast food. Sometimes making a meal is as easy as biting into a nectarine or peeling a banana.

DINNER

Dinner tonight is homey, comforting, and soul soothing, and it is one of the most spectacular presentations you may have ever encountered. Fully Raw Lasagna is a truly amazing dish. Be warned: It takes more time to put together than the other dinners this week, but the results are s-o-o-o-o worth it! And I thought you might be ready for something more impressive and challenging.

If you have time or have company coming over, this is your dish. Because it is so similar to the look and taste of real lasagna, it's perfect to serve and share with family, guests, or friends who may be new to raw food. Some won't even guess that it's not cooked!

EXERCISE

One workout I love (besides running) is boxing. It's a short circuit and intense training session that focuses on all areas of the body, but especially the upper body. I take boxing classes three or four times a week in addition to running. Perhaps you can try a boxing class or another similar high-intensity short circuit class today for approximately an hour! Be sure to drink lots of water and push yourself only as much as you are willing to go without getting overheated or nauseous.

VULNERABILITY IS POWER!

As we move through these diet days together, I can only imagine that you will feel carefree at times and super emotional at other times. Keep in mind that you are not just shedding physical baggage, but also emotional baggage. Eating cleansing foods may bring up surprising emotions. Part of going Fully Raw is learning how to process and handle these emotions as they come up. Sometimes you

THEY CALL ME A KNOCKOUT! HA!

I HAVE BEEN A LONG distance runner for about ten years. I have run for about an hour almost *every single* day for the past decade. I don't think I have missed more than ten days per year. I love moving my body. It energizes me. It makes me breathe deeply. It makes me relax. It's my *me time,* and I get a surge of self-love and motivation when I do this for myself. Not only that, but staying physically active really helps me to maintain my figure and keep everything in my body functioning like clockwork.

I can run all day and still feel energized. My legs are super strong. However, I have not spent as much time on my upper body. I have dabbled in yoga, acro-yoga, and even Pilates, but I have always come back to running.

Being a long distance runner for so long, I realized that my upper body is weak and that I really didn't have too much variety in my workout, so I decided it was time to mix it up—I just didn't know how. I took some more yoga classes as well as Pilates and barre, but still felt like something was missing. I like to feel an emotional release when I excercise. For me, it's not just physical, but also emotional. When a dear friend recommended boxing, I laughed, but then I thought about it seriously.

I decided to go for one class and see if I liked it. That first class kicked my butt! I am not kidding. I was red, dripping sweat, and nauseous. My knuckles were slightly blistered and every muscle in my body was sore. I felt invigorated.

Boxing showed me my weakness, and it made me want to really work on it and get better. *That* is what made me want to stick with it.

I am already starting to notice toning in my arms, a more sculpted stomach, and more upper body strength. I never used to be able to do a burpee (page 252). Now I can do 30 to 40 in a row. For me, that's improvement.

I started off by using the bag, and now I am training privately with professionals and learning self-defense. This has helped me more than I can possibly express. I love feeling that I am strong enough to defend myself in any threatening situation.

I'm not where I want to be just yet, but I am so inspired. My accuracy and precision are developing, and I am no longer weak. I am alternating running days with boxing days, and I am trying to balance my lower body and upper body workouts. I feel amazing and I sleep better at night. For people who think that you can't be active like this on a raw food vegan lifestyle, I am proof that it *can* be done. My diet gives me abundant energy and enthusiasm to be able to be this active, and for that I am so grateful.

may feel insecure, frustrated, upset, or hopeless. That's okay. It's beneficial to allow yourself the vulnerability to feel and heal so that you can release these pent-up emotions. When you release them, you accelerate the cleansing process and move forward in love and joy.

Health is not just about food; it encompasses *all* the components of life that allow you to truly shine! This includes emotional stability, mental clarity, physical relaxation/excitement, and spiritual peace. The thing that generally scares us the most is being exposed: Being stripped naked, letting go of ego, and showing humility. But to let someone see your pain, your hurt, your heart . . . that only makes you *real*. What you think is weakness is actually *power*. The one thing others can never take away from you is your ability to accept and love yourself just as you are at this very moment. If people try to derail you, love them. Humble yourself. Forgive wholeheartedly. Give freely. Look towards the sun and leave behind your shadow! Have courage to show compassion. What makes you vulnerable makes you beautiful. Let yourself be deeply seen, love with your whole heart, live Fully Raw, and repeat after me: *I am the source of love!*

DAY 7

MENU

Cucumber Mint Water (page 98)

Lemon Ginger Blast (page 111)

Sour Punch Smoothie (page 126; choose any one)

Spring Alive Salad with Strawberry Vinaigrette (page 176)

Triple-Layer Neapolitan Torte (page 226)

WAKE UP

Start the day with 32 ounces of Cucumber Mint Water. Cucumbers are filled with water and electrolytes, giving them a profoundly hydrating effect in your body. Potassium, an electrolyte, helps to regulate the amount of sodium in your system, ensures smooth muscle movement, and has a cleansing effect on your digestive tract. Eating cucumbers every day is one of the best ways to give your skin "the glow." Mint is a refreshing palate cleanser. It's perfect to eliminate bad breath. It is also very calming to your system. So if you wake up with anxiety, drinking a minty refresher like this will help you relax and get your day started right!

BREAKFAST

For breakfast this morning I recommend a Lemon Ginger Blast. Last night's dinner was heavier than most of the dinners in this program. Because dinner was substantial, a light breakfast will feel especially refreshing. Time to get the day started right so that you can feel your best no matter what is going on!

I love the Lemon Ginger Blast because it is not sweet, but rather savory, sassy, and green. Don't let the color scare you. Unlike some other green vegetable juices, here the refreshing lemon juice and cleansing ginger balance the stronger flavors of the greens. Think of this juice as "life-enhancing." It alkalizes and hydrates your body, calms your stress levels, balances hormones, and helps regulate chemical imbalances and reduce stomach irritability, digestive issues, congestion, excess mucus, headaches, and hangovers. This is my go-to juice for a quick fix. It's my all-purpose full-body repair formula!

IT'S ABOUT THE JOURNEY *AND* THE DESTINATION

Watch your progress. It may not be as fast as you wish, but it's happening. Progressing gradually produces deeper, more long-lasting changes in your body chemistry than a crash diet does. As it changes, your body is moving towards a New You! Taking all of that in—in your thinking, your actions, and your desires—takes time. Relax and go with the flow. Enjoy! If you aren't enjoying yourself, then it will be very difficult to stay on the path. Be sure to have fun on the journey.

LUNCH

Lunch is your choice of one of the five Sour Punch Smoothies made with Granny Smith apples. All are light, sweet, and highly nutritious. I have found that Granny Smith apples are excellent at balancing the strong flavors of dark leafy greens, especially the sulfuric compounds found in kale and other cabbage-family vegetables. Granny Smiths are filled with fiber to get your digestive system going, and they help push out toxins. If you're looking for veggie options, these are the smoothies to get you started. Try Hide-the-Spinach Tropical Smoothie—the more apple (or other fruit) you add, the sweeter and tangier it will be. Or you can try the Tart Start, which is loaded with bright mint, nutritious kale, and refreshing grapefruit juice. To start, I recommend using just a few leaves of kale. As you get more accustomed to drinking green smoothies, you will feel more comfortable adding in more greens to make it taste stronger, and you may even begin to desire that taste in the long run!

Smoothies are quick and easy to take on the go. Make one in the morning and take it with you to school or work. As long as you can keep it in a refrigerator or in a cool place, or carry it in a thermos, it will last for a few hours until you are able to drink it.

DINNER

Are you ready for a bowl of exquisite springtime sweetness? My Spring Alive Salad with Strawberry Vinaigrette is an avalanche of spring garden greens dressed with a luscious fat-free strawberry "vinaigrette" and loaded with starbursts of tropical carambola, heirloom tomatoes, kiwi wheels, strawberry slices, and naturally rich pecans. This gorgeous palate of color and texture will leave you feeling fresh, light, and happy! I call the dressing "vinaigrette" even though it contains no vinegar, but the natural brightness of strawberries and oranges makes processed vinegar completely unnecessary. Ain't nature grand?!

DESSERT

You've completed your first week and you deserve a treat. So tonight I'm going to feed you in style. Get your eyes adjusted and your taste buds ready for something truly gorgeous and delicious—no, it's not the new you! It's my Triple-Layer Neapolitan Torte: three scrumptious layers of dates and nuts, carob-rich banana cream, and strawberry raspberry mousse. All of it is 100 percent raw and 100 percent nutritious. One of the miraculous things about eating Fully Raw is that everything you make is equally good for you—even dessert. It doesn't matter if you are eating your fresh, wholesome fruit in the form of a juice or a smoothie, a soup or a salad, a cake or a pudding—all of it is made from the same healthy ingredients. Indulge without guilt!

My Story
MY FULLY RAW AWAKENING

FOOD IS MORE THAN JUST something you eat; it's everything and anything you ingest—food for the mind, soul, spirit, or body. Everyone wants to live happily and to feel 100 percent confident in their bodies. I believe I have found that, and I want to share with you how I did so, and how I have kept it.

On July 15, 2007, I stopped eating cooked foods. I was 18 years old, and I suffered from hyperglycemia, the precursor to type 2 diabetes. I was underweight and I regularly endured migraines, nausea, chronic fatigue, depression, dry itchy skin, high and low blood sugar levels, days of vomiting followed by extreme dehydration, and hopelessness. I did exactly what the doctors told me to do, and I never gave a thought to any type of treatment other than those prescribed by my doctors. I depended heavily on drugs, everything from allergy medicine to sleeping pills to Mucinex to focus pills, some of which had nothing to do with my diagnosis. And I followed my doctors' advice about what to eat. My diet consisted solely of things from packages, things labeled "sugar-free," "carbohydrate-free," or "for diabetics," all with scores of ingredients that I couldn't pronounce.

In high school I took so many sick days I almost didn't graduate. By senior year I had the highest GPA in our class and I was determined to give a speech at our graduation, but I felt too frail, too sad, and too sick. I was depressed because I didn't know if I was going to be able to hold myself together until the end of the year.

I had just finished one of my hospital stints, and I was in Whole Foods digging through a batch of granola, when I heard a voice behind me and felt a tap on my shoulder. "Excuse me, are you a raw foodie?" I jumped up, startled. "What?? What is that?" A man in his early 40s looked me straight in the eye and started talking to me about how he ate at least ten pounds of fruits, vegetables, or their juices in a day, how he had been a "raw foodie" for nearly 18 years. He said he had gone for 90 days on juice alone. I couldn't believe my ears. I stood there with my mouth open . . . It was unlike anything I had ever heard before.

It's not every day that an older male stranger comes up to an 18-year-old girl in the grocery store and starts talking about eating fruits and vegetables—or at least this had never happened to me before. His name was John Rose, and little did I know then that we would become close friends.

I listened to everything he said, and barely said a word. I wasn't really sure what to say or what to believe. Ironically, I had never heard of such a thing as a raw foodie. I was too sick to eat fruit, and doctors had told me not to eat any sugar because it would spike my blood sugar levels. The information he was sharing was so different that it seemed crazy that it could potentially help me and change my life. I actually felt afraid. But I was old enough to know that things that scared me wouldn't necessarily hurt me, and might actually have the potential to help make me better. I took his card, and went home.

I grew up in a family of Latin American and Middle Eastern influences. My father is Ecuadorean, and my mother is Lebanese. I barely ate any fruits or vegetables as a child. If I had a vegetable, it was mixed in with some type of a meat dish, and fruit was practically unseen except for maybe a watermelon in the summertime. My diet consisted of South American dishes of chicken, beans, rice, and churrasco (steak), and Arabic dishes such as grape leaves, kabobs (meat on a stick), kibbe naye (raw meat), rice with vermicelli, baba ganoush, hummus, olive oil, olive oil, and more olive oil. One could practically say that I grew up drinking olive oil, because I did. When I was sick, my mother would sometimes give me a cup of olive oil and tell me to drink it because it would help me feel better. This was a "remedy" passed down through our family for generations.

That night, as we sat around the dinner table, I told my family that I had met a man who ate only fruits and vegetables, and he didn't cook them. It quickly came up that he must be "a rabbit man," and that was that. After dinner I went to bed. Around 3 a.m., I woke up vomiting, dehydrated, and barely able to walk, with crazy blood sugar levels and a pounding head. My parents immediately took me back to the hospital. I had never gotten out of the hospital one day and gone back the very next day. I knew I was getting worse. I felt worse. I was 5 feet, 6 inches tall and weighed 87 pounds. I felt alone. I felt helpless. I had hit rock bottom. Three days later when I was released, I decided to call Mr. John Rose. I wasn't sure what I needed from him, but I was ready to try anything.

We met at Whole Foods the next day, and he sat with me for more than three hours, explaining the condition of my body to me, why I was experiencing blood sugar issues, and how my health was plummeting. He explained that the root of my problem was my diet. The foods that I had been eating my whole life were making me sick. He told me that taking animal products out of my diet and eating a diet of raw, ripe, organic, whole fruits and vegetables would help me feel much better.

At first I told him my doctors would not permit me to eat any sugar, including fruit, due to my blood sugar issues. But John explained that the sugars in fruit are far different than the sugars found in refined complex carbohydrates. My body was crying for purity, and I was "junking" it up. He told me, "Try it for one day. Call me tomorrow, and tell me how you feel."

After a day of eating peaches, I had energy, I had no migraines, and I was excited to be eating fruit. It was the beginning of the rest of my life. We met and talked for three hours every day that week and he opened my eyes about health.

Not too long after that I found out about Dr. Douglas Graham, who taught that eating raw isn't optimal if the balance of fat in your diet is too high. Although I was not a high-fat raw vegan, I still ate more fat than I needed. Dr. Graham's right-hand (wo)man, Lennie, told me that anything more than two tablespoons of nut butter in a day was too much, and I remember feeling shocked. Now, my perceptions have completely shifted. Since then, I have interned with Dr. Graham in both Washington State and Costa Rica, and I have been an avid 80/10/10 proponent for over ten years. I run seven miles a day, and I love to visit organic farms. I am dedicated to spreading the message about living a low-fat raw vegan lifestyle, and it was my motivating factor in writing this book!

If I am eating fats like nuts, seeds, avocados, or coconut, I typically use them in my dressings or in a dessert. I rarely snack on nuts or seeds in the middle of the day. I like to feel light and energized on my feet during the day, so I eat more fruits or greens. In the evening, I like to wind down, and eating some calorie-dense fat helps to slow me down a bit. Eating a handful of nuts or seeds a day or every other day is a delicious treat, but keep in mind that English walnuts, hemp seeds, chia seeds, and flaxseeds sport the most desirable omega-6:3 ratio. If you ever want to exclude fats from your dressings, you are absolutely free to do so.

EXERCISE

Today is a day of rest. Be sure that you are getting enough sleep and feeling fully recouped. If you want some exercise today, I recommend an hour-long walk, an hour of yoga, or a slow 30-minute jog.

WEEK 2

KITCHEN EQUIPMENT

Sharp chopping knife

Cutting board

High-speed blender, such as Vitamix

Vegetable juicer

Citrus juicer

Supply of large drinking vessels (I use quart-size Mason jars)

Big salad bowl

Platter or plate

DAY 8

MENU

Berrylicious Water (page 98)

Cotton Candy Juice! (page 114)

Melon meal of watermelon and cantaloupe

Fruit platter of pears, apples, and nectarines followed by a Rainbow Salad with Cherry Tomato–Beet Top Dressing (page 117)

WAKE UP

Start the day with 32 ounces of Berrylicious Water. It's the start of Week 2, so you should be getting used to drinking (and hopefully enjoying) your fruit-infused waters in the mornings. Once you find the combinations you like, you will easily be able to put new mixes together that sound good to you or that you enjoy. Remember that morning is a time to cleanse and invigorate. Drinking water after sleeping all night rehydrates your system. It gets you ready to start the day.

MEDITATION/MORNING ROUTINES

Starting your day off with the right mental attitude is just as important as starting the day eating nutritious foods. When I first wake up in the morning, I write down my dreams in my dream journal to help me make the transition from the subconscious thinking I have been doing in deep rest to the more actionable thoughts of wakefulness. I find writing down my dreams helps me harness their energy and integrate them seamlessly into my thoughts for the day. In this journal, I also write down my affirmations. Affirmations are phrases that you say to yourself to help you infuse your interactions with a sense of confidence, security, self-love, and well-being. Sometimes, I write these affirmations on my mirror or put them on sticky notes. Some of my favorite affirmations are phrases like, "I am beautifully and wonderfully made," and "I am health." You can create or pick whatever affirmation resonates with you and repeat it daily.

BREAKFAST

Today's breakfast is 32 ounces of Cotton Candy Juice! I call it *cotton candy* because it creates sweetness in your life that radiates to the world . . . and because the color looks like cotton candy! This light pink drink is so delicious that you can't help but smile. How can you not love a juice that makes you happy? When you become happy with your food choices, you feel more confident in your skin. When you feel more confident in your skin, you begin to love yourself. This juice is like a love potion, helping to instill self-love, which, as we know, is the basis for being able to truly and deeply love others. Are you ready to fall in love? I know that you will love this juice recipe!

LUNCH

Today's lunch is a meal of sliced watermelon and cantaloupe. Depending on the size of the watermelon, I might eat anywhere from a third to a half. If I were combining it with cantaloupe, I would probably eat around a half of the cantaloupe and a quarter of the watermelon. A meal of melon in the middle of the day is extremely satisfying and hydrating. The added moisture aids in digestion and helps keep all of the fluids throughout your body flowing. Remember you are 60 percent water, and the moisture in your cells is constantly being depleted. Raw food in general is the most hydrating food you can eat, and melons are the superfoods of hydration!

WATERMELON AND LYCOPENE

Lycopene, which is associated in most people's minds almost exclusively with tomatoes and tomato products, constitutes the red pigment in watermelon. It is taken in pill form to prevent heart disease, cardiovascular disease, and cancer of the prostate, breast, lung, bladder, ovaries, and colon. Among fresh fruits, watermelon now accounts for more intake of lycopene (by weight of fruit eaten) in the U.S. than any other fruit, including tomatoes.

DINNER

For dinner we're going to start with an appetizer of pears, apples, and nectarines (1 or 2 of each), or any fruit of your choice, followed by a Rainbow Salad with Cherry Tomato–Beet Top Dressing. Creating delicious dressings is the secret of *any* salad. In the recipe section of this book there are more than a dozen oil-free dressings that use fresh vegetables and fruits to make tangy, flavorful, satisfying dressings. When you find a few that you like, it's okay to rely on them the way you would a trusted friend. They will be there to bolster your well-being whenever you need them!

EXERCISE

Play outside today! Get a jump rope and do 5 sets of 100 jumps (page 250) . . . more if you can! Do 100 jumping jacks (page 250), 100 squats (page 251), 3 sets of 20 jumps to the sky (page 251), 3 sets of 20 push-ups (page 252), and 3 sets of 30-second sprints. Let nature be your gym and have fun!

DAY 9

MENU

Orange Lemon Refresh*Mint* Water (page 99)

Beet Carrot Ginger Juice (page 106)

Mono-meal of grapes

Fruit platter of apricots, peaches, and berries,
followed by Mango Gazpacho (page 145)

Walnut "Fudge" (page 233)

WAKE UP

Start the day with 32 ounces of Orange Lemon Refresh*Mint* Water. It is normal to feel thirsty when you wake up. While you sleep, most of your bodily processes are still functioning, and in the process using water. Because it has been a long time since you have taken in any liquid, your body is craving something hydrating to start the day. Drinking anything orange in the morning feels sunny to me, and when I combine it with mint, it's pure refresh*mint*. It's the beginning of your daily life cycle: hydrate, cleanse, refresh, and restore!

EXPRESS APPRECIATION FOR WHERE YOU ARE IN YOUR JOURNEY

It's important as you move along from day to day that you stay focused on all of the positive energy around you. When you take on challenges, like a new diet, it's easy to get down on yourself when you sense you aren't getting the immediate results that you want, or feel like you aren't making progress. Truth is, change takes time. You are pursuing health and that's not an overnight accomplishment; it's a work in progress. I know you will get there! When you get to the place of being truly healthy, you will know it, too! You will

feel good, you will see that you look good, and you will recognize with every molecule of your being that *life is invigorating*. As you travel this path, take time to honor your progression (whatever it is) by expressing appreciation for the people, places, and things in your life that mean something special to you. No matter in what frame of mind you find yourself, living with gratitude will always bring you back to center and point you in the right direction.

BREAKFAST

Today's breakfast is 32 ounces of Beet Carrot Ginger Juice. This juice recipe is unbelievably simple, and versatile enough to go in most any direction. So feel free to spruce it up, or add a twist. The basic juice is three parts carrot to one part beet with one thumb of ginger. If you want to make it brighter, add the juice of a lime or two, and even a small pinky of jalapeño. Talk about a sweet fireball! It goes down cool, and leaves you feeling hot!

LUNCH

Today's lunch is a mono-meal of grapes. Grapes are easy to take with you no matter where you go. They are a fast and travel-friendly food, whether you are going to the office, school, or an outdoor event. After our sweet and spicy juice this morning, grapes are pure refreshment, light and clean. Grapes are loaded with glucose, which means they are great at satisfying hunger. Usually a bag of grapes from the grocery store weighs about 2 pounds, which is a good amount for a meal. It will give you about 600 calories worth of fuel, which is just what you want in the middle of the day. Of all fruits, grapes are one of the most cleansing, aiding with nausea, weight loss, digestion, and clear skin. Grapes are bite-size and it

DINNER

Dinner tonight starts with a plate of apricots, peaches, and berries (or any fruit that is in season), followed by Mango Gazpacho. Many restaurants offer combo-meals of soups and salads; consider this dinner to be fruit with a side soup. You want your fruit platter to be ample, at least a pound total, and if you're really hungry go for 2 pounds or more. If you feel that this is too much fruit for you, then you can either just eat the fruit with some greens on the side (or wrap your fruit in your greens), or you can make yourself a traditional vegetable gazpacho. Please always feel free to use whatever fruit is local and in season.

NURTURE YOURSELF

As you continue on your Fully Raw journey, here are some other things you can do to make sure you always feel your best:

1. DRINK. Although you'll be getting lots of water from the fruits and vegetables you're eating, if you're thirsty, drink water to stay hydrated. I almost always have my glass water bottle with me, or a fruit-infused water.

2. GET PROPER SLEEP. This is important because your body repairs and restores when you are sleeping.

3. EXERCISE. Get your body moving by running, walking, practicing yoga, swimming, boxing—whatever you love.

4. GET SOME DAILY SUNSHINE or spend time in nature. I find that if I spend at least 20 minutes a day in the sun or outside, my mood is immediately elevated, I breathe better, I feel more relaxed, and I even get in a dose of vitamin D. While in the sun: pray, meditate, think of things that you love, and be present in the moment.

is easy to pop them without thoroughly chewing; so be sure to take the time to chew them well. If you don't chew grape skins well enough, they can cause minor bouts of diarrhea. Another option is to blend your grapes in a blender with a squeeze of lemon juice for a light lemon grape smoothie.

RUN BEFORE DINNER

I typically get my workouts in between lunch and dinner. Sunset runs are my favorite because they serve as a type of meditation time at the close of my day and help get me "grounded" and ready to wind down for the evening. Also, a good workout gets me hungry. I always tell people, you have to "earn your meal!"

5. DO SOME DRY SKIN BRUSHING, which proponents say improves circulation. It brushes off all of those dead layers of skin, revealing that new glowing skin you have coming up. Do this in the shower before you turn the water on, and brush in a circular motion towards your heart.

6. IF YOU WISH, START USING ESSENTIAL OILS. These oils, like peppermint and lavender, are great for energizing your body, clearing nasal passages, fighting colds or coughs, helping your skin, aiding your sleep, and more. I love Young Living and DoTERRA oils, and I use a variety of them daily. I love my oils.

7. JOURNAL. Keep yourself motivated, inspired, and on track. Write down your goals. Find inspirational quotes that you love and read yourself affirmations daily. Write daily. When I first went raw I wrote down everything: what I ate and what I did, and I noted all the changes my body was going through. This helped me when I needed encouragement. Your most powerful voice of encouragement comes from within.

8. GET SUPPORT. Sometimes, you're just going through a rough time and you need to hear an encouraging voice. Find one or two friends who support you 100 percent. Allow them to be there for you, and you be there for them.

DESSERT

Want something a little sweet? How about a piece of walnut fudge? *Fudge?* You've got to be kidding! Who eats fudge on a diet? You do—at least this fudge. An ingeniously delicious blend of dates, figs, carob powder, and a hint of cinnamon, this is guiltless candy. And it is made—start to finish—in less than 15 minutes. The recipe makes enough for you to have a nutritious sweet treat for the rest of the week.

EXERCISE

Stretch for 10 minutes then take a 30- to 40-minute jog. If you cannot jog, then speed walk. If you do not feel like jogging, then try a fast-paced 50-minute bike ride.

DAY 10

MENU

Orange Blueberry Kiwi Water (page 99)

The Invincible Hulk (page 100)

Fruit platter of mango, berries, and peaches

Fully Raw Pad Thai (page 206)

WAKE UP

Start the day with 32 ounces of Orange Blueberry Kiwi Water. It's sweet and unique! Simply slice your kiwis, add sliced oranges if desired, add in your blueberries, and pour in your water. I find that I like to make this combination at night and let it sit overnight in the fridge. It tastes crisp and sweeter in the morning!

GET SUPPORT!

No sitting and sulking! You are doing this because you *love yourself* and believe that you can be a better *you.* Attitude is everything, so start adjusting your attitude to be encouraging, inspiring, and motivating, not only to yourself, but also to others. Encourage your friends to join you or reach out to others in meet-up groups or online to go Fully Raw with you. Hold each other accountable and offer support. Enjoy the process and the ride. This will make it more exciting and enjoyable for you.

BREAKFAST

Today's breakfast is 32 ounces of The Invincible Hulk. The Invincible Hulk gives you an insanely nutritious green vegetable kick that will keep you going strong all morning long. This juice is sweetened with apples and sparked by lemon to help balance the intensity of the greens. Pure kale or spinach juice can be a bit intense if you are not used to it. But this combo makes the mean green energy machine go down smooth and easy.

LUNCH

Today's lunch is a fruit platter of mango, berries, and peaches or any other fruit that is in season. Remember, you want to eat to your heart's content. You *can* eat until you are satisfied. You don't need to starve yourself or restrict calories, and you also don't need to stuff yourself until you can't move. I usually eat a pound or two of fresh fruit for lunch. For this platter I would eat 1 to 2 mangoes, 2 to 3 peaches, and 1 pound total of strawberries or blueberries and/or raspberries. Eat consciously, chew your food, enjoy each bite, and decide when you feel satisfied enough to stop eating. Eat for nourishment *and* pleasure.

THE REAL SCOOP ON POOP

An important thing to watch during your days is your elimination. Many people are very concerned with what goes *into* their bodies on a daily basis, but not many think about what is coming *out*. For optimal flow, you want to be urinating every 2 to 3 hours and pooping at least 2 or 3 times per day. Get active, eat Fully Raw, and get your bowels (and everything else!) moving.

DINNER

Dinner tonight is Fully Raw Pad Thai. I love this dish because it is so special to prepare. If you love to spend time and have fun in the kitchen, this dish is almost therapeutic to make. The smells, the chopping, the colors—all combine to give you a very rich and unique kitchen experience. I originally came up with the recipe with my mother, and we laughed, tasted, and had fun together in the kitchen creating it. It reminded me of how we used to have fun making treats when I was young. For those who love to cook and miss your time in the kitchen creating meals, you don't have to feel that way. Preparing raw live foods is just as special, colorful, taste-filled, and fun as cooking—if not more so, because it is centered around health and loving yourself. If you want to see the video of my mother and me making this dish, you can find it by searching "FullyRaw Vegan Pad Thai" (no quote marks) on YouTube. Make, share, eat, and enjoy!

FOOD BULLIES

I have talked about this on YouTube but I feel it is so important, and such a common issue that derails people as they start eating raw, that I wanted to write about it here as well. We've all had to deal with bullies in our lives, and unfortunately there are many types of bullies out there. In the past nine years of eating Fully Raw I have met many people who try to bully me, or criticize me about my food choices, my lifestyle, and my weight. People have picked on me about everything from my boobs to my beliefs. I've dealt with it all. I encounter food bullies every day and I want to share with you how I deal with them.

A food bully is someone who does not respect or support your food choices and your healthy lifestyle practices. Bullies will try to coerce you, intimidate

My Story
WHAT I EAT IN A TYPICAL DAY

WHEN YOU'RE LEARNING HOW TO live a raw foods lifestyle (and I say *lifestyle* because to me it's not just a diet), it's really helpful to see what others who are living similarly are eating. So I want to share with you what I might eat in a typical day.

I typically eat two or three meals a day, totaling 2,200 to 2,500 or more calories, with the majority of my calories being eaten early in the day. (That's a lot of calories, but remember, I run about 7 miles each day.) We are using energy all day, so it's important to replace that fuel with carbohydrates that your body can use immediately. This is why I like to eat fruit during the day and vegetable salads at night.

As you have seen, I always start my day off with a glass of fruit-infused water such as Orange Blueberry Kiwi Water (page 99). I usually just cut up whatever fruits I have, put them in a jar, fill the jar with water, and then let it sit overnight in the refrigerator. When I wake up in the morning, it's chilled and flavor-filled—my favorite way to start the day!

Then, I like to make myself approximately 32 ounces of juice in the morning before I head out, for example a Beet Carrot Ginger Juice (page 106). Yum! I pretty much consider myself a master juicer at this point. I *love* juice!

Lunch is generally any fruit that I can get my hands on! Sometimes I'm rushed and will eat a mono-meal of just one type of whole fruit for convenience. Sometimes, I will take the time to cut up a variety of fruit in a bowl and enjoy it even more. A typical lunch would be a rainbow fruit bowl of mango, papaya, berries, grapes, and pineapple. I really like to encourage people to eat whatever fruit is available and in season. Eat until you are satisfied. Don't be afraid—if you pay attention to how you feel, you won't overeat. Eat until you are full and *enjoy* and cherish each bite!

I always start off my dinner with a small plate of fruit and then follow it up with a large rainbow salad. An appetizer might be 2 mangoes and 3 pints of raspberries, followed by a rainbow salad of a bed of kale and romaine topped with bell peppers, purple cabbage, carrots, berries, more mango, and a small amount of avocado, then tossed with a dressing such as Red Pepper–Hemp Seed Orange Dressing (page 168). I make my dressings each night because I really love to eat fresh, minimally processed dressings.

So what about protein? Am I getting enough nutrients in my day? Those are two of the most frequently asked questions that I hear. You can definitely get enough protein eating raw and vegan, and it comes primarily from eating an abundance of dark leafy greens every day and a good amount of fruit— yes, even fruit has protein in it. The trick is eating *enough* of it to be able to benefit from its protein. See page 258 in the Appendix for a more in-depth discussion of protein.

As for getting enough nutrients, I find it puzzling that the people around me can eat junk food all day and never question where their nutrients are coming from, but when they see me eating *only* fruits and veggies, the most nutrient-dense foods on the planet, they feel fine expressing concern about my nutrition. I always say, "Tell someone you eat junk food, they think you're normal. Tell someone you eat raw fruits and veggies, they think you're crazy." I don't know about you . . . but I think I'll go for crazy.

you, prod you, or harass you. Food bullies frequently put up the facade of being very knowledgeable about health, but you will find that they are not open-minded about different health alternatives. Though they may seem to be very strong and resolute in their beliefs, it is often because they struggle with their own health or body image. Bullies want to hurt you only because it makes them feel better about themselves. You will encounter food bullies in four main settings:

1. YOUR FAMILY When a family member is unsupportive, it is usually because you are going through a change that is unfamiliar. My family freaked out when I started eating Fully Raw because it was not a part of their culture and they were concerned for my health. Plus, I didn't know how to talk to them about it. We had to sit down and talk about what was happening and learn to understand one another again. I found it was a great help to make some meals together. Once your family understands, they will calm down and become much more supportive.

2. SOCIAL SETTINGS When you change your lifestyle and your close friends do not, you will likely encounter some degrees of separation. When I made the switch I had to be very careful to make sure my friends did not see my new eating habits as a rejection or criticism of the way they ate. And then there's peer pressure—when you do not want to drink or smoke, your friends may not understand your new health choices. You want to keep your existing friendships by loving your friends unconditionally, but also find new friends with similar interests and passions.

3. INTIMATE RELATIONSHIPS I know many couples who eat differently. It can be a challenge, but you don't stop loving someone just because he or she does or doesn't eat meat or dairy. Communicate with each other and love.

4. INTERNET BULLIES Many of us connect online with others who have similar interests and passions. It's easy to get wrapped up in gossip online, but does it really help anybody? Never judge and don't believe everything you read. When you read something nasty it reflects more on the speaker than the person being gossiped about.

The best way to handle a food bully is to focus on yourself and be the best person you can be. Have confidence in what you are doing. Also, speak kindly about others, and focus on what you can control. Be the bigger person. Love your body, and show compassion. Communicate so that others can understand what you are doing, but when you really disagree, keeping quiet can say more than a pointed, hurtful jab. Practice patience; understand that your journey may not be their journey. No matter who you are you have the right to stand up for yourself, to act respectfully, to live healthfully, and to live the life you want.

EXERCISE

Class day! Find a class that you want to take, whether it be yoga, Pilates, or any other fitness class. Enjoy it!

DAY 11

MENU

Lemon Rosemary Water (page 98)

Cantaloupe Mint Sorbet Smoothie (page 131)

Fruit platter of nectarines, peaches,
    and cherries

Pineapple and strawberries followed by
    Rainbow Salad with Red Pepper–Hemp Seed
    Orange Dressing (page 177)

WAKE UP

Start the day with 32 ounces of Lemon Rosemary Water. Make this water the night before to allow it to infuse overnight. Rosemary is an evergreen in the mint family. It has an extremely refreshing mentholated piney aroma that wakes up your taste buds and helps to fight bad breath. When paired with lemon, rosemary brings out its floral qualities; the combination is absolutely divine! According to legend, Aphrodite wore a drapery of rosemary when she ascended from the sea, and if that doesn't make this stuff divine, I don't know what does!

YOU ARE WORTHY!

Always remember that you are worthy. You have so much goodness to offer the world, and you deserve all of the goodness that life has to offer you. If you fall short of a goal, pick yourself up, dust yourself off, and keep moving forward. One of the benefits of falling is the strength you gain by picking yourself back up. Look at the positives of learning from shortcomings. Recovering from a setback makes you more resilient and stronger; it's strength training for your character! If you don't do something perfectly or if you have a weak moment, tell yourself that it is okay. We are human, and that's a great thing to be. Remember, the most successful people are the ones who fail the most. Long-term success is not about how much you've done perfectly from the start, but how resourceful and resilient you are as you move ahead. Remember *why* you started this journey and hold that inspiration in your heart. If you didn't love yourself, you wouldn't be *here* now. Repeat after me: *I am worthy.*

BREAKFAST

Today's breakfast is 32 ounces of Cantaloupe Mint Sorbet Smoothie. This two-ingredient recipe is the definition of simplicity. Cut, peel, and remove seeds of an entire ripe cantaloupe. You know when your cantaloupe is ripe because it will smell fragrant when sniffed at its blossom end (the end with the little round flat scar, not the one that's indented; that's the stem end) and it will give to gentle pressure at both ends. Place your cantaloupe in the blender with a small handful of mint and blend. I freeze the cantaloupe pieces before blending to make the smoothie more like a sorbet. Welcome to heaven!

LUNCH

Today's lunch is a fruit platter of nectarines, peaches, and sweet cherries or any other of your favorite fruits. Remember that stone fruits are lower in calories than other sweet fruits (see the chart on page 18), so a 600-calorie meal of nectarines or peaches alone is 8 to 11 pieces of fruit, depending on their size or weight. A 600-calorie meal of just cherries would be about 7 cups.

DINNER

Dinner tonight begins with an appetizer of ripe pineapple and strawberries, followed by a Rainbow Salad with Red Pepper–Hemp Seed Orange Dressing. A half of one pineapple with approximately a pound of strawberries will satisfy your hunger before your salad. Please remember that there is no wrong way to build a rainbow salad. Bring them to life and color them with whatever fruits or veggies you have!

EATING OUT AT RESTAURANTS

I would like to share funny story that happened at my sister's birthday one of the earlier years that I was eating raw. She invited me to come to her birthday party at a restaurant with everybody there, and she asked me to eat with everybody else and be "normal." She didn't want the entire evening to revolve around people talking about my new diet. I totally understood where she was coming from—she wanted the attention for the evening and I was totally cool with that. So I called up the restaurant and asked them if I could bring my own food because I had just gotten over hyperglycemia. They were very nice and agreed, so I packed up my own lunchbox with salad fixings and asked the restaurant to simply bring it out on a plate along with everyone else's food so that it would not create a scene. They were happy to do this. When they brought out the food during the dinner, everybody saw my salad and wanted what I was having. Too bad it was just for me!

At the end of the dinner, the chef came out and asked who was the one who brought her food to the restaurant. I raised my hand and she thanked me. She said that she had not had the opportunity to be creative with food in five years and that she had so much fun making my salad. Well, I was flattered, and everyone at the table started laughing because my sister's face turned red. It was a good lesson for me—that I should always just be myself, and that we never know how our lives will touch others', and how we could be inspiring people to be healthy, even if we are going against the status quo.

EXERCISE

Start your exercise with 100 squats (page 251). Do 5 sets of 25 jumping jacks (page 250). Do 3 sets of 20 jumps to the sky (page 251), and plank for 3 sets of 1 minute (page 252). After that, go for a 20-minute walk, jog, or run.

MONEY MATTERS

MONEY IS A SENSITIVE TOPIC for many people, so I will try to give you as many helpful tips as I can for spending less and eating better. I want to help you find ways to get healthy that are realistic and affordable to you. So here's the question: Are you willing to invest in your health? The only thing that you truly own is your body . . . If you don't take care of your body, where will you live? And how much is that worth? I'll give you a hint . . . you are priceless. So then, how much is too much to spend on food?

When you consider what the average cooked-food-eating American spends on food each week ($150 to $175), you are actually saving a lot of money when you go raw. I personally spend less than $160 a week on food and I eat quite a bit. If I then subtract from that all the money I save on gas and electricity by not cooking, on unnecessary doctor bills by improving my health, and on restaurants by choosing homemade food, I am spending way less than the average on my body and my health, which is what eating is all about.

You can eat the best fruit possible rather expensively, or you can be very minimalistic and eat for practically free. I ate raw in college for $60 a week because I wanted it badly enough. My health was worth it. I used to spend thousands on medical bills, and now I spend nothing.

Many of you know that I started my organic food co-op nearly eight years ago after I overcame chronic hyperglycemia, and it is now a thriving non-profit feeding hundreds of families each week. We save families thousands of dollars a year. This is now where I get all of my produce. I recommend that you find a local co-op to help you afford produce. There are many different styles of food co-ops to choose from. My co-op, Rawfully Organic, uses the buyers'-club model where hundreds of local people join together to buy high-quality fruit and vegetables at near wholesale prices. If you don't have a co-op, here are several other ways that you can save money:

BUY IN BULK. You save money buying by the case and can get up to a 30 percent discount from some suppliers. I get my cases at Rawfully Organic, but you can get a discount by asking your local grocer to simply order you some cases. Take advantage of your resources. Shop around and find the stores that have the best deals in quantity, quality, and price.

LOOK FOR PRODUCE BUYING CLUBS or CSAs (community supported agriculture) that support farmers in your area.

SHOP AT FARMERS' MARKETS and make deals with your farmers! A secret is to go at the end of the day and get the ripe fruit that won't be salable tomorrow. At that time, the farmers are looking to sell what they have, so they will discount it for you . . . bonus!

VARIETY VS. QUALITY: Buy the cheap things, like organic bananas, in bulk. Then put aside money for some specialty items like bell peppers, berries, or dates. Balance in this lifestyle is key, and it will make you enjoy it more.

VOLUNTEER! If you have the time, do a little work in exchange for food. You can volunteer part-time at local farms, at the farmers' market, or at your local co-op.

BUY WHAT IS IN SEASON, and buy as much local produce as possible: It is always cheaper!

SPEND YOUR MONEY ON ORGANIC PRODUCE where it counts. Some produce, like celery, apples, strawberries, peaches, peppers, tomatoes, cucumbers, potatoes, and blueberries, have a particularly high amount of residue from insecticides and herbicides. Fruits and veggies like avocado, corn, pineapples, cabbage, mangoes, papayas, kiwi, grapefruit, cauliflower, and sweet potatoes contain the lowest pesticide residues of all produce. It is fine to buy these items conventionally farmed, which will cost you much less. For more, see The Dirty Dozen and the Clean Fifteen (page 85).

GROW YOUR OWN GARDEN! Create your own abundance. Food grows on trees—literally! This is real sustainability. If you don't have a garden, find a community garden, or perhaps even neighbors who grow food and are willing to share their bounty with you. Remember that you are "voting" with your dollar: Every time you buy produce, you are supporting something. Support the kind of food you believe in!

DAY 12

MENU

Strawberry Grapefruit Water (page 99)

Refresh*Mint* Juice (page 117)

Banana Blackberry Basil Smoothie (page 132)

Awesomesauce Burritos (page 194)

Fruit Parfait with Orange Nut Crème (page 231)

WAKE UP

Start the day with 32 ounces of Strawberry Grapefruit Water. I cannot express enough how much I *love* drinking my fruit water in the morning. It cleans out my stomach, gives me healthier looking skin, increases digestion and elimination, and increases the production of blood cells. Adult bodies are made of 60 percent water and the combination of fragrant sweet strawberry and tangy bittersweet grapefruit make this refreshing water irresistible!

Flowing water is revered as a symbol of humility and service. Water nurtures and sustains all living things. It seeks nothing for itself, and it always flows to the lowest spot. Be like water, be humble, nurture yourself and others.

BREAKFAST

Today's breakfast is 32 ounces of the Refresh*Mint* Juice. This can be a great morning juice to wake you up. Mint is one of the most pleasant herbs to break your nightlong fast because it restarts your system and makes you feel light and tingly inside. The menthol in mint aerates the tissues in your mouth, giving you a cooling sensation every time you inhale. Also, mint calms the muscles in the stomach, which is why it is a classic remedy for indigestion.

LUNCH

Today's lunch is 32 ounces of Banana Blackberry Basil Smoothie. This recipe is unique. It's deep blue, almost black, and it's *powerful!* The bananas in the smoothie are a good source of potassium and pure carbohydrate, making the drink sweet. The blackberries are filled with antioxidants and cancer fighting properties. The basil infuses the drink with a mouthwatering herbal essence that is intoxicating. I have a friend who loves basil so much that she carries some in her pocket and keeps some at work, so that she can chew its leaves throughout the day! If you use frozen bananas, this smoothie is like an amazing ice cream shake. I *love* eating ice cream for lunch!

DINNER

Dinner tonight is Awesomesauce Burritos. These burritos are absolutely one of my favorite Fully Raw dishes. They're not like typical burritos wrapped in tortillas. Instead, I use collard greens! The flavors are fresh, rich, juicy, and intense.

When I first went Fully Raw, it was very difficult for me to get my family to adjust to me eating this way. They resisted it because it was different. These Fully Raw Burritos were one of the first recipes that I made for them that they loved and were able to share with me. If you want your family and loved ones to join you in this journey, sometimes you have to make transitional foods for them. Enjoying food with others is a bonding experience. For more information on how I shared my Fully Raw lifestyle with my family, see page 64.

DESSERT

Ready for an amazing creamy easy-as-pie dessert? Tonight we're having Fruit Parfait with Orange Nut Crème—layers of brightly hued berries alternating with stripes of orange-scented mousse that tastes like a healthy orange Creamsicle. This recipe is an ultimate craving buster. It's one of only a few of my recipes that use super-rich macadamia nuts. When whipped up, the orange-macadamia-date mousse is a little taste of heaven. Mixed with layers of colorful fruit, you can feel confident serving this at any event, and people will beg for more.

EXERCISE

Hit up a high-intensity cardio class like boxing. Go all out. Give it your all for one complete hour. Take a 20-minute walk to calm down and refuel with raw fruits and veggies!

DAY 13

MENU

Cucumber Blackberry Basil Water (page 98)

Fully Raw Veggilicious Juice (page 113)

Fruit platter of oranges, kiwi, and mango

Fully Raw Fettuccine Alfredo (page 202)

WAKE UP

Start the day with 32 ounces of Cucumber Blackberry Basil Water. A little light, a little sweet, and a little blue—whether you need a morning pick-me-up or just some TLC for that beautiful self of yours, this delicious mix is good for the soul! Water is the universal solvent, so whenever you soak sliced up fruit or veggies or herbs, all of their aromatic volatile compounds (and their water-soluble nutrients too) infuse into the water. And remember that the best part of drinking infused waters is that you get to eat the fruits and veggies at the end.

DEALING WITH NEGATIVE EMOTIONS

I am not an angry person, but some mornings I wake up more irritated, frustrated, or anxious than other mornings. Usually the feeling is amorphous and hard to grasp, but when I think about it I can usually track it to one of several reasons. Sometimes it's because I just didn't get enough sleep, or that I am having unresolved issues with members of my family or one of my friends. Sometimes I am emotional about a random encounter I had the previous day, or I am dealing with some difficult challenge professionally. Whatever the cause, the only way to clear unwanted emotions is to face them and own them. Celebrate them! Handling anger and frustration is just as important as expressing feelings of joy, forgiveness, and love. If you don't express them, negative emotions have a way of hanging around as stiff muscles, headaches, or an upset stomach. Even after years of cleansing, emotions can remain stuffed deep down inside of us. You want to release them by dealing with the problems up front. If that is impossible, writing a letter (like to that irritating frenemy)—you don't have to send it—gets those emotions on paper and out of your heart. Often writing out your feelings can make it easier to own them, understand them, and see them in perspective. Then it's only one more emotional baby step to forgive and move on. Consider committing yourself to transforming your anger into love, pain into compassion, darkness into light, fire into water. Living fully encompasses your body, mind, *and* soul! The choice to heal is always ours. Let go and love! *After the rain, the rainbow.*

My Story
HOW I MADE FRIENDS IN COLLEGE

EATING FULLY RAW in college was a challenge—I lived in an 8- by 8-foot dorm room with no kitchen and no sink, produce stacked up under my bed, washing my fruits and veggies in the girls' bathroom sink (gross)—and I definitely paid my dues. The logistics were difficult, for sure, but the social stigma of eating so differently from everyone else around me was really hard. I'll never forget how I got the girls in my hall to accept not just me but also my lifestyle.

The girls in my dorm would frequently make fun of me behind my back, but I never said anything, until the day I overheard girls whispering and giggling about the fact that I ate so many bananas. I thought to myself, "Aw, no, I don't want to be 'that girl.'" So I walked back; there were about twenty of them sitting in the dorm room talking about me. I introduced myself, since they really did not know me, and asked if they wanted to come into my room and watch a movie and I would make smoothies for everyone. Most of their jaws dropped. As they came back to my room and we began to talk, I explained why I was doing what I was doing and how it changed my life. That is how I became good friends with all the girls in my hall.

From then on, a lot of them would stop by for a piece of fruit or to ask if I could make a smoothie to help them to feel better after a night of drinking. I learned that if I kept my lifestyle to myself, people would think there was something wrong with me, but if I shared it, then I was giving people the opportunity to understand the experience of this beautiful way of life. This has helped me tremendously: having a great time with others while getting them to understand what I am doing. When you share your lifestyle, you give everyone an opportunity to love it as much as you do.

BREAKFAST

Today's breakfast is 32 ounces of Fully Raw Veggilicious Juice. If you have ever had V8 vegetable juice, you'll love the Fully Raw version! Everyone knows they need to eat their veggies, but sometimes it can be too difficult, too intimidating, or just too much work to get all of the vegetables you want to eat. The Fully Raw Veggilicious Juice is made from eight vibrantly colored vegetables: tomatoes, carrots, beets, spinach, celery, watercress, romaine, and parsley. Blending all of these colors adds vitality to your life. But unlike commercial V8, which is made from vegetable concentrates and added flavors, plus lots of salt, this juice is 100 percent fresh raw veggies, and I use the whole vegetable, including the greens on the carrots and beets. Raw fresh vegetables are naturally rich in minerals, including sodium, so there is no need to add extra salt!

LUNCH

Today's lunch is a fruit platter of mango, oranges, kiwi, or any other desired fruit. Eating these foods should be natural to you now and no longer a struggle. Eat the fruits that you love. Make it exciting.

DINNER

Dinner tonight is Fully Raw Fettuccine Alfredo. This recipe is higher in fat than my typical dishes; however, it's okay to eat a little more fat every now and then. As you cleanse your body, you may find that heavier dishes like this one make you feel a bit sluggish. That's okay. Making a dish like this one for yourself, or to share with others, is fun and decadent on occasion. Even though Fully Raw Fettuccine Alfredo is one of my richer dishes, it is still lower in fat than regular Fettuccine Alfredo, and it is salt-free, gluten free, and scrumptious!

THE SKINNY ABOUT FAT

Fats are essential for health, and though we are all familiar with the problems that eating too much fat causes, it is wrong to think of fats as all bad. Fats are required for the absorption of fat-soluble vitamins, which include A, D, E, and K. They play an important role in regulating our internal bodily temperature and insulating us from excessive cold and heat, and they are an essential part of our nervous system, keeping the electricity that flows through our brains and nerves on course. Some of my favorite healthy Fully Raw fat sources are avocados, durians, and young coconuts. Note that I eat only *whole* foods, which means no oil, ever. Not olive, coconut, flax, or any other.

EXERCISE

Have fun outside today! Go for an hour-long hike or jog. Spend time in nature, meditating, envisioning, and planning ahead. Practice deep breathing. Get your heart rate up but don't push yourself too much.

DAY 14

MENU

Raspberry Cucumber Lime Water (page 99)

Orange Spinach Basil Smoothie (variation on page 130)

Fruit platter of mango, oranges, and kiwi

Pineapple Cucumber Gazpacho (page 146)

Mediterranean Tabouli (page 205)

Fully Raw Cherry or Peach Cobbler (page 240 or page 242)

WAKE UP

Start the day with 32 ounces of Raspberry Cucumber Lime Water. I have heard people call fruit-infused waters, glistening with berries and slices of citrus or cucumbers, "spa waters," as if they were some sort of elitist potion. I find that funny because you don't need to go to a spa to take care of yourself. You should feel free to fill every day with acts of self-love. Nourishing your body is a basic principle of respecting what nature gave you and an essential element in loving yourself. Nourish, hydrate, replenish, and restore. You are as sweet and as flowing as the water you drink.

LEARNING TO LOVE YOURSELF

It's not always easy to love ourselves. What does it mean to love yourself? It means much more than just accepting yourself as you are. It also means making wise decisions for yourself, and sometimes denying immediate gratification to focus on what you know will be more beneficial in the long run. It means not sabotaging yourself. Indulging in food or practices that may feel good momentarily but that cause discomfort and require repair down the road is a formula for future suffering. As you practice wise food choices, perform daily meditations and positive affirmations, engage in consistent exercise, get adequate periods of deep sleep, surround yourself with supportive friends, and practice acts of compassion on a daily basis, a feeling of calm and love for yourself and others will bloom. When you find yourself caught in moments of confusion or desperation, ask yourself, "What is it that I really want?" At the end of the day, if you pursue what makes you happy *in the long run,* you will find that deep down you are happier right now.

BREAKFAST

Today's breakfast is 32 ounces of Orange Spinach Basil Smoothie. This delicious smoothie was one of the very first recipes that I shared on FullyRaw.com and at my Houston co-op, Rawfully Organic. Everyone went *crazy* over this smoothie that miraculously gives you all of the veggie power of a green smoothie with the ease of a sweet, fresh fruit shake. All we did was zap a cup of spinach leaves and big handful of basil with a pint of fresh orange juice. It quickly became the most popular start-your-day-on-the-go meal among my group of friends. We would even text and email pictures of each other drinking this smoothie! (What were we thinking?) Before long, we were riffing on the basic formula, making up our own recipes and sharing them with each other. That's the beautiful thing about learning a basic recipe: You can rely on it forever to help you invent a lifetime of diverse, delicious meals. Once you have a tried and true recipe in your food memory bank, you can feel comfortable improvising, substituting seasonal ingredients, and tweaking flavors. Then you can share your successful experiments and your recipe-concocting power with others!

LUNCH

For lunch today I suggest a beautiful platter of sliced mango, navel oranges, and kiwi, or any other fruit you like. Setting up a platter of beautifully ripe fruit should be natural to you by now, and hopefully no longer a struggle. Eat the fruits that you love. I always try to think about color complementation when I set up a fruit platter. Today's color combo is subtly lovely, encouraging the yellow-orange of mango flesh to play shyly with the brighter, more extroverted red-orange of the ripe navel oranges. Both of these warm sunny colors are brightened by being juxtaposed with the neon coolness of acid-green kiwi—gorgeous! I can't emphasize enough how important it is to make even a simple platter of fruit or a tossed salad look vibrant. If you're not excited about what you're eating, the day just never seems to get off the ground. Eat bright and fly!

The fruit platter is followed by a hydrating, satisfying Pineapple Cucumber Gazpacho, made like a typical gazpacho with tomato, bell pepper, cilantro, lemon, and a hot spike of jalapeño pepper, then sweetened and enlivened with fresh pineapple. It's like a big bowl of pineapple salsa, only better, because it's made only with wholesome fruits and vegetables and not a speck of fat so you can afford to indulge!

DINNER

Dinner tonight is Mediterranean Tabouli. This recipe was my first hit on YouTube. It is like traditional tabouli, except the bulgur has been ingeniously replaced with finely chopped cauliflower. One of the things that my family loves to do most in the kitchen, other than prepare food, is dance. When we make food together, we play music and we sing and we dance. When I was first getting started on YouTube, my mother suggested that I not only make tabouli, but also that I show everyone that I can belly dance so that I could share more than one aspect of my culture. My mother was once a professional belly dancer, and she taught me everything I know about belly dancing when I was growing up. I had a wonderful time filming the video, and I will never forget it. As you make this dish, I encourage you to play music, dance, and enjoy the flavors of life!

DESSERT

Fully Raw cobblers are a wonder of deception! They really look and taste like Grandma's fruit cobbler. And the best part is that a cobbler is quick and easy to assemble and ready to eat right away. All you do is make a streusel-like crust of dates and nuts in a food processor, pack it into a pan, then top it with fresh fruit and add a little more of the date-nut crumble. If you like, you can finish it with a pureed glaze of dates and peaches or cherries, depending on the kind of cobbler you're making. Grandma is going to be s-o-o-o envious!

EXERCISE

Today is a rest day. Catch up on sleep. Hydrate and stretch. If you want to work out, go for a 30-minute walk or slow-paced jog.

WEEK 3

KITCHEN EQUIPMENT

Sharp chopping knife

Cutting board

High-speed blender, such as Vitamix

Vegetable juicer

Food processor

Mandoline or spiral slicer

Platter or plate

Supply of large drinking vessels
    (I use quart-size Mason jars)

Big salad bowl

Rubber spatula

Springform pan

Cake platter, if desired

My Story
MY FAMILY

MY JOURNEY WITH MY FAMILY has been both beautiful and challenging. When I first went Fully Raw, my parents thought I was crazy. My mother had the hardest time of all. She felt like I was abandoning my Lebanese culture, but she also worried that I wasn't getting enough nutrition, especially protein. By the time I left for college, we were not on speaking terms.

This was an otherwise great time in my life. I was getting to know my body and getting to know and love myself on a completely different level. My medical bills went from over $25,000 a year to zero. I looked healthier—I had put on the weight that I needed, my skin was glowing, my hair was growing back (it had started to fall out)—my digestion was improving, I was making straight A's in school, and I was happy.

Being Fully Raw cleansed not only my body but also my mind. I read books like *The Biology of Belief* by Bruce Lipton and *Nonviolent Communication* by Marshall Rosenberg, which began to give me the tools I needed to create solid relationships with my mother, myself, and everyone I loved.

When I came home from college six months later, my mother and I began to really work things out. I had grown up hiding my emotions and keeping things to myself because I thought people would never accept me for who I was. Now that I had accepted myself I was able to express my joy and love for her, and she began to listen.

Fast-forward eight years. I had launched a 21-day challenge on my YouTube channel, the same challenge that became the inspiration for this book. My mother signed on, and told me she wanted to watch the videos and do it all on her own, without my help. That challenge became a powerful turning point in our lives. Since then, my mother has lost 25 pounds and has come off all of her anxiety medications. She looks wonderful! We have grown so close that I now call her one of my best friends.

It was easier for my father to accept my lifestyle. One morning I was making a mango smoothie, and he asked me why I was eating "poor people food." My response was, "*What?* This mango cost three dollars at Whole Foods!" My father grew up in poverty in Ecuador and Mexico, where people who ate fruit and farmed vegetables were considered poor, because they could not afford steak, expensive cheese, and wine. To him, fruit was poor people food.

I showed him research showing that poor populations often were healthier and lived longer than wealthier people who consumed animal products, processed foods, and alcohol. He immediately saw that what I was doing was about health and happiness. He was also intrigued to see me eating mangoes, his favorite fruit growing up. From that day forward my father has shared a smoothie with me every single morning. He no longer eats red meat or dairy and he has gotten much healthier.

My lifestyle change was not a big cultural shock for my sister and brother. At first, they thought their little sis was going a bit crazy, but then they came to understand. They knew that I would do anything I put my mind to. My sister actually went Fully Raw with me for six months when I first started and she came to love how she felt. She still eats one Fully Raw meal a day. She loves my lifestyle and supports me 100 percent. My brother eats whatever he chooses, some raw, mostly not. But he loves any food that I put in front of him!

DAY 15

MENU

Strawberry Lemon Rosemary Water (page 99)

Fully Raw Jungle Juice (page 119)

Mono-meal of watermelon, cantaloupe, or honeydew

Nectarine and Cherry Tomato Soup (page 150) with a Beautiful Beet Salad with Cherry Tomato Vinaigrette (page 177)

WAKE UP

Start the day with 32 ounces of Strawberry Lemon Rosemary Water. I find that when infusing water with firm fruit, like strawberries, apples, or pears, slicing the fruit thinly allows the water to absorb more fruit flavor. Drinking fruit waters is *better* than drinking plain water. It's delicious, more nutritious, and stunningly beautiful. Although I try to give you lots of choices, providing a different flavored water every day of the diet, most of you will find a handful of flavors that appeal to you more than others. A good way to subtly alter the aroma of your fruit waters is to add a snip of fresh herbs. Start a small herb garden in your backyard, on your porch, in your window, or in a pot where you can easily pluck a few sprigs to add to your water; then you will have the aroma of fresh herbs to refresh you every day!

START FRESH

As you begin your day, think about starting fresh. Each day is a new beginning, with no mistakes in it. You have infinite opportunities to perform great works for others and for yourself! All you have to do is embrace them to change the world every day!

BREAKFAST

Today's breakfast is 32 ounces of Fully Raw Jungle Juice. This is one of our signature juices at Rawfully Organic, which I also sell as part of my line of Fully-Raw Juice. This juice is a delicious blend of grapes, tangelos (or tangerines or oranges), cilantro, apples, kale, pineapple, and lime. It has a full spectrum of colors and benefits for your body. The name came to me when my cousin told me about a crazy college party that he went to where "Jungle Juice" was served. To make Jungle Juice, each student dumps a bottle of booze into the house bathtub when he or she arrives. Whatever the mix is in the bathtub at serving time becomes that party's Jungle Juice. I thought this was the most ridiculous idea ever, until I realized I could concoct a Fully Raw version by juicing all of my favorite ingredients into one super juice! Jungle Juice was born! Surprise—it came out tasting incredible! I don't know what drinking a bar's worth of booze will do for you, but I can guarantee that this juice is like a party in a jar!

LUNCH

Today's lunch is a simple mono-meal of melon. You can choose watermelon, cantaloupe, or honeydew. Sometimes I find the easiest way to eat a melon is to cut it in half, clean out the seeds if it's a cantaloupe or honeydew, and scoop out the edible flesh with a spoon. If you have time to remove the rind and cut the melon into chunks, you can bring it with you in a jar or container. When mono-mealing I eat until I am satisfied and feel completely hydrated. Depending on the size of the melon, I usually eat half a watermelon or a whole cantaloupe or honeydew for lunch.

MELON BELLY

When eating mono-meals of melon, people often tell me that they feel bloated or too full. I like to call this "melon belly." A few hours later, they tell me that they feel starving, as if they hadn't eaten anything at all. Remember that melons are extremely high in water but very low in calories. It's normal to feel very full when you finish eating them, but because they will pass through your stomach quickly, it's okay to eat a bit more even after you feel full in order to be satiated longer. On hot days, a meal of melon is the most refreshing lunch possible!

DINNER

Dinner tonight is a Nectarine and Cherry Tomato Soup followed by a Beautiful Beet Salad with the Cherry Tomato and Basil Soup recipe used as a dressing. For tonight's soup, if you do not have access to nectarines, you can substitute papayas, peaches, mangoes, pineapple, or oranges.

CHERRY TOMATOES MAKE THE *BEST* DRESSINGS

Cherry tomatoes are my favorite fruit for salad dressings. They are savory, a little salty, and rich in flavor—a delicious base for a tangy dressing to make any green or vegetable salad more epic. Cherry tomatoes also create a thicker sauce than regular beefsteak tomatoes or even plum tomatoes because they have less water than other varieties. Because they are small, you get more individual fruits per pound, which gives you more skin surface, so a blend of fresh cherry tomatoes has a bit more texture than dressings blended from larger tomatoes. You can never have too many cherry tomatoes!

EXERCISE

You're in the last week of the challenge, so you want to finish strong! Give it your *all* this week and really be dedicated to your workouts and eating practices. Find a cardio class to do today. You can even find intensive workouts on YouTube for free. One hour. Go all out!

DAY 16

MENU

Orange Kiwi Mint Water (page 99)

Carrot Apple Ginger Juice (page 107)

Mono-meal of persimmons or bananas

Rainbow tacos (see opposite) with Orange Avocado Cilantro Picante (page 154)

Fully Raw Pumpkin Pie Brownies (page 236)

WAKE UP

Start the day with 32 ounces of Orange Kiwi Mint Water. Our bodies do most of their active cleansing in the hours immediately after waking, therefore, we reap more benefits from the water consumed during that time. For maximum health, focus on cleansing your body as soon as you wake, refreshing every cell in your system.

BREAKFAST

Today's breakfast is 32 ounces of Carrot Apple Ginger Juice. This is a delicious juice with the potent combo of savory carrots, tart-sweet apples, and pungently aromatic ginger. If you want, you can boost the goodness by substituting orange juice for part of the apple and fresh turmeric for some of the ginger, and adding a zesty spike of lime and an incendiary kick in the pants from a dash of cayenne pepper. I call this spiced up version my Hot Tropic Fireburst Juice!

LUNCH

Today's lunch is a simple mono-meal of 5 to 8 persimmons or bananas, depending on your size and activity. I usually eat 6 of these fruits for lunch, 7 or 8 if I have been particularly active. If you are not able to get either of these fruits (although I can't imagine that you can't get bananas), other options include 3 to 5 large mangoes, 1 large papaya, 2 pounds of grapes, or 5 to 6 apples.

RIP AND DIP

That's what I often say when my friends ask me what I am doing for dinner. Tonight's tacos are a good example. To eat them I could cut them with a knife and fork, but I prefer ripping off bite-size pieces, dunking them into a bowl of dressing, and munching away! It's so easy and enjoyable! Rip and dip, Baby!

DINNER

Dinner tonight is rainbow tacos with Orange Avocado Cilantro Picante. *Yum!* The "tacos" are made just like the Macho Tacos on page 196. All you do is lay romaine leaves, curled edges up, on a large platter and fill them with diced colorful bell peppers, diced celery, shredded carrots, or any other veggie of your choice. You can use Swiss chard leaves or kale if you prefer those to romaine. Fold them like tacos, drizzle them with your picante sauce, and enjoy! You can also use the picante sauce as a dip for your tacos or serve it as an appetizer. I often make dressings in such large volumes that they look like soups. And since my salad dressings

BUILDING FRIENDSHIPS

I KNOW THAT FRIENDSHIPS BASED solely on food are not real friendships. Friendships must be well rounded. If a person truly cares about you, he or she won't stop being your friend or loving you because of what you eat. When I stopped eating meat, and then all animal products, and then anything cooked, many of my friends thought I was crazy. It was difficult for me to enjoy my life fully when my friends didn't understand what I was doing, and when our relationships turned critical from both sides. I quickly realized that what I truly wanted in my life more than anything were solid, and beautiful, healthy relationships. So rather than meet friends for lunch, I started inviting them to do other things. Like going for a run in the park. Or enjoying a movie together. Or going to a concert—things that do not revolve around food. This has gotten me out of many awkward social situations and has allowed me to become closer with my friends.

are nothing more than pureed fruits and vegetables, they are much more versatile than traditional oil and vinegar dressings. I have always said that I am a saucy woman, meaning that I love a lot of dressing on my dishes.

DESSERT

It's been a long day and I think we deserve an epic dessert. What do you say to Fully Raw Pumpkin Pie Brownies? A few years ago, I dressed up as a pumpkin for a YouTube video and made my first pumpkin pie recipe. It was *so* good that my mother said it was even better than my grandmother's hand-me-down pumpkin pie recipe. Each year at pumpkin time I have tried to outdo the last year's dessert, and this pumpkin pie remix is a definite winner. It's heavenly! If you don't have persimmons, you can substitute papaya or simply leave it out. At serving time you want this dessert to be firm enough to cut with a knife, which means you should make it far enough ahead to allow it to firm up in the freezer for an hour or so before serving. If you don't want to use nuts or seeds for the crust, you can use dried mulberries instead.

EXERCISE

Stretch for 20 minutes, then go for a 30-minute run. Do high intensity. Run with music, get your blood flowing, heart pumping, and adrenaline rushing. Do a 10-minute walk as a cooldown.

LOVE THE BODY YOU HAVE

Body shaming is unacceptable no matter who you are or what you look like. People get caught up making fun of people on the Internet because of how they look. It's important to understand that the Internet isn't faceless. We are all real people. My body is mine and I am proud of it. I am still filling out and my body is still changing. I love the body that God gave me. I try to take care of it the best way that I can, eating Fully Raw and living healthfully. It's the only body I have. One of my favorite quotes is, "If you don't take care of your body, where will you live?" I am so happy in my skin and I want you to be too. We are all people.

We are all different shapes and sizes, and we are all beautiful. What matters most is how you treat your body, what you feed your temple, and how you feel! Never give anyone the power to make you feel inferior. Let us be fearless and support one another so that we can all achieve greater health. Being a vegan is *not just* about loving animals and the environment. It's about loving yourself, and it's about showing kindness and compassion to everyone around you, especially the person who lives right here, inside your skin.

DAY 17

MENU

Blueberry Grape Water (page 98)

The Glow Stick (page 120)

Fruit platter of mango, berries, and peaches

Raw Vegan Chili, Baby! (page 186)

Fully Raw Chocolate Pecan Pie (page 210)

WAKE UP

Start the day with 32 ounces of Blueberry Grape Water. You don't need precise amounts for this one; simply throw a handful each of blueberries and grapes into a jar, fill it with water, and chill it overnight, if you can. You will awaken to a magical violet surprise!

SELF-SABOTAGE

I know you want to move forward and create positive change in your life. If you didn't, we couldn't have come this far together. So why do we stay stuck in places of negativity and unfulfilling behavior? I think for most of us it is because we are scared of change. We would rather continue to suffer where we are rather than move to greener pastures. The lesson in the old adage about the grass being greener on the other side is that you should be content where you are, but I challenge you to flip it around. Sometimes that greener pasture *really is* a better place to be. I encourage you to take the plunge into the plush greenery that awaits you. Self-sabotage can manifest as overeating, undereating, not sleeping, avoiding responsibility, making poor food choices—any choice that you consciously (or even unconsciously) make that is detrimental to your health, body, mind, or life. If you want to feel better and look better and do better, dedicate yourself to making choices that will positively benefit you, and move forward day by day with that focus in mind.

BREAKFAST

Today's breakfast is 32 ounces of The Glow Stick. This juice is great if you are looking to load up on vegetables. Remember that when you turn fresh produce into juice the fiber is extracted, producing a lighter and more refreshing lunch, rather than one that fills you up. The Glow Stick is about equal parts carrot and apple, invigorated with fresh ginger. The result is sunrise bright, slightly sweet, and utterly refreshing.

GETTING THE GLOW

Eating any wholesome ripe fruit or crisp fresh vegetable will help give you the "Glow." I like to remind people that no one fruit or veggie is more important than another. There is no magic bullet, no secret ingredient that will give you unbridled health all by itself. When living a healthy lifestyle, balance is the key ingredient. You do not need one nutrient more than another; you need *all* of them. The easiest way to make sure you are getting a broad balance is to eat a rainbow spectrum of fruits and veggies, either in a series of mono-meals or in combination with one another. Concentrate on consuming a wide variety of produce over time, and you will be rewarded with long-lasting health benefits.

LUNCH

Today's lunch is a fruit platter of mango, berries, and peaches, or whatever is bright and ripe and in season. For me, lunch today would be 3 or 4 small mangoes, 1 to 2 pints of berries, and 1 or 2 peaches. If you are feeling really hungry or you have been particularly active, eat more. Aim for approximately 650 to 700 calories with this meal to keep you satisfied until dinner.

IT'S NOT A STARVATION DIET; IT'S THE FREEDOM DIET

When people think "diet," they think about depriving themselves of food or radically limiting their food options. When eating Fully Raw, you are not eating "junk" foods that pack on the pounds; you are eating clean foods that naturally help you get slimmer. Whenever you diet, it's important that you eat enough and feel satisfied after each meal, so that you can create a sustainable and healthy lifestyle for yourself. If a diet doesn't sustain you physically, it is doomed to failure. Always eat raw fruits and vegetables until you feel satisfied. If you are hungry for more, eat more. Know when your body feels hunger and strive to be conscious enough to recognize the difference between filling yourself and overeating.

DINNER

Dinner tonight is Raw Vegan Chili, Baby! This dish is rich and savory, so get ready for some serious satisfaction! Before you pour on the red tomato sauce, you will be able to see how beautiful and colorful this dish really is. You can make a large batch of this chili and share with family and friends, or take it to an event. It's also great to take to work for lunch, or for dinner. Because it is not cooked, the flavors will be much more intense than regular chili. The chili lasts for approximately 2 to 3 days in the refrigerator. If you want to warm it up a bit you can always add in a bit more cayenne pepper or even let it sit in the sunshine for 30 minutes. There's no better way to release natural flavors than letting food sit in the sunshine.

COMPARE AND CONTRAST

A 6-cup serving of Raw Vegan Chili has 295 calories. A 2-cup serving of cooked chili with beans has 573 calories. If you were to eat 6 cups of cooked chili, you would be consuming 1,720 calories in one meal—most or all of the calories you would need for a day! Oy!

DESSERT

Tonight's dessert is Fully Raw Chocolate Pecan Pie. This is probably my favorite dessert recipe. It's rich and creamy, and it looks divine! In order to become firm enough to slice, the pie needs some time to freeze, so plan accordingly. But unlike most of my other Fully Raw desserts, which are lower in fat, this one is rich enough to stay smooth and creamy no matter how long it stays in the freezer. This recipe is absolute perfection! Enjoy!

EXERCISE

Start your workout with 100 squats (page 251). Do jumping jacks (page 250) for 3 full minutes. Do 3 sets of 20 jumps to the sky (page 251), and plank (page 252) for 3 sets of 1 minute. After that, go for a 30-minute walk, jog, run, bike, or swim.

DAY 18

MENU

Pineapple Cucumber Mint Water (page 99)

Collard Orange Pineapple Smoothie (page 130)

Fruit bowl

Spinach Soup (page 148) followed by Rainbow Salad with Red Bell Pepper–Hemp Seed Orange Dressing (page 177)

WAKE UP

Start the day with 32 ounces of Pineapple Cucumber Mint Water. If you want to add a little lemon, go right ahead. The pineapple has a tendency to take over, so make sure to use more cucumber than pineapple, especially if you are going to chill it overnight.

WHAT WILL YOU DO ON DAY 22?

As we near the end of the 21-day diet plan, it's important to think ahead. What will you do when the challenge is over? Will you continue to eat raw? Will you try to eat one or two Fully Raw meals a day? How will you apply what you have learned to your everyday life? Start thinking about what success looks like to *you*. Write down your goals and make a plan to move forward. With a little planning, a little motivation, and faith, you can make it happen!

My Story
GROWING FULLY RAW
& RAWFULLY ORGANIC

WHILE I WAS IN COLLEGE, I worked for Dr. Douglas Graham in Seattle during the summers, interning at his fasting and raw food retreats. I also studied in Costa Rica with my university, visiting the beaches every weekend and eating the best fruit in the world. I was having the time of my life living on my own, experiencing my Hispanic heritage, and becoming truly healthier.

Back in Houston, where I attended Rice University, I joined twelve other students in starting up a farmers' market on Tuesday afternoons in the university parking lot. At first only a few farmers came, but that was all we really needed. I got close to some of these farmers and they became like family, especially the Gundermanns. Joan Gundermann ran their stand along with her children, who were my age. Within no time I was spending weekends at their farm, picking and having fun and loving being a part of their extended family.

The Gundermanns primarily grew greens and peaches in season. Because the majority of my calories were coming from fruit, I still needed to go to the grocery store to buy cases of produce. It was very expensive, and so I decided to try to start an organic produce buying club so that my close friends and I could all afford organic produce in bulk. Through a friend of a friend I got the number for a wholesale organic produce distributor in Houston. After much begging and pleading, I got him to agree to a weekly delivery to my house of a minimum order of 40 cases. Of course I had no idea what I was getting myself into. Allow me to put this into perspective: One case

of bananas is 40 pounds, one case of lettuce is 24 heads, and one case of apples is 100 apples. I had just committed myself to 40 cases a week and I only had two or three people who wanted to do this with me. So I called up as many people as I could and got about 12 people to join in on my first bulk order. I remember that day: When the truck left, we had produce stacked up to the ceiling in my mother's living room.

When my neighbors saw the truck arrive, they peeped their heads outside of their windows, and some even came over to ask what was going on. I explained that I had just started a produce co-op in my garage, and that we wanted to get as many neighbors involved as we could. The next week I had 40 people picking up produce from my garage and before I knew it, the co-op had grown to 100 people picking up produce every week.

I was juggling school and managing this new business, which we named Rawfully Organic, as a side passion. A few months later we were kicked out of my garage because people could not drive through the streets in our neighborhood on co-op days. Instead, the neighborhood association put us in an open area of a neighborhood parking lot. We now had 300 families picking up produce each week, and the grocery store a few streets away began to complain that we were taking away their business!

The most beautiful part about our co-op is that it is based upon community. Each co-op day, volunteers help sort the boxes, and everyone comes together to share beautiful affordable produce. The relationships I have formed through the co-op have changed my life, and we continue to feel like family seven years after we started.

It wasn't long before word spread that the co-op needed a home, and I had offers from people all over the city who wanted Rawfully Organic as part of their community. I was fortunate to be able to choose three locations, and I had so much volunteer help that within a few years we were able to expand from one market a week, servicing a couple hundred families, to three markets each week and over 15,000 registered members. Today, the co-op still runs three days a week serving three different local communities, but now we have far more families participating weekly and thousands more volunteers involved. We are so blessed to have such a beautiful community that supports the local farmers and distributors who bring us abundant top-quality organic produce at affordable prices.

I am still extremely close with the Gundermanns. They are like family to me and I've even become godmother to one of the newest children in their family. When I first started Rawfully Organic, they had 50 acres of land planted in fruit and vegetables. Now they grow produce on over 500 acres for the co-op and for the city of Houston. I always say that we vote with our dollars. What we purchase says a lot about how we want our world to be. Rawfully Organic has changed the environment around Houston, creating a greener and more peaceful footprint on our planet.

I have evolved as well. Although I run the co-op and I distribute fresh produce, I quickly realized that while people love fresh food, they don't always know what to do with it or how to prepare it. At first, I would print out recipes on sticky notes and post them on boxes every week so that people would know what to do with the produce in their order. But not everybody picked up each week, and I began to get many requests from people asking for the recipe cards from the previous week. This was too much for me to keep up with, so I decided to start my own YouTube channel so that I could put all of the recipes in an archive. Before I knew it, my YouTube videos were getting a lot of hits, and I even had people in Japan emailing me telling me how much they loved my recipes. I learned to tailor my content to a much larger audience so that I could educate more people on the benefits eating a raw vegan lifestyle. I had named the co-op Rawfully Organic because it was full of raw food and all the produce was organic. I called the YouTube channel FullyRaw. So while Rawfully Organic was responsible for feeding people actual produce, FullyRaw was responsible for educating the world about this beautiful lifestyle. They became like a married couple, two companies working together to reach people wherever they may live and inspire them to eat Fully Raw.

Rawfully Organic and FullyRaw have recently given birth to their new child, called FullyRaw Juice. This is my juice company, which uses fresh produce from local Texas farmers to create raw cold-pressed organic juices. They are unpasteurized and made only with nature's goodness.

My story continues to change as my friends and family and I continue to grow. I'm dedicated to this lifestyle and I'm dedicated to helping feed people good food and healthful information. This has changed my life, and I hope that it will change yours.

BREAKFAST

Today's breakfast is 32 ounces of Collard Orange Pineapple Smoothie. This smoothie has a tropical twist. It may look green, but it actually tastes sweetly of pineapple and orange. It's deceivingly good!

Collard greens (the non-heading form of cabbage) are highly nutritious, like kale, and extremely versatile for preparing raw foods. One cup of chopped raw collards has less than 12 calories but contains 12 percent of your recommended daily allowance for folate, 36 percent of your daily vitamin A, 21 percent of your vitamin C, and 197 percent of your needed vitamin K! It also gives you 2 percent of your protein for the day as well as good amount of calcium (8 percent) and manganese (10 percent). Take advantage of the nutrition of collards in smoothies and salads, or even use them to make delicious burrito wraps!

LUNCH

Today's lunch is a big, luscious fruit bowl. This is similar to a fruit platter, but in my fruit bowls everything is cut into smaller-than-bite-size pieces, so that you can get several pieces of fruit in each bite. You want a total of 2 quarts of cut fruit. The combo is completely up to you. I like to make the salad about 75 percent acidic, less-sweet fruits (mango, berries, oranges, pineapple, persimmons, pears, and/or apples) and 25 percent sweeter fruits (bananas, dates, figs, mulberries). Make sure you fill up your bowl, and taste the sweetness!

DINNER

Dinner tonight is Spinach Soup followed by a Rainbow Salad with Red Pepper–Hemp Seed Orange Dressing. This savory dinner is rich in red colors, which means it's naturally high in anti-inflammatory anthocyanins and carotenes. Something else that you may consider doing is using a portion of your spinach soup as a second salad dressing or as a dip for dousing bites of your rainbow salad.

If you are still hungry for something sweet after eating dinner, then perhaps you didn't eat enough fruit during the day or before dinner. Melt a few dates in your mouth afterwards as a sweet treat. You can also pit the date and replace the pit with an almond or your nut of choice and eat a few of those.

EXERCISE

Today is all about cardio! Find a class that you love and participate for 1 hour. Another option is to run for an hour. See how many miles you can complete. You can also choose to bike. Stretch accordingly.

DAY 19

MENU

Lemon Grapefruit Water (page 98)

The Holy Grale (page 118)

Cherry Nectarine Delight (page 138)

Raw Zucchini Pasta with Fresh Tomato Marinara Sauce (page 200)

Fully Raw Apple Pie (page 223)

WAKE UP

Start the day with 32 ounces of Lemon Grapefruit Water. This citrus blend is super detoxifying and helps to boost your metabolism. Citrus helps to stimulate digestion and alkalize you bodily fluids on a cellular level. A study published in the *Journal of Medicinal Food* in the spring of 2006 found that grapefruit is particularly helpful in boosting metabolism, improving insulin resistance, and accelerating weight loss.

BREAKFAST

Today's breakfast is 32 ounces of the Holy Grale. GRapes + kALE = GRALE. It's *so* delicious that you'll forget how good it is for you! The sweetness of the grapes is balanced by the intriguingly bitter savory qualities of kale. If you have never had *real* grape juice, you are in for a pleasant surprise. Forget the dark purple and cloying candied sweetness of commercial grape juice. Freshly squeezed grape juice is pale green, slightly tinged with red if you are using dark skinned grapes, and the flavor is naturally sweet and ever so slightly astringent.

SKIP THE WINE; DRINK THE GRAPES

Grape juice is said to be more beneficial than drinking wine. It's not fermented, it's fresh, and it contains many nutrients that help to build and restore your blood cells. In addition, the resveratrol, which has reputed antioxidant properties, resides in the grape skins, so you don't need to drink a drop of alcohol to enjoy its health benefits.

LUNCH

For lunch today we're going to have a Cherry Nectarine Delight. This smoothie is sweet and tart! It is loaded with natural fiber, which gives a rather thick consistency. If you prefer it a bit more fluid, add a little fresh coconut water. And if you want to tone down its natural tartness, you can add a banana or two. For most of the U.S., cherries and nectarines are in season only in the summer. If you do not have

access to fresh nectarines or cherries, use frozen organic fruit, which you will find in the freezer case of your local market, or do what I do and freeze any excess ripe summer fruit for use anytime of the year. Do not feel that using frozen fruit is a compromise. Commercially frozen unsweetened fruit is frozen at its peak of ripeness, often riper than the fresh fruit that appears in most markets. And because freezing is a preservation process, there is no need for added preservatives.

YOUR OPINION MATTERS

"You can be the ripest, juiciest peach in the world, and there is still going to be somebody who hates peaches."

—Dita Von Teese

Remember as you navigate your journey of health to always stay true to yourself. Each decision you make matters. If something doesn't feel right to you, then don't do it. You are responsible for your well-being. You may get criticism and comments, but the opinion that matters the most . . . is yours.

DINNER

Dinner tonight is Raw Zucchini Pasta with Fresh Tomato Marinara. I don't think there is any dish in my raw food repertoire that I enjoy more frequently than this one. The secret is using thinly sliced zucchini for your pasta. I *love* zucchini pasta, and so do my family and friends, even those who eat no other raw food dishes. Zucchini pasta is better for you than pasta made from flour, because it is 100 percent fresh vegetable, not a highly processed paste. It's juicier, lower in carbohydrates, and higher in vitamins and minerals. And because it is raw,

every strand of this "pasta" is naturally "al dente" (the Italian term for perfectly cooked, slightly chewy noodles). You can eat a pile of zucchini pasta and push away from the table feeling refreshed and satisfied, instead of stuffed, constipated, and regretful. Zucchini pasta is fast and easy to prepare, and the tomato sauce doubles as a dressing that you can also use on salads. Fantastico!

DESSERT

Tonight's dessert is a miracle—Fully Raw Apple Pie! I grew up on my grandma's apple pie and I loved it, but I have to admit (sorry, Gran) that I love this raw version even more. As long as apples are available (which is almost year-round), this pie is a spectacular dessert. And considering how impressive it is, it is pretty darn easy to assemble. There are only five ingredients: apples (any variety you like), pitted fresh dates, dried figs, cinnamon, and nutmeg. I have used a range of apple varieties for this pie and

I can't tell you which ones are better than others. I love them all!

EXERCISE

Today is about precision and accuracy. Do you like sports? Perhaps play a sport of your choice like tennis, basketball, volleyball, boxing, or swimming. If you don't feel comfortable doing this, then get a jump rope and do 5 sets of 100 jumps (page 250) . . . more if you can! Then do 100 jumping jacks (page 250), 100 squats (page 251), 3 sets of 20 jumps to the sky (page 251), 3 sets of 20 push-ups (page 252), and 3 sets of 30-second sprints. Turn up the music and have fun!

DAY 20

MENU

Strawberry Cucumber Basil Water (page 99)

Bugs Bunny Juice (page 122)

Fruit platter of oranges, kiwis, grapefruit, mango, papaya, and berries

Stuffed Red Peppers with Avocado Salsa (page 198)

WAKE UP

Start the day with 32 ounces of Strawberry Cucumber Basil Water. Similar to the Pineapple Cucumber Mint Water you had the day before yesterday, this is another infused water that takes advantage of the color and nutrition inherent in various parts of a plant. Fruits provide us with quick energy, jewel-like color, and lots of vitamins. Cucumbers and green vegetables are rich in minerals; and basil and other aromatic leafy herbs contain phytonutrients that help us fight infection and inflammation.

BELIEVE IN YOURSELF

"A bird sitting in a tree is never afraid of the branch breaking, because her trust is not on the branch but on her own wings. Always believe in yourself."

—Unknown

As we near the completion of our 21-day diet, think about how you will move forward after Day 21. Most of us have trouble maintaining motivation once the impetus of daily menus and inspirations are gone. I want to challenge you to keep the momentum going! Just like the quote above, you need to trust in yourself to make healthy decisions. Over the last three weeks, you have proven that you have the power to change your life in incredibly powerful ways. Trust in your own wings and you will fly!

BREAKFAST

Today's breakfast is 28 ounces of Bugs Bunny Juice! This juice is made from carrots, apples, and greens, perfect for bunnies, and not so bad for us other mammals, too! Just look at the amazing variety of fruits, vegetables, juices, smoothies, salads, entrees, and desserts that you have eaten in the past three weeks! The number of Fully Raw recipes available online and in print is increasing all the time, and as time passes, I promise that I will be creating more and more for you to enjoy! Eat what feels good to you, and you will find happiness in health!

BE RAINBOW BRIGHT!

Dreams come true when you are true to yourself. Be crazy, be colorful, be thoughtful, be silly, be weird . . . *be yourself!* May your self-love bring you to brighter health. Life is too short to be anything but happy!

LUNCH

Lunch today is a rainbow fruit platter with a half-dozen different fruits. When you eat this much variety, you don't need to include a ton of each fruit to make a meal. For example, you could eat 2 each of oranges, mangoes, and kiwis, 1 each of grapefruit and papaya, and 2 big handfuls of berries scattered over the top. A gorgeous platter like this weighs in at about 3 pounds of trimmed edible fruit and delivers about 700 calories of rainbow-licious goodness!

WHAT'S UP, DOC?

Bugs was on to something. Munching down a bunch of carrots is a great way to get your B vitamins, vitamin A, and a mine's worth of minerals—calcium, copper, iron, magnesium, phosphorus, potassium, sodium, and zinc. It gives you nearly half of the dietary fiber you need for the whole day, and it ain't so bad on protein, either.

DINNER

For dinner we're having Stuffed Red Peppers with Avocado Salsa, a Kodachrome platter of ripe red peppers stuffed with a salad of greens, tomatoes, cilantro, avocado, and green onions. Although stuffing the peppers is not difficult, if you want to serve this as a more casual meal, you can chop everything up, toss it with the avocado salsa, and serve it in a big bowl as a salad.

EXERCISE

Today, go for an hour-long walk. Keep your heart rate up. If you want to jog you can do that too. Stretch accordingly.

DAY 21

MENU

Raspberry Blueberry Blackberry Water (page 99)

Coconut Banana Smoothie with a Speck of
    Cinnamon (page 133)

Spicy Mango Basil Salad (page 185)

Fully Raw Sweet Corn Salad (page 180), or
    Macho Tacos (page 196) if it's not corn season

Fully Raw Strawberry Shortcake (page 215)

WAKE UP

Start the day with 32 ounces of Raspberry Blueberry
Blackberry Water. I love how the colors of these
berries bleed into the water, especially after sitting
for a period of time. I find it best chilled overnight.
This is what I call my berrylicious water! It's rich in
antioxidants, flavor, and more!

EVERY ENDING IS A NEW BEGINNING

The end of a journey is always the beginning of a
new one! The journey *is* the destination, and there
is never an end. When we culminate a journey we
may experience emotions of sadness, but these are
inevitably mixed with emotions of joy and gratitude.
Learn to trust and open your heart to acceptance
and faith. You will love. You will get hurt. You will
laugh, and give, and cry, and heal, and smile! You
will experience sadness and joy. Good health and
balance become an essential part of your happiness
no matter who you are, where you live, or what you
eat. *Love yourself,* and everything else will fall into
place.

BREAKFAST

Today's breakfast is 32 ounces of Coconut Banana
Smoothie with a Speck of Cinnamon. This smoothie
is such a treat. It tastes like a banana coconut crème
pie in a jar! The main ingredient is bananas, with just
enough coconut, a hint of vanilla, and a sprinkling of
cinnamon to add a special warming touch. I usually
use around 6 bananas, sometimes more. Although it
makes a particularly powerful breakfast, feel free to
make this for lunch or a casual quick dinner. Enjoy
anytime!

WHERE DO YOU GO FROM HERE?

Now that you are winding up, go back through these
past 21 days and select the recipes you enjoyed the
most. Make these recipes the foundation of what you
will eat most frequently in your everyday routine.
This book is full of fabulous Fully Raw recipes and
in the past three weeks you have experienced a lot of
them. Use the ones you liked the most to start you off
on a lifetime of healthful, delicious meals that you
can enjoy without worrying about calories, without
guilt over bingeing on unhealthy junk, and without obsessing over whether or not you are getting
enough nutrients. When you eat Fully Raw, you will
find how easy it is to stick with a healthy diet every
single day.

LUNCH

Today's lunch is a Spicy Mango Basil Salad, a fragrant and colorful combination of plush golden
mango flesh punctuated by shreds of vibrant green
basil leaves and flecks of cayenne. If you prefer, you
can simply leave out the cayenne.

DINNER

Dinner tonight is Fully Raw Sweet Corn Salad. This recipe is one of the most savory salads I know, and I *love* it. It's festive, it's colorful, it's flavorful, and it's filling! This dish is best when you have fresh seasonal corn. Raw sweet corn is much tastier than cooked corn. If it's not corn season, I suggest holding off on this one and substituting Macho Tacos. I usually make more of this than I can eat, because when confronted by recipes this delicious my eyes get bigger than my stomach. If you are prone to a similar visual-gastric discrepancy, you can store your leftovers in the refrigerator in a tightly closed container for two to three days. It's great to take to work the next day or have for dinner another night. When leftovers are this good, nobody complains. They're fabuloso!

EMBRACING MY HERITAGE THE FULLY RAW WAY

I am half Lebanese and half Ecuadorean. I think my instantaneous love affair with the Sweet Corn Salad stemmed from its similarity to the dishes that my Ecuadorean cousins make. Their love for each other is palpable in the food they share. As soon as I took my first bite of this flavorful salad, that love infused into me. In addition, it was one of the dishes that helped to get my family to start eating more salads with me. It is so similar to the dishes that we grew up on that they barely noticed they were eating raw food. I have learned to replicate many dishes that my family already enjoyed. I encour-age you to do the same. I haven't yet run across any cooked vegan dish that I couldn't make raw. Perhaps this will be a great idea for my next book . . . stay tuned!

DESSERT

Dessert tonight is Fully Raw Strawberry Shortcake. This is my most EPIC dessert! Who doesn't love strawberry shortcake? And many people find it even better than the original because it doesn't contain dairy, chemicals, or processed ingredients. You can make this from scratch in about 30 minutes and enjoy it immediately with a spoon. But if you want a cake that you can slice, you will need to put it in the freezer to firm for about 4 hours, so plan accordingly. The creamy strawberry filling is made with almond milk, frozen bananas, and cashews. If you want to reduce the fat in the filling, you can replace the coconut or cashews with frozen bananas. Just be aware that the banana crème will soften faster than the nut crème, so you will have to serve it within 10 minutes of removing it from the freezer; the nut version can thaw for 30 minutes without losing its shape. Have fun making the layers of this cake. It is truly a masterpiece, and it has *love* all over it.

EXERCISE

Participate in your favorite cardio class. Go *all* out! You made it to the end. Hopefully, this last day is the first day of your new beginning! Keep working out from here on. Consistency is key to getting the results that you want and discovering true health!

PART TWO

THE FULLY RAW KITCHEN

Shopping, Equipment, and Recipes

GETTING STARTED

Eating Fully Raw can be as simple or as complex as you wish it to be. You can go Fully Raw with nothing more than a sharp chopping knife and a cutting board, or you can load up your kitchen with tons of fun tools and gadgets. I lived through college eating Fully Raw on $60 a week with no blender, no kitchen, and only the girls' bathroom sink to wash my vegetables. I now have a "fully loaded" kitchen that allows me to be more creative and make extravagant dishes for my family and friends. Keep in mind that I didn't purchase all of these things at once. It has taken me years to truly build up my kitchen. Just like learning about this lifestyle, creating the perfect kitchen with tools is a process. I have learned to have fun with it and to enjoy each bite.

SHOPPING AND STORAGE TIPS

I always recommend that you first shop at local farmers' markets or co-operatives for fresh produce. This not only helps you to save money, but also supports your local farmers. It also ensures that you get the highest quality produce possible. Shop locally and seasonally; local, seasonal produce is more nutritious and higher in vitamins than produce that is shipped across the world or held in storage for long periods of time.

Learn how to store your produce properly to help it last the longest with the least amount of waste. I've been living Fully Raw for nine years now and I have lots of experience with ripening fruit, rotating produce in my fridge, and getting the most amount of flavor with the least waste. Here are my top six tips to help make your produce last just a little bit longer:

1. BAG YOUR GREENS TO KEEP THEM FRESH. To keep your greens from wilting, spray them with a little water and put them in plastic food storage bags. I use biodegradable bags and twist the tops to keep moisture in without locking out all of the air. This will make your greens last up to a week longer.

2. ROTATE YOUR FOOD. Fruits and vegetables are *real food:* They are perishable; they are not going to last forever. You need to use them or you're going to lose them. I pick up produce from my local co-op once or twice a week. I always put my older produce in the front of the fridge and the newer stuff in the back. This keeps me eating riper fruit first and encourages me to use my vegetables before they deteriorate.

3. STORE FRUITS AND VEGGIES SEPARATELY. Many fruits do better outside of the fridge, particularly sweet or tropical fruits like mangoes, persimmons, pomegranates, bananas, melons, and avocados. Those fruits need to be stored at room temperature to ripen properly. Tomatoes too! The flavor of tomatoes is killed by cold storage. Keep them on the counter and they will always taste amazing! More-perishable fruits and vegetables like berries, greens, cucumbers, bell peppers, cauliflower, and squashes need to be refrigerated. Put the stems of herb bunches in a jar of water, just like you would do with cut flowers; that way the stems can draw up the water and keep the leaves fresh and vibrant. If you are going to chop produce ahead of time, try to do it as close as possible to the time you are going to eat, and store it in tightly closed containers to keep it from drying out. Of course, it is always best to eat fresh produce as soon as it is cut or juiced, but we do the best we can. Always put cut food, smoothies, and juices near the top of the fridge where it is colder.

4. KEEP YOUR REFRIGERATOR AT 40°F. To make sure that your refrigerator is running efficiently, be careful not to block the air vents, and don't leave the door open any longer than needed. Keep more perishable food near the top. Air vents are on the top of the fridge, and the cold air flows from top to bottom. So things stored on the top shelf keep coldest. For instance, berries that are very perishable will last about a day longer on the top shelf than they will in the drawer at the bottom of the fridge.

5. PREPARE AS NEEDED. Fresh is always best. You are going to get the most nutrients and the least waste when you prepare as you go. You will have less spoilage when you prepare your food right before you eat it. Fruit is fast food. Eating raw can be as easy as peeling a banana or biting into an apple. If you want to prepare your meals the night before, that is okay. It will keep you from depending on less nutritious food that you might pick up on the go. Juices

and smoothies will begin to oxidize after a few hours, so it is best to consume those as soon as possible.

HOW DOES THE PRODUCE CRISPER IN YOUR FRIDGE WORK?

Crisp plant cells are packed with water. Most fruits and vegetables are at least 70 percent water, and for delicate leaves, like lettuces, losing as little as 5 percent moisture causes wilting. The crisper drawer in your refrigerator is designed to hold in moisture, but not too much, since water droplets lingering on the surface of vegetables can encourage rotting. To get just the right amount of moisture, crisper drawers are vented. By adjusting a lever or dial on the drawer, you control the amount of air and moisture flowing in and out. For vegetables, especially leafy vegetables, keep the vent a third to halfway open to ensure a moist environment and allow some ventilation. To lengthen the storage life of fully ripened fruit, keep the vent closed to minimize the amount of oxygen flowing into the compartment. It may sound strange, but ripe fruit breathes, taking in oxygen and respiring carbon dioxide. Closing the crisper vent slows down respiration and increases the storage life of ripe fruit.

6. TOSS YOUR TIRED PRODUCE. Raw produce does go bad, so do not worry if you lose a piece of fruit occasionally or find a rotten spot that needs to be cut off. That's okay. You can compost it and give it back to the earth. Real food is alive and it does not last forever. You want to eat your food when it has life so that it brings you life.

THE DIRTY DOZEN AND THE CLEAN FIFTEEN

ORGANIC PRODUCE IS PREFERABLE when you are eating Fully Raw, because the residues of pesticides, insecticides, and herbicides are greater in conventionally grown produce. The Environmental Working Group (a non-profit organization that monitors environmental issues) assembles a yearly report, called *The Dirty Dozen*, that lists the fruits and vegetables that show the highest residues of toxins. You should always buy organic when shopping for the following fruits and vegetables:

1. Apples
2. Celery
3. Cherry tomatoes
4. Cucumbers
5. Grapes
6. Nectarines
7. Peaches
8. Potatoes
9. Snap peas, imported
10. Spinach
11. Strawberries
12. Sweet bell peppers

On the other hand, the EWG has identified the following produce as *The Clean Fifteen*. It is relatively safe to buy these items grown conventionally, which can save you money:

1. Avocados
2. Asparagus
3. Cabbage
4. Cantaloupe
5. Cauliflower
6. Eggplant
7. Grapefruit
8. Kiwi
9. Mangoes
10. Onions
11. Papayas
12. Pineapple
13. Sweet corn
14. Sweet peas, frozen
15. Sweet potatoes

SELECTING THE RIGHT EQUIPMENT

People are always asking me what kind of equipment they will need to successfully live a Fully Raw life, and I tell them that it doesn't have to be particularly extravagant. I first started eating Fully Raw while living in a college dorm room, with just a knife and a cutting board. Over the last eight years I have collected many kitchen tools and gadgets and now have a fully equipped kitchen that allows me to be more creative. Here are some of my favorites:

GOOD KNIVES High-quality knives perform better and last longer. Even though good knives may be expensive, considering their life spans and the joy you will get working with them, they will cost less in the long run than budget knives. Japanese knives are my personal favorites, and I absolutely adore Shun knives. Made in Seki City, the home of samurai swords, Shun knives are comfortable to hold and miraculously maintain their edge. I probably sharpen mine about once a year, and they slice through any food like butter.

LARGE CUTTING BOARD Nothing is more frustrating than chopping a meal's worth of veggies on a tiny cutting board. Most of my boards are 20 by 15 inches, which I find ample. I prefer wooden boards, preferably a hard wood, like mango, for their look and feel, and because they cause less wear and tear on my knives. I know that some experts say that plastic cutting boards are safer to use, because they are harder and therefore do not absorb bacteria as readily, but a study done in 2009 at the University of California at Davis showed that wood tended to pull bacteria down below the surface of the cutting board, where they didn't multiply and eventually died. They found even old wooden boards with deep grooves had low bacteria levels. On the other hand, plastic boards were easily sterilized on their surfaces, but bacteria tended to stay in the grooves.

HIGH-SPEED BLENDER I love my Vitamix blender. I can make anything with this blender: juices, smoothies, dressings, pie fillings, even nut butters. High-speed blenders are much more powerful than standard blenders, powerful enough to break down the toughest vegetable fibers. Smoothies that contain fibrous leafy greens like kale and collards are made instantly smooth. I do not have a lot of experience with other brands, but high-speed blenders that get good reviews from my friends include top-of-the-line Blendtec, Breville, and Ninja models. These blenders also get high rankings in consumer comparison tests.

JUICER Although blenders and juicers both turn raw produce into smooth drinkable liquids, juicers filter out most of the fiber, yielding a beverage that is lighter, cleaner, and more concentrated. It is possible to make juice from very soft high-moisture fruits (like melons, tomatoes, and citrus) using a high-speed blender and a strainer, but for all other fruits and vegetables you will need some type of juicer.

There are two categories of juicers, and two types within each category. The one you chose depends on what you want to juice most often, how much you want to spend, and how much noise you can tolerate.

HIGH-SPEED JUICERS
Centrifugal Centrifugal juicers grind up produce, shredding the fiber and releasing the juice held within. The shreds and the juice are flung onto the sides of a straining basket spinning at a minimum of 3,000 rpm. The pulp is caught inside the basket and the juice is forced through the strainer in the same way that a washing machine rids damp clothes of water in the spin cycle. The juice comes out of a spout, leaving the pulp behind. Most centrifugal juicers can make about 2 quarts of juice before the basket needs to be cleaned. Centrifugal juicers are very good at juicing hard fruits and vegetables, like carrots, apples, celery, cucumbers, and beets. The downside: They are pretty loud and do not do a good job breaking down softer fruits and leafy greens. Two popular centrifugal juicers are the Omega 1000 and 9000 models.

Centrifugal ejection Like the centrifugal juicer, but with a slant-sided strainer basket that makes the basket self-cleaning, this juicer separates pulp from juice, sending the juice out one spout in the front and the pulp into a collection bin at the back. These juicers need to spin faster in order to eject the pulp, around 6,300 rpm. More efficient at extraction than regular centrifugal juicers, these machines also excel at juicing hard produce. Upside: the larger feed tube allows you to produce juice faster. Downside: these are the noisiest of all styles, and do not do well with soft fruit and greens. Popular models are the L'Equip 110.5 and the Omega Big Mouth.

SLOW JUICERS

Masticating Unlike high-speed juicers, which pulverize ingredients and spin at super speed in a centrifuge, masticating juicers chop the ingredient with a blade into small pieces, which are moved along a perforated cylinder by a rotating auger that crushes the produce and pushes it up against a screen, forcing out the juice. Masticating juicers work at much slower speeds, but they extract far more juice than centrifugal machines. Because of their slower speed, these do not oxidize the juice nearly as much as high-speed models, yielding better-tasting, more nutritious juice. Masticating juicers will juice everything except wheatgrass, they are relatively quiet, and very efficient. The downside: they're slow. Popular brands are Breville Juice Fountain, Omega 8004, Omega Vert, Hurom, and Champion.

Twin-gear press Produce is crushed with high force between two screws that turn against one another, forcing out its juice. These are the slowest type of juicers (90 rpm), and they cause the least amount of oxidation. They are efficient at juicing everything and are extremely quiet. They are also very expensive, and the feed tubes tend to be small. Popular brands are Green Power, Green Star, and Samson Ultra.

Personally, I prefer masticating machines. I use both an Omega Vert and a Hurom.

CITRUS JUICER Sometimes called a manual juicer, this juicer has a ridged reamer sized to fit inside a cut lemon, lime, or orange. Citrus juicers can be mechanized so that a motor turns the reamer as you simply press the cut citrus against it, or they can be hand operated.

FOOD PROCESSOR You don't really need one but you will find that a food processor makes some recipes, like pies or gazpacho, much easier. It works a lot like a blender but is better when you want some more texture in your finished product. I use Cuisinart.

MANDOLINE This slicing tool used to be found only in professional kitchens, but now low-cost options for home cooks are readily available. It is very helpful when you have to slice a lot of produce—apples for pie, or carrots, cucumbers, and radishes for a rainbow salad. A mandoline consists of two flat surfaces laid end to end, one of which holds a blade. You slide your vegetable along the non-blade surface towards the blade's edge. As the vegetable passes over the blade, a slice is taken off, which falls into the gap under the blade onto your work surface below. The blade side of a mandoline is adjustable, allowing you to make slices of different thicknesses.

SPIRAL SLICER This is a great tool for turning vegetables and fruit into noodles. There are two styles. The one I use has a cradle for holding the produce and a hand crank. A simpler and less expensive style is the cone spiral slicer, which is useful only with cylindrical vegetables, like zucchini, yellow squash, and cucumbers. You will need the larger hand-cranked model if you want to spiralize spherical produce, like apples or pears. (For more information, see How to Make Zucchini Noodles, page 201.)

STRAINER If you're going to make juice, you also want a good stainless steel strainer to remove traces of pulp that get through the juicer. No one likes bits of vegetable in their juice.

LARGE WOODEN BOWLS I serve and eat out of large wooden salad bowls. These hand- and machine-crafted bowls are all-natural and beautiful. No two are exactly alike, so each of mine really feels like it is *my personal bowl,* and when I eat out of it or serve with it, the meal feels special.

WOODEN UTENSILS I stopped using metal utensils years ago. I do not like the feel of them clinking against my teeth. I prefer wooden spoons and forks for all the same reasons I prefer wooden bowls. They are relatively inexpensive and last for years.

MASON JARS I prefer glass for food storage, and for drinking and storing flavored waters, juices, and smoothies. Glass is safe and doesn't react with the nutrients and acids in your juice. Mason jars come in a variety of sizes and have volume marks on the outside, making it easy to know exactly how much you are making and consuming.

A WORD ABOUT THE RECIPES

I love to prepare food, and I love to create recipes, but I must confess, I really don't *follow* recipes very often anymore. To me, recipes are maps. Like all maps, they tell you how to get somewhere. In the case of recipes, the destination is hopefully somewhere really healthy and delicious. As when using a map to travel somewhere for the first time, when you first prepare a dish, you have to follow the recipe (map) really closely. In fact, the first time through you usually pay closer attention to the recipe than to the food that is right in front of you. Once you've made something a few times, you don't need to look at the recipe as often or follow it as closely. And once you've made the dish a lot, you pretty much know how to get where you're going and you probably don't even look at the recipe anymore. That's mostly where I am.

Once a driving route is familiar, your map can serve as a guide to other local points of interest, or an alternate route. That's also what happens with recipes. The cool thing about knowing a recipe well is that it frees you up to experiment.

Usually my recipes are so forgiving that a little bit more or less of something doesn't matter. When your ingredients are pure and fresh and ripe, the results are still going to be delicious. You just might have a little bit less or more to eat. You will see in the recipes that follow that I often give multiple measures for each ingredient. For instance, I might call for 3 or 4 medium apples, and then tell you that number of apples equals about 2 pounds. I do this because you might find that your apples are smaller that day, or larger, and I want you to be able to adjust accordingly. Once you have made a juice, or smoothie, or salad a few times, you will automatically know how many apples to use and you won't need to be tied to the dishes.

I encourage you to get comfortable with substitutions. When the ingredients in my recipes are not available to you, try replacing them with something similar that is fresh and in season. I've stumbled across some really amazing recipes that way!

The kitchen techniques I use are very simple, and if any of them are unusual (like opening a young coconut, or making spiral-cut zucchini noodles), I give you specific directions on the pages near the recipe. Most of the techniques you will be using involve a knife. I use only common knife cuts and chopping techniques. If you are unfamiliar with knife cuts, here are the ones I use:

CHOP Cut in even-sized randomly shaped pieces, sometimes modified by a size indication, like finely or coarsely. *Finely chopped* means about ⅛-inch pieces. *Coarsely chopped* means about ½-inch pieces. Just plain *chopped* means something in between.

CHUNK Chop in large even-sized randomly shaped pieces. Usually ¾ inch or larger.

SLICE Cut in thin, broad pieces. If the thickness of the slice matters it is specified.

STRIPS Cut in thin, broad pieces that are longer than they are wide.

DICE Cut in small cubes. Start by making strips the width you want the dice to be. Cut the strips lengthwise the same thickness that you made the strips. Line the strips parallel to one another and cut across again in pieces that are the same thickness.

JULIENNE Cut in rods, like french fries. Start by making slices the width you want the julienne to be, then cut the slices the same thickness lengthwise into strips.

CHIFFONADE Cut in threads, usually done to leaves (of herbs and greens). Remove the tough center stem from the leaves. Stack a few leaves on top of each other and roll up lengthwise. You will have something that looks like a cigar. Hold the roll tightly closed and slice crosswise, as thinly as possible. As the rolled-up pieces are sliced, the roll will unfurl into dozens of skinny ribbons, called "chiffonades."

SHRED Run across the teeth of a shredder into tiny curls; can be coarse or fine.

RIBBONS AND BITS: WORKING WITH STURDY SALAD GREENS

Because all my dressings are made from pureed vegetables and fruit and are completely oil- and vinegar-free, they are as nutritious as any of the other ingredients in the salad. I want lots of dressing to cling to the salad ingredients. That means I want to expose the dressing to as many cut surfaces as possible, so I always slice my salad greens really well. I chop curly kale, frisée, and escarole into tiny bits. For flat leaves, like lacinato (dinosaur) kale, collards, chard, or bok choy, I use the classic slicing technique called chiffonade described above.

RECIPES

JUICES & SMOOTHIES

JUICES VS. SMOOTHIES: WHAT'S THE DIFFERENCE?

Fiber is the difference. Fiber, technically known as *cellulose*, is the main thing that gives the leaves and stems and roots and fruit of plants their form. Take their fiber away and fruits and vegetables are nothing more than, well, juice! Both juicers and blenders crush the fibers of fruits and vegetables, which liquefies them. The only difference is that juicers strain out the crushed fiber, giving you juice, and blenders leave it in, giving you smoothies.

Fiber is indigestible. When you eat a whole piece of fruit or vegetable, your teeth crush its fiber through chewing, exposing the nutritious tissue held between the fibers, which contains all of the vitamins and minerals and protein and carbs that the plant has to offer to your digestive system. Fiber itself cannot be broken down by the digestive enzymes in your stomach and intestines, and therefore has no nutritional value. Fiber does add bulk to your stools and helps you poop, but that's not really nutrition.

By eliminating all the fiber, juicing speeds up digestion, distributing the nutrients in the fruit and/or vegetable throughout your body more quickly. This is helpful if you have digestive problems or sensitive digestion, and when you are on a cleansing or healing program, because juice feeds your body on a cellular level more directly than any other form of eating. A word of warning: The speed at which the nutrients in juice are absorbed can cause a momentary spike in blood sugar if you are juicing fruits alone. This is great for a jolt of energy, but you should be aware that a rapid rise in blood sugar or unstable blood sugar can give you weird mood swings and plummeting energy loss in response to the sugar high.

Unlike juices, smoothies contain everything that is in the whole fruits and vegetables—their nutrients, their fiber, and sometimes even their skins and seeds. Because the fiber has been pulverized by a blender, it is much easier on your digestion than when the fruit or vegetable is eaten whole. As opposed to juice, a smoothie's fiber slows its movement through your digestive tract so the nutrients are absorbed more gradually. This allows a slow, even release of nutrients into your blood and regulates blood sugar levels. The fiber also makes smoothies more filling than juice; but cup for cup, juices are more concentrated, and therefore pack more nutrition into a serving than smoothies.

WHICH ONE IS BETTER?

Both juices and smoothies have benefits, so I don't believe that one is better than another. There is a time and place for each in your day-to-day diet.

I like to drink juices in the morning because they are lighter and digest more quickly and easily. They wake up my system, give me fuel after a good night's sleep, and hydrate me after "fasting" throughout the night. I drink juices if I do a juice fast/cleanse, or sometimes I will blend juices with seeds for my salad dressings. Also, if I feel like drinking something light, I tend to go for a juice.

I like to drink smoothies anytime I want something that will keep me full. I will sometimes have a smoothie for breakfast, but more often for lunch or dinner. I find for most people, drinking smoothies regularly helps them maintain a Fully Raw diet because it is a nearly effortless way to get a complete meal. We do need fiber for our bodies to function optimally.

JUICES VS. SMOOTHIES AT A GLANCE

JUICES (JUICING)	VS.	SMOOTHIES (BLENDING)
Made in a juicer.		Made in a blender.
Removes the pulp (fiber).		Retains the pulp (fiber).
A nutritionally concentrated food—all of the indigestible parts are removed.		A whole food—the entire food is pulverized into a drink.
Light and refreshing.		Thick and filling.
Better for cleansing and healing.		Better for sustaining an everyday healthy lifestyle.
Drains quickly from the stomach. Better to drink if you're not as hungry and want a concentrated source of nutrition.		Digests gradually. Keeps you fuller longer.
You cannot live on juices alone.		You could live on smoothies alone (though this is not recommended).
Gives you a rush of energy.		Delivers a steady flow of energy over several hours.
Quicker absorption of nutrients.		Gradual, even absorption of nutrients.
Undiluted fruit juices can spike your blood sugars if you are not careful or if you have blood sugar issues.		Ratio of fiber helps stabilize your blood sugar.
Cannot juice low-moisture fruits and veggies (i.e., bananas and dates) or nuts.		Can blend low-moisture ingredients, and add concentrated green powders. Some veggies are not as good for blending as they are for juicing (i.e., carrots and beets).
Good for tough fiber vegetables like carrots, beets, and celery.		Tough fibers do not blend completely, yielding gritty results.
Less cost efficient—takes more produce to make a serving.		Cost efficient—utilizing the whole fruit or vegetable means nothing is wasted.
More concentrated. You get more micro-nutrients per ounce of juice than you do in a smoothie. For example, you can juice 2 bunches of kale with 8 apples, half a pineapple, and 2 or 3 oranges for 32 ounces of juice that you can drink in one meal. Many people would find it difficult to eat those same ingredients blended into a smoothie because of the fiber.		Less concentrated; however, smoothies are a more complete meal made from whole foods. Many will argue that it is unnatural to juice since juicers did not exist 100 years ago, but that blending basically replicates the action of very thorough chewing and helps you better extract and absorb nutrients.

JUICING AND BLENDING CAVEATS

When you are juicing, don't get too stressed about rinsing everything or cutting it beforehand. The screen in the juicer will separate out any dirt along with excess fiber, and if you are using organic produce, which is always preferable, you don't need to worry about pesticides and herbicides.

Also, it isn't usually necessary to cut everything in tiny pieces unless you have a very challenged/older juicer. Newer juicers such as the Breville are designed so that you can throw in an entire romaine leaf or apple, and the machine can easily mow it down.

If you are juicing multiple types of vegetables and fruits, run roots such as ginger and beets through the juicer first so that the rest of the juices will wash down the flavor and zest of the roots. I also typically run greens through the juicer before fruit. That way the fruit juices wash down all of the green juice.

While green juices and smoothies are delicious and nutritious, you should aim to drink them as soon as possible after processing to avoid nutrient degradation. Slower juicing and minimal blending are best, because higher speeds introduce more oxygen and thus oxidation. Additionally, some important health benefits of leafy greens come only when mixed with specific bacteria in our mouths during chewing, so please don't think you can drink all your greens!

One last thing: *Be sure to "chew" your juices and smoothies*. Don't just gulp them down. Taste them, drink them slowly, and mix them with your saliva. Carbohydrate digestion starts in the mouth, and you want to be sure that you are absorbing all of the nutrients that you can.

INFUSED WATER: BASIC RECIPE

Makes about 1 quart (32 fluid ounces)

As everyone knows, drinking lots of water is an essential part of weight loss and maintenance. Although you can always drink your water unadulterated and plain, infusing cold water with sliced or juiced produce is my preferred way to take my daily dose. Slices of fruit and veggies not only give water a sweet and aromatic flavor, but also add vitamins and other nutrients.

Most of my infused waters contain some citrus juice for a positive alkalizing effect on bodily fluids. You can get the same effect by adding sliced citrus fruit or whole berries to the water. Unlike lemons and limes, you can't squeeze the juice out of a berry, so it takes some time for the flavor and nutrients from berries, or slices of pineapple or kiwi, to infuse the water. Whenever possible, I try to plan ahead and chill my morning water overnight to help bring out the flavors of the sliced and whole ingredients. Remember that you can always eat the fruit after you drink the water . . . it's the best part!

Use the chart of recipes and ingredients on page 98 as a quick reference anytime.

HERE'S WHAT YOU NEED:

Fruit (see chart)

Vegetables (see chart)

1 quart cold spring or filtered water

EQUIPMENT

Sharp chopping knife

Cutting board

32-ounce Mason jar or large glass for drinking, preferably chilled

HERE'S WHAT YOU DO:

Choose your combination of fruit and/or vegetables from the chart on page 98. Combine them with 1 quart cold water and chill overnight for fullest flavor, or drink after a brief resting period.

INFUSED WATER RECIPES AT A GLANCE

Add 1 quart of cold water to the indicated fruits and vegetables.

RECIPE	FRUIT	VEGGIES	METHOD
Berry	1 cup blueberries or blackberries 1 cup raspberries or sliced strawberries	None	Chill overnight
Berrylicious	1 to 2 cups mixed blackberries, blueberries, raspberries, and/or sliced strawberries 1 lemon, sliced or squeezed	None	Chill overnight
Blueberry Grape	1 cup blueberries 1 to 2 cups grapes	None	Drink immediately or chill overnight
Cucumber Blackberry Basil	1 cup blackberries	Large handful fresh basil 1 cucumber, sliced	Chill overnight
Cucumber Mint	None	1 cucumber, sliced Large handful fresh mint	Drink immediately or chill overnight
Lemon	3 lemons, sliced or squeezed	None	Drink immediately or chill overnight
Lemon Cucumber	1 to 2 lemons, sliced or squeezed	1 cucumber, sliced	Drink immediately or chill overnight
Lemon Grapefruit	1 lemon, sliced or squeezed 1 grapefruit, sliced or squeezed	None	Drink immediately or chill overnight
Lemon Rosemary	2 lemons, sliced or squeezed	Small handful fresh rosemary	Chill overnight
Lime	1 to 3 limes, sliced or squeezed	None	Drink immediately or chill overnight
Lime Berry	1 lime, sliced or squeezed 1 cup raspberries or sliced strawberries	None	Drink immediately or chill overnight

RECIPE	FRUIT	VEGGIES	METHOD
Orange Blueberry Kiwi	1 kiwi 1 cup blueberries 1 orange, sliced or squeezed	None	Chill overnight
Orange Kiwi Mint	2 oranges, sliced 1 kiwi, sliced	Small handful fresh mint	Drink immediately or chill overnight
Orange Lemon Refresh*Mint*	1 to 2 oranges, sliced or squeezed 1 lemon, sliced or squeezed	Small handful fresh mint	Drink immediately or chill overnight
Pineapple Cucumber Mint	1 cup sliced pineapple	Small handful fresh mint 1 cucumber, sliced	Drink immediately or chill overnight
Raspberry Blueberry Blackberry	1 to 2 cups mixed raspberries, blueberries, and blackberries	None	Chill overnight
Raspberry Cucumber Lime	1 cup raspberries 1 lime, sliced or squeezed	1 cucumber, sliced	Drink immediately or chill overnight
Strawberry Cucumber Basil	1 cup strawberries, sliced	1 cucumber, sliced Large handful fresh basil	Drink immediately or chill overnight
Strawberry Grapefruit	1 cup sliced strawberries ½ to 1 grapefruit, sliced	None	Chill overnight
Strawberry Lemon Rosemary	1 cup sliced strawberries 1 to 2 lemons, sliced or squeezed	1 small handful fresh rosemary	Chill overnight
Tangerine Blueberry	1 to 2 tangerines, sliced ½ to 1 cup blueberries	None	Chill overnight

THE INVINCIBLE HULK

Makes about 3 ½ cups (28 fluid ounces)

This big bad green boy is incredible! It's brimming with so much power it just might split your seams! Did you know that dark green leafy veggies are loaded with phytonutrients that are associated with cancer prevention? This recipe calls for a lot of different greens. If you don't have them all, it is fine to double up on some of the others.

HERE'S WHAT YOU NEED:

1 medium thumb (about 1 inch) fresh ginger

3 large romaine leaves

3 kale leaves, including stems, preferably lacinato (dinosaur) or curly kale

1 bunch (about 8 ounces) spinach leaves

Juice of 1 lemon (about 2 tablespoons)

10 sprigs fresh parsley or cilantro, leaves and stems

3 green apples (about 1 ½ pounds), peel, seeds, and all

4 celery stalks, with leaves if they have them

2 unwaxed cucumbers (about 20 ounces)

EQUIPMENT

Sharp chopping knife

Cutting board

Citrus juicer

Vegetable juicer, preferably a slow (masticating) model (see page 88)

32-ounce Mason jar or large glass for drinking, preferably chilled

HERE'S WHAT YOU DO:

Rinse all ingredients as needed. Cut them so they fit easily into the feed tube of your juicer.

Start by juicing the ginger, followed by the romaine, kale, and spinach. Juice the lemon next.

End by juicing the herbs, apples, celery, and cucumbers to help clean the ginger and leafy fibers out of the juicer.

Drink immediately, or refrigerate for up to 24 hours in a closed container.

How to Juice Lemons

To juice a lemon, you could just run it through your all-purpose juicer along with the other ingredients (cut off the peel first). Or use a handheld citrus juicer: Cut the lemon in half crosswise, then grind the cut sides against the cone of the juicer to extract the juice.

MY WATERMELON JUICE SECRET

Makes about 1 quart (32 fluid ounces)

What's my watermelon juice secret? In addition to watermelon being spectacularly hydrating and packed with nutrients, the secret to watermelon juice is that you barely have to juice it. Watermelon is so packed with juice and low in tough fibers that a second in the blender releases all of the goodness the fruit has to give. All you do to turn it into juice is pour it through a strainer into your drinking jar to separate the little bit of fiber that's in the liquid.

HERE'S WHAT YOU NEED:

½ medium watermelon

Large handful of fresh basil leaves

Large handful of fresh mint leaves

EQUIPMENT

Sharp chopping knife

Cutting board

High-speed blender, such as Vitamix

Strainer

32-ounce Mason jar or large glass for drinking, preferably chilled

HERE'S WHAT YOU DO:

Cut the rind off the watermelon, and cut the flesh into large chunks. Blend the watermelon flesh in the high-speed blender. Strain to remove any pulp. I typically strain twice to make sure it's super smooth.

Put the herbs in the jar and pour your watermelon juice over them.

Drink after steeping for 30 minutes or more. Or refrigerate for up to 24 hours in a tightly closed container. Shake before serving.

BEETLE JUICE

Makes about 3 ½ cups (28 fluid ounces)

Beet and apple are a committed couple ("Meet the Beetles!"). They complement one another in so many ways—flavor (earthy pyrazines in beets and tangy malic acid in apples), color (the deep down purple red of beets and the yellow/green/red striation of apple skins), nutrition (mineral-rich vegetables and vitamin-laden fruit). Everyone knows both are awesome alone, and together they can't be beet (sorry!). You get subtle differences in the flavor and pungency of the finished juice by changing up the varieties of apples. I've listed some of my favorites in the matchmaking chart below. Repeat after me: Beetle Juice! Beetle Juice!! Beetle Juice!!!

HERE'S WHAT YOU NEED:

2 small beets, including leaves and stems

2 large romaine leaves

3 to 4 apples (about 2 pounds), preferably Fuji, Stayman, Gala, or Honeycrisp, peel, seeds, and all

3 celery stalks, with leaves if they have them

EQUIPMENT

Cutting board

Sharp chopping knife

Vegetable juicer, preferably a slow (masticating) model (see page 88)

Strainer

32-ounce Mason jar or large glass for drinking, preferably chilled

HERE'S WHAT YOU DO:

Rinse all ingredients as needed. Cut them so that they fit easily into the feed tube of your juicer.

Run all ingredients through your juicer. Remove any remaining bits of fiber (which will look like foam) by pouring the juice through a wire strainer.

Drink immediately, or refrigerate for up to 24 hours in a tightly closed container.

Juicing Advice

It is best to run the softer juicy fruits through the juicer first and then the harder vegetables. Soft fruits tend to get stuck and create juice build-up. The vegetables then clear out the strainer and wipe away any fiber build up. This is especially true for older juicers such as the Green Star, Champion, or Omega.

Go Easy on the Beets

If you're new to using beets, go light on them. They're highly cleansing. The more greens you add, the stronger tasting your juice will be. Beets are naturally sweet and highly detoxifying. They are best juiced with apples, pineapples, oranges, and greens.

POPULAR APPLE VARIETIES

The number of apples you use depends on their size and how hungry you are. Any apple can be juiced. If you want your juice sweeter, choose more red apples. If you like it tart, go for green.

VARIETY	DESCRIPTION	SEASON
FUJI	Red with yellow spots to dark red; tend to be large, low acid and very sweet	Mid-August through December
PINK LADY	Pink blush with green or yellow background; crisp and tangy with mild sweetness	Late October through December
HONEYCRISP	Red with orange or yellow undercoat; nice balance of tart and sweet with a honeyed floral fragrance	Year-round
GRANNY SMITH	Large, green, tart, and fragrant	Year-round
BRAEBURN	Red and russeted with green and brown; fragrant, nice balance of sweet and tart	October through December

BEET CARROT GINGER JUICE

Makes about 3 ½ cups (28 fluid ounces)

Root vegetables are naturally sweet and packed with a lot more juice than you might expect. This spectacular color-rich, hearty juice is filled with flavor and a hefty helping of nutrition: 176 percent of the daily value for vitamin C and more than 45 times the daily value for vitamin A plus significant amounts of vitamin B1 (67 percent), vitamin B3 (72 percent), vitamin B6 (105 percent), manganese (140 percent), and potassium (149 percent). The ginger complements the sweetness of the juice with a spicy zip that wakes you up to the wonders of a new day!

HERE'S WHAT YOU NEED:

3 medium beets

3 pounds carrots

1 medium thumb (about 1 inch) fresh ginger

Juice of 1 lime (about 2 tablespoons)

EQUIPMENT

Sharp chopping knife

Cutting board

Citrus juicer

Vegetable juicer, preferably a slow (masticating) model (see page 88)

Strainer

32-ounce Mason jar or large glass for drinking, preferably chilled

HERE'S WHAT YOU DO:

Rinse all ingredients as needed. Cut them so that they fit easily into the feed tube of your juicer.

Run the beets, carrots, and ginger through your juicer. Remove any remaining bits of fiber (which will look like foam) by pouring the juice through a wire strainer. Mix in the lime juice.

Drink immediately, or refrigerate for up to 24 hours in a tightly closed container.

CARROT APPLE GINGER JUICE

Makes about 3 ½ cups (28 fluid ounces)

You will "fall" in love with this simple and delicious juice! Although most fruit is highly seasonal, apples, carrots, and ginger store exceptionally well, making seasonality less of an issue. In fact, if you live in a Northern climate or other regions that make it difficult to procure ripe fruit in season, this juice is your best friend. It is perfect to drink when chilly weather approaches, lending its warming spice to the changing winds. The ginger gives it a radiant heat that makes you feel all nice and warm inside.

HERE'S WHAT YOU NEED:

1 large thumb (about 2 inches) fresh ginger

3 apples (about 1 ½ pounds), preferably Honeycrisp or Pink Lady, peel, seeds, and all

1 pound carrots, including a few green tops if they have them

Juice of ½ lemon (about 2 tablespoons)

EQUIPMENT

Sharp chopping knife

Cutting board

Citrus juicer

Vegetable juicer, preferably a slow (masticating) model (see page 88)

Strainer

32-ounce Mason jar or large glass for drinking, preferably chilled

HERE'S WHAT YOU DO:

Rinse all ingredients as needed. Cut them so that they fit easily into the feed tube of your juicer.

Run all ingredients except the lemon juice through your juicer. Remove any remaining bits of fiber (which will look like foam) by pouring the juice through a wire strainer. Stir in the lemon juice.

Drink immediately, or refrigerate for up to 24 hours in a tightly closed container.

SUNBURST JUICE

Makes about 3 ½ cups (28 fluid ounces)

This vibrant juice is designed to make you *burst* with energy, goodness, and life! Its benefits are off the charts: It is high in bromelain (helps with protein digestion and inflammation), vitamin C and vitamin A (potent antioxidants), vitamin K (essential for blood coagulation) and . . . sparkle! A big glass of this juice in the morning helps with inflammatory conditions like arthritis, and with acne, indigestion, and migraines. It is a powerhouse of simple carbohydrates that keeps you energized. My special Sunburst Juice will bring sunshine into your life!

HERE'S WHAT YOU NEED:

3 kale leaves, preferably lacinato (dinosaur) or curly kale, including stems

3 apples (about 1 ½ pounds), peel, seeds, and all

½ large pineapple (about 1 pound), leaves and rind removed (see page 136)

Juice of 3 juice oranges

Juice of 1 lime (about 2 tablespoons)

EQUIPMENT

Sharp chopping knife

Cutting board

Citrus juicer

Vegetable juicer, preferably a slow (masticating) model (see page 88)

Strainer

32-ounce Mason jar or large glass for drinking, preferably chilled

HERE'S WHAT YOU DO:

Rinse all ingredients as needed. Cut them so that they fit easily into the feed tube of your juicer.

Run all ingredients except the citrus juices through your juicer. Remove any remaining bits of fiber (which will look like foam) by pouring the juice through a wire strainer. Stir in the citrus juices.

Drink immediately, or refrigerate for up to 24 hours in a tightly closed container.

Juice Your Pineapple Last

Pineapples are exceptionally high in fiber that can clog up your juicer, so it is important to juice the pineapple last.

Pineapple Tip: Maximize Sweetness

Pineapples are delicious, but only if they're evenly ripe. A trick that I use to maximize a pineapple's sweetness is to let it sit on the kitchen counter for 1 to 2 days, then twist off the top, flip the pineapple upside down, and place it in the refrigerator for another 2 days. This allows all of the ripe sugary juices from the bottom to make their way to the top of the fruit and turn the fruit completely sweet. If you get mouth irritation from pineapple, combine it with other fruit, which will dilute the bromelain, a protein-digesting enzyme in fresh pineapple.

MY SECRET SOULSHINE JUICE

Makes about 3 ½ cups (28 fluid ounces)

This delicious blend of tart sweet apples and rich nutritious kale is amazingly refreshing and filling. The main ingredients are supported by a bright spark of citrus and a savory sodium kick from the celery and cucumber. Just take a sip and feel your soul begin to shine!

HERE'S WHAT YOU NEED:

½ head romaine

Leaves from 1 bunch lacinato (dinosaur) or curly kale, including stems

6 apples, preferably Honeycrisp or Pink Lady (about 3 pounds), peel, seeds, and all

6 celery stalks

1 unwaxed cucumber (about 10 ounces)

Juice of 2 lemons or 4 limes (about ½ cup)

EQUIPMENT

Sharp chopping knife

Cutting board

Citrus juicer

Vegetable juicer, preferably a slow (masticating) model (see page 88)

Strainer

32-ounce Mason jar or large glass for drinking, preferably chilled

HERE'S WHAT YOU DO:

Rinse all ingredients as needed. Cut them so that they fit easily into the feed tube of your juicer.

Run all ingredients except the lemon juice through your juicer. Remove any remaining bits of fiber (which will look like foam) by pouring the juice through a wire strainer. Stir in the lemon juice.

Drink immediately, or refrigerate for up to 24 hours in a tightly closed container.

LEMON GINGER BLAST

Makes about 3 ½ cups (28 fluid ounces)

This juice is a health tonic with a BLAST of antioxidants . . . AKA the *real* flu shot. If I am feeling under the weather, this is my immediate go-to juice to quickly get back up and running! The recipe calls for a lot of different greens; if you don't have them all, it is fine to double up on some of the others.

HERE'S WHAT YOU NEED:

1 large thumb (about 3 inches) fresh ginger

1 bunch cilantro (about 3 ounces), leaves and stems

½ head romaine

4 kale leaves, preferably lacinato (dinosaur) or curly kale, including stems

6 sprigs fresh flat-leaf (Italian) parsley

4 celery stalks

1 unwaxed cucumber (about 10 ounces)

Juice of 1 ½ lemons (about 6 tablespoons)

EQUIPMENT

Sharp chopping knife

Cutting board

Citrus juicer

Vegetable juicer, preferably a slow (masticating) model (see page 88)

Strainer

32-ounce Mason jar or large glass for drinking, preferably chilled

HERE'S WHAT YOU DO:

Rinse all ingredients as needed. Cut them so that they fit easily into the feed tube of your juicer.

Run all ingredients except the lemon juice through your juicer. Remove any remaining bits of fiber (which will look like foam) by pouring the juice through a wire strainer. Stir in the lemon juice.

Drink immediately, or refrigerate for up to 24 hours in a tightly closed container.

How Can You Tell if Your Citrus Is Ripe?

You can tell when lemons, limes, oranges, or grapefruit are ripe by the thinness of their skins. Pinch the fruit between your thumb and first finger, and you should be able to feel the resiliency of the fruit under the skin. Citrus doesn't ripen as well after it has been picked off the tree. Quality fruit is allowed to sit on the tree until it is fully ripe, which is when it will be easier to digest, have more nutrients, and taste even sweeter and more incredible!

SWEET POTATO PIE JUICE

Makes about 3 ½ cups (28 fluid ounces)

This juice is fabulous for helping to balance hormones—for both women and men. A single sweet potato contains 369 percent of the daily value for vitamin A, 5 percent of vitamin C, 13 percent of potassium, and 8 percent of magnesium. It also contains 2 grams of protein, which means this recipe will give you about 4 percent of your daily value for protein. The sweet potatoes' starch and fiber tend to clog the juicer, which is why I recommend juicing them near the end.

HERE'S WHAT YOU NEED:

4 large pears or medium apples (about 2 pounds), peel, seeds, and all

2 medium orange-fleshed sweet potatoes (about 1 ½ pounds)

1 medium thumb (about 1 inch) fresh ginger (optional)

Juice of 1 lemon (about ¼ cup)

EQUIPMENT

Sharp chopping knife

Cutting board

Citrus juicer

Vegetable juicer, preferably a slow (masticating) model (see page 88)

Strainer

32-ounce Mason jar or large glass for drinking, preferably chilled

HERE'S WHAT YOU DO:

Rinse all ingredients as needed. Cut them so that they fit easily into the feed tube of your juicer.

Run all ingredients except the lemon juice through your juicer. Remove any remaining bits of fiber (which will look like foam) by pouring the juice through a wire strainer. Stir in the lemon juice.

Drink immediately, or refrigerate for up to 24 hours in a tightly closed container.

FULLY RAW VEGGILICIOUS JUICE

Makes about 3 ½ cups (28 fluid ounces)

Still drinking packaged juices? What if I told you that even bottled juices such as V8 have artificial flavors and chemicals that are detrimental to your body? But not mine! This eight-vegetable juice is pure, delicious, and more nutritious than the packaged stuff. If you are used to commercial vegetable juices that are loaded with pulp, you will find my version far more refreshing, but still hearty enough to fill you up. A large serving is a complete meal, providing many of your daily nutrients.

HERE'S WHAT YOU NEED:

1 medium beet

Large handful of baby spinach leaves

8 sprigs fresh flat-leaf (Italian) parsley

3 large romaine leaves

8 sprigs watercress

2 large ripe tomatoes (about 1 ½ pounds), stems removed

2 celery stalks

2 large carrots (about 5 ounces), with tops if possible

EQUIPMENT

Sharp chopping knife

Cutting board

Vegetable juicer, preferably a slow (masticating) model (see page 88)

Strainer

32-ounce Mason jar or large glass for drinking, preferably chilled

HERE'S WHAT YOU DO:

Rinse all ingredients as needed. Cut them so that they fit easily into the feed tube of your juicer.

Run all ingredients through your juicer. Remove any remaining bits of fiber (which will look like foam) by pouring the juice through a wire strainer.

Drink immediately, or refrigerate for up to 24 hours in a tightly closed container.

COTTON CANDY JUICE!

Makes about 3 ½ cups (28 fluid ounces)

This juice is a crowd pleaser. I serve it at my food co-op in Houston, and sell it under the brand FullyRaw Juice, my raw juice company. Its natural sweetness and beautiful candy pink color give it its name. But don't let its sweetness fool you. This juice has potent nutrition.

HERE'S WHAT YOU NEED:

1 medium thumb (about 1 inch) fresh ginger

1 small slice red beet

2 to 3 apples (about 1 pound), preferably Honeycrisp, peel, seeds, and all

½ pineapple (about 12 ounces), leaves and rind removed (see page 136)

EQUIPMENT

Sharp chopping knife

Cutting board

Vegetable juicer, preferably a slow (masticating) model (see page 88)

Strainer

32-ounce Mason jar or large glass for drinking, preferably chilled

HERE'S WHAT YOU DO:

Rinse all ingredients as needed. Cut them so that they fit easily into the feed tube of your juicer.

Run all ingredients through your juicer. Remove any remaining bits of fiber (which will look like foam) by pouring the juice through a wire strainer.

Drink immediately, or refrigerate for up to 24 hours in a tightly closed container.

Picking the Perfect Pineapple

Pineapples don't ripen (increase in sweetness) once they are picked, and fully ripe pineapples are too juicy and perishable to ship without bruising. For that reason, most pineapples are ripened most of the way on the tree and then air-shipped from the tropics. Buying a fully green pineapple is not advised. The bottom is the ripest part. So the higher the golden color advances up the rind, the more evenly the fruit inside will be flavored. Golden color and a pleasant pineapple aroma coming from the base are the best ways to judge ripeness. The ease with which a leaf can be pulled from the top proves nothing about ripeness, despite the enduring popularity of the practice.

CUCUMBER GRAPE JUICE

Makes about 3 ½ cups (28 fluid ounces)

There are three juices that I make with grapes, and this is my favorite. Real grape juice is amazingly sweet and clean tasting. Its benefits include increased energy, improved digestion, and stress relief. Because of its unabashed natural fruitiness, grape juice is stellar as a complement to green vegetables, like cucumber, that have an assertive chlorophyll flavor. Cucumber balances the grape with a light savory quality that creates a smooth drink.

HERE'S WHAT YOU NEED:

2 pounds seedless grapes, large branches removed

3 unwaxed cucumbers (about 30 ounces)

EQUIPMENT

Sharp chopping knife

Cutting board

Vegetable juicer, preferably a slow (masticating) model (see page 88)

Strainer

32-ounce Mason jar or large glass for drinking, preferably chilled

HERE'S WHAT YOU DO:

Rinse the cucumbers and grapes. Cut the cucumbers so that they fit easily into the feed tube of your juicer.

Run the grapes and then the cucumbers through your juicer. Remove any remaining bits of fiber (which will look like foam) by pouring the juice through a wire strainer.

Drink immediately, or refrigerate for up to 24 hours in a tightly closed container.

REFRESH*MINT* JUICE

Makes about 3 ½ cups (28 fluid ounces)

Cool, crisp, refreshing, hydrating, and a special treat to share with family and friends: I love this juice because it can be drunk as a nutritious meal or as a non-alcoholic version of a mojito. It is absolutely gorgeous, and the sweetest green juice you will ever taste. Serve it for any special occasion, and people will love it!

HERE'S WHAT YOU NEED:

4 romaine leaves

1 large bunch (2 ounces) fresh mint

4 green apples (about 2 pounds), peel, seeds, and all

1 honeydew melon, peel and seeds removed

1 unwaxed cucumber (about 10 ounces)

Juice of 1 lemon (about ¼ cup)

EQUIPMENT

Sharp chopping knife

Cutting board

Citrus juicer

Vegetable juicer, preferably a slow (masticating) model (see page 88)

Strainer

32-ounce Mason jar or large glass for drinking, preferably chilled

HERE'S WHAT YOU DO:

Rinse all ingredients as needed. Cut them so that they fit easily into the feed tube of your juicer.

Run all ingredients except the lemon juice through your juicer. Remove any remaining bits of fiber (which will look like foam) by pouring the juice through a wire strainer. Stir in the lemon juice.

Drink immediately, or refrigerate for up to 24 hours in a tightly closed container.

THE HOLY GRALE

Makes about 3 ½ cups (28 fluid ounces)

This two-ingredient recipe comes straight from heaven. It's just grapes plus kale ("Grale"—get it?). It is sweet and refreshing and mighty nutritious. Because the juicer eliminates all pulp and debris, it is fine to throw in the whole bunch of grapes—stems, branches, seeds, and all. Adding a few leaves of kale to any fruit juice boosts the nutrition ante heartily. Just four large kale leaves deliver about 453 percent of your daily vitamin A, 454 percent of your vitamin C, and a whopping 1,998 percent of vitamin K, plus significant amounts of your needed minerals, including calcium (34 percent), copper (170 percent), iron (18 percent), magnesium (27 percent), phosphorus (21 percent), and potassium (32 percent) . . . all for a mere 111 calories and just 2 grams of fat.

HERE'S WHAT YOU NEED:

4 large kale leaves, preferably lacinato (dinosaur) or curly kale, including stems

2 pounds seedless grapes, large branches removed

EQUIPMENT

Sharp chopping knife

Cutting board

Vegetable juicer, preferably a slow (masticating) model (see page 88)

Strainer

32-ounce Mason jar or large glass for drinking, preferably chilled

HERE'S WHAT YOU DO:

Rinse the kale and grapes. Cut the grape clusters and kale so that they fit easily into the feed tube of your juicer.

Run the kale and grapes through your juicer. Remove any remaining bits of fiber (which will look like foam) by pouring the juice through a wire strainer.

Drink immediately, or refrigerate for up to 24 hours in a tightly closed container.

FULLY RAW JUNGLE JUICE

Makes about 1 quart (32 fluid ounces)

Fully ripe fresh fruit is nature's candy, and this juice tastes like candy in a jar! Not only is it sweet, but it is incredible good for you. Resveratrol, a micronutrient in grape skins, has shown to be important in the expression of genes responsible for longevity. Both tangelos and grapes are significant sources of vitamin C, which has been shown to reduce inflammation and boost the immune system. Cilantro and kale both contain antioxidants (retinol and carotenes) that help protect against malignancies. Because this juice is also high in B vitamins, it has the power to relieve a substantial amount of stress held in your body.

HERE'S WHAT YOU NEED:

1 pound seedless green, red, and/or black grapes, stems removed

Juice of 4 or 5 tangelos (or the juice of 6 tangerines or 4 oranges), depending on size

½ bunch cilantro (about 1 ½ ounces), leaves and stems

5 apples (about 2 ½ pounds), preferably Honeycrisp or Fuji, peel, seeds, and all

3 to 4 large leaves lacinato (dinosaur) or curly kale, including stems

½ pineapple, leaves and rind removed (see page 136)

Juice of 1 lime (about 2 tablespoons)

EQUIPMENT

Sharp chopping knife

Cutting board

Citrus juicer

Vegetable juicer, preferably a slow (masticating) model (see page 88)

32-ounce Mason jar or large glass for drinking, preferably chilled

HERE'S WHAT YOU DO:

Rinse all ingredients as needed. Cut them so that they fit easily into the feed tube of your juicer.

Run all ingredients except the lime juice through your juicer. Strain to remove any pulp. Stir in the lime juice.

Drink immediately, or refrigerate for up to 24 hours in a tightly closed container.

THE GLOW STICK

Makes about 3 ½ cups (28 fluid ounces)

This recipe provides nutrients that give your skin that *glow!!!* Plus it contains antioxidants that help protect your skin when you're in the sun. Sweet and clean, the Glow Stick assists you with weight loss, hydration, and detoxification. Did I already mention it gives you beautiful skin?

HERE'S WHAT YOU NEED:

1 ½ pounds carrots

1 small thumb (about ½ inch) fresh ginger, cut in chunks

2 apples (about 1 pound), peel, seeds, and all (optional)

Juice of 5 oranges or 7 tangelos

EQUIPMENT

Sharp chopping knife

Cutting board

Citrus juicer

Vegetable juicer, preferably a slow (masticating) model (see page 88)

Strainer

32-ounce Mason jar or large glass for drinking, preferably chilled

HERE'S WHAT YOU DO:

Rinse all ingredients as needed. Cut them so that they fit easily into the feed tube of your juicer.

Run all ingredients except the orange juice through your juicer. Remove any remaining bits of fiber (which will look like foam) by pouring the juice through a wire strainer. Stir in the orange juice.

Drink immediately, or refrigerate for up to 24 hours in a tightly closed container.

BUGS BUNNY JUICE

Makes about 3 ½ cups (28 fluid ounces)

When people mock raw food dishes by calling them rabbit food, this recipe is what they are talking about. It has all the awesome nutrition of a sun-drenched vegetable patch—the perfect blend of vitamins and minerals, a ton of energy, and just the right amount of protein. Did you ever wonder why Bugs Bunny is always outsmarting and outrunning that gun-toting wabbit-hunting meat-eating Elmer Fudd? Maybe it's what he's eating!

HERE'S WHAT YOU NEED:

5 green apples (about 2 ½ pounds), peel, seeds, and all

3 romaine leaves

½ bunch (4 ounces) spinach, leaves and stems

3 celery stalks

2 pounds carrots

Juice of 1 lemon (about ¼ cup)

EQUIPMENT

Sharp chopping knife

Cutting board

Citrus juicer

Vegetable juicer, preferably a slow (masticating) model (see page 88)

Strainer

32-ounce Mason jar or large glass for drinking, preferably chilled

HERE'S WHAT YOU DO:

Rinse all ingredients as needed. Cut them so that they fit easily into the feed tube of your juicer.

Run all ingredients except the lemon juice through your juicer. Remove any remaining bits of fiber (which will look like foam) by pouring the juice through a wire strainer. Stir in the lemon juice.

Drink immediately, or refrigerate for up to 24 hours in a tightly closed container.

SMOOTHIE: BASIC RECIPE

Makes 1 quart (32 fluid ounces)

The chart that follows on page 124 contains more than 20 variations to this basic recipe, and the variations are also written out in recipe form. Each smoothie is unique and awesome, but they are all made pretty much the same way: Discard big fruit pits and stems (little seeds like apple seeds can go right in the blender; they will get blended up like everything else), chop your ingredients into chunks (they can be fairly large; 2 to 3 inches across is fine), and add to the blender. Then cap and turn on the blender (I give detailed blending instructions in each recipe). That's it!

HERE'S WHAT YOU NEED:

About 2 quarts chopped fruits and veggies
    (see chart, page 124)

Other flavoring ingredients (optional; see chart)

EQUIPMENT

Sharp chopping knife

Cutting board

Citrus juicer, if needed

High-speed blender, such as Vitamix

32-ounce Mason jar or large glass for drinking,
    preferably chilled

HERE'S WHAT YOU DO:

Have all of your ingredients well chilled.

Put all ingredients in the blender and blend until smooth, starting on the slowest speed and gradually working up to the fastest. Blend on the highest speed until the mixture is uniformly smooth and the sound of the blender is moderately high pitched and steady.

Reduce the speed of the blender to the lowest setting before turning it off.

Drink immediately, or refrigerate for up to 4 hours in a tightly closed container. Shake before serving.

SMOOTHIE RECIPES AT A GLANCE

Use this table as a quick reference for making a smoothie. Detailed recipes are given in the following pages.

SMOOTHIE RECIPE	FRUITS	VEGGIES	OTHER
Antioxidant Power	¾ pound cherries, stemmed and pitted 4 nectarines, pitted 1 pint blueberries	None	None
Banana Blackberry Basil	4 bananas, peeled 1 pint blackberries	6 fresh basil leaves	None
Banana Celery	7 bananas, peeled	3 celery stalks Spinach (optional)	None
Banana Granny	3 to 4 bananas, peeled 1 to 2 Granny Smith apples, cored	2 to 3 celery stalks Spinach (optional)	None
Bananatarine	3 to 4 bananas, peeled 3 to 4 nectarines, pitted	None	None
Cantaloupe Honeydew	½ honeydew, peeled and seeded ½ cantaloupe, peeled and seeded	None	None
Cantaloupe Mint Sorbet	1 cantaloupe, peeled, seeded, and frozen 2 limes, juiced Blueberries, for garnish	6 fresh mint sprigs	None
Cherry Nectarine Delight	1 cup seedless grapes ¾ pound cherries, pitted 4 nectarines, pitted	None	None
Coconut Banana	5 to 6 bananas, peeled	None	Seeds from ½ vanilla bean ¼ teaspoon cinnamon 1 cup coconut water
Collard Orange Pineapple	6 oranges, juiced ½ pineapple, peeled and cored	2 to 3 collard leaves, stems removed	None
Cucumber Melon	½ honeydew, peeled and seeded	1 cucumber	None
Granny Eat Your Strawberries!	2 to 3 Granny Smith apples, cored 10 to 12 strawberries, greens removed	1 head butter lettuce	None

SMOOTHIE RECIPE	FRUITS	VEGGIES	OTHER
Hide-the-Spinach Tropical	1 cored pineapple ring ½ orange, peeled and seeded ½ to 1 cup frozen blueberries ½ Granny Smith apple, cored 1 banana, peeled and frozen	1 cup spinach 4 to 5 fresh mint leaves	None
Honey Dew Be Mine	1 honeydew, peeled and seeded	None	None
Honeydew Grape	½ honeydew, peeled and seeded 2 cups seedless green grapes	None	None
Honeydew Nectarine	½ honeydew, peeled and seeded 3 nectarines, pitted	None	None
Kale Granny	2 to 3 Granny Smith apples, cored	3 kale leaves, stems removed	up to ¼ cup water
Orange Spinach Basil	6 oranges, juiced	6 ounces spinach leaves 6 fresh basil leaves	None
Pineapple Honeydew	½ honeydew, peeled and seeded ½ large pineapple, peeled and cored	None	None
Super Sweet Pink	½ pineapple, peeled and cored 2 to 3 blood oranges, peeled and seeded 2 cups strawberries, with greens	None	2 to 3 cups coconut water
Tart Start	1 grapefruit, peeled 1 Granny Smith apple, cored 1 banana, peeled and frozen	8 kale leaves, stems removed 4 to 5 fresh mint leaves	None
Totally Tropical	2 mangoes, peeled and pitted ¼ pineapple, peeled and cored 3 bananas, peeled	2 to 3 kale leaves, stems removed	1 cup coconut water
Tropical Cherry	½ pound cherries, stemmed and pitted ½ pineapple, peeled and cored	None	None

SOUR PUNCH SMOOTHIES

Makes about 1 quart (32 fluid ounces)

Granny Smiths are a raw fooder's go-to apple. They're available all year-round, and of all the common apple varieties they're the highest in antioxidants, especially when you eat the whole fruit. They also have the perfect balance of sweet and tart—a sour punch that fights for health! Here are five awesome Granny Smith smoothie recipes. Drink up, and don't forget to thank Granny!

HERE'S WHAT YOU NEED:

TART START

1 large ruby red grapefruit, peeled

8 lacinato (dinosaur) or curly kale leaves, rinsed, tough stems removed

4 to 5 fresh mint leaves

1 Granny Smith apple (about ½ pound), cored and cut in chunks

1 banana, peeled and frozen firm, cut in chunks

HIDE-THE-SPINACH TROPICAL SMOOTHIE

1 ring fresh pineapple (1 inch thick), cored and rind removed

½ orange, peeled, seeded, and cut in chunks

1 cup spinach, rinsed

½ to 1 cup frozen wild blueberries

4 to 5 fresh mint leaves

½ Granny Smith apple, cored and cut in chunks

1 banana, peeled and frozen firm, cut in chunks

BANANA GRANNY SMOOTHIE

3 to 4 bananas, peeled, frozen if desired, and cut into chunks

1 to 2 Granny Smith apples, cored and cut in chunks

2 to 3 celery stalks, with leaves if they have them, cut in chunks

Spinach, as desired (optional, for added creaminess!)

KALE GRANNY SMOOTHIE

2 to 3 Granny Smith apples, cored and cut in chunks

3 large lacinato (dinosaur) or curly kale leaves, rinsed, tough stems removed

A bit of water (no more than ¼ cup)

GRANNY EAT YOUR STRAWBERRIES!

2 to 3 Granny Smith apples (about 1 ½ pounds), cored and cut in chunks

10 to 12 strawberries, greens removed

1 head butter lettuce, rinsed

EQUIPMENT

Sharp chopping knife

Cutting board

Citrus juicer, if needed

High-speed blender, such as Vitamix

32-ounce Mason jar or large glass for drinking,
    preferably chilled

HERE'S WHAT YOU DO:

Have all of your ingredients well chilled.

Put all ingredients in the blender and blend until
smooth, starting on the slowest speed and gradually working up to the fastest. Blend on the highest
speed until the mixture is uniformly smooth and the
sound of the blender is high pitched and steady.

Reduce the speed of the blender to the lowest setting
before turning it off.

Drink immediately, or refrigerate for up to 4 hours
in a tightly closed container. Shake before serving.

Granny Trivia

Granny Smith apples were first cultivated
by accident in Australia in the mid-19th
century, and are now grown extensively
in both the Southern and Northern hemi-
spheres. Since the hemispheric growing
and harvesting seasons complement one
another (harvest in the north is in the fall
and in the south is in the spring), fresh
Granny Smiths are available year-round,
although they are not always local.

Eating Apple Seeds

I know some of you are concerned that
apple seeds contain cyanide. True, but the
amount is so small that it is not harmful. In
fact, research has shown that the amount
of cyanide in apple seeds may be healthful
due to its immunological effect!

SUPER SWEET PINK SMOOTHIE

Makes about 1 quart (32 fluid ounces)

This smoothie is a *love bomb!* Whether you are on the go, coming back from a workout, or simply just enjoying the day, this amazing elixir is one of the easiest and most delicious smoothies you can make. It's fun and fast, and it's filled with electrolytes and simple sugars to keep you fueled and smiling. Not to mention that its warm sunset hues croon "love!" Whether it is because of how much you love this smoothie or how good you will feel after you drink it, I know that you will cherish it! Calories: 450; Cost: $6; Benefits: endless!

HERE'S WHAT YOU NEED:

2 to 3 cups (depending on desired thickness) fresh young coconut water (from 2 to 3 young coconuts, see page 35), or store-bought raw coconut water

½ pineapple (about 12 ounces), leaves and rind removed, cored and cut in chunks (see page 136)

2 to 3 blood oranges (or juice oranges), peeled, seeded, and cut in chunks

2 cups fresh strawberries, with greens

EQUIPMENT

Sharp chopping knife

Cutting board

High-speed blender, such as Vitamix

32-ounce Mason jar or large glass for drinking, preferably chilled

HERE'S WHAT YOU DO:

Have all of your ingredients well chilled.

Put all ingredients in the blender and blend until smooth, starting on the slowest speed and gradually working up to the fastest. Blend on the highest speed until the mixture is uniformly smooth and the sound of the blender is high pitched and steady.

Reduce the speed of the blender to the lowest setting before turning it off.

Drink immediately, or refrigerate for up to 4 hours in a tightly closed container. Shake before serving.

The Magic of Strawberry Greens

I never remove the greens from strawberries, provided they are fresh and firm. Strawberry leaf is said to relieve gastrointestinal problems and joint pain.

COLLARD ORANGE PINEAPPLE SMOOTHIE

Makes about 1 quart (32 fluid ounces)

Here is another cool way to use greens! I know you are used to adding a few kale leaves to your smoothies for extra nutrition (gotta love that boost of minerals), but I bet you have never thought of trying collard greens in a smoothie before. You'll be *amazed* at this quick, hearty, and delicious treat, but you really shouldn't be surprised. Kale and collard are vegetal cousins. They both are members of the Brassicaceae family, better known as the cabbage family, and they have very similar flavors and nutritional content. Throw them in the blender with some fruit and be amazed at how creamy and delicious this blend can taste. ***Note:*** You need a very strong blender like a Vitamix for the collards; otherwise, the blend may come out somewhat chewy!

HERE'S WHAT YOU NEED:

2 to 3 collard leaves, tough stems removed, coarsely chopped (about 3 cups; or substitute 4 kale leaves, 2 celery stalks, ½ head romaine, or 2 cups spinach)

Juice of 6 juice oranges (about 2 cups)

½ large pineapple (about 1 pound), leaves and rind removed, cored and cut in chunks (see page 136)

EQUIPMENT

Sharp chopping knife

Cutting board

Citrus juicer

High-speed blender, such as Vitamix

32-ounce Mason jar or large glass for drinking, preferably chilled

HERE'S WHAT YOU DO:

Have all of your ingredients well chilled.

Put all ingredients in the blender and blend until smooth, starting on the slowest speed and gradually working up to the fastest. Blend on the highest speed until the mixture is uniformly smooth and the sound of the blender is high pitched and steady.

Reduce the speed of the blender to the lowest setting before turning it off.

Drink immediately, or refrigerate for up to 4 hours in a tightly closed container. Shake before serving.

VARIATION

ORANGE SPINACH BASIL SMOOTHIE

Follow the preceding recipe, using 6 ounces spinach leaves (about 3 packed cups) and 6 basil leaves instead of the collards; eliminate the pineapple.

CANTALOUPE MINT SORBET SMOOTHIE

Makes about 1 quart (32 fluid ounces)

This fruity minty cooler is guaranteed to chill you out! The proper consistency for the perfect smoothie is somewhere between liquid and solid. This one leans toward the solid side, which is why I call it a sorbet smoothie—sort of like a bowl of sherbet and sort of like a shake. It's perfect when the weather is uber hot and you long for some edible air conditioning. Be sure to wait until your cantaloupe is soft at the end and smells potent; the taste will be significantly sweeter.

HERE'S WHAT YOU NEED:

1 ripe cantaloupe (about 2 pounds), peeled, seeds and pulp removed, frozen, and cut in chunks

Leaves from 6 fresh mint sprigs

Juice of 2 limes (about ¼ cup)

Blueberries and more mint sprigs, for garnish

EQUIPMENT

Sharp chopping knife

Cutting board

Food processor

Rubber spatula

Large bowl and spoon

HERE'S WHAT YOU DO:

Put the cut-up cantaloupe in a gallon-size sealable bag and freeze until the chunks are solid, at least 2 hours.

Pulse the frozen melon chunks with the mint and lime juice in a food processor until the mixture is finely chopped. Run the processor (without pulsing) for 10 to 30 seconds more, until the sound of the processor is even. You shouldn't hear any clicking, which indicates that there are still some larger chunks.

Scoop the sorbet smoothie into a bowl or jar with a spatula and top with a few more mint sprigs and a few blueberries. Best savored in the sun!

Cleaning a Cantaloupe

When your cantaloupe is ripe, trim off the rind, getting as close to the flesh as you can but without leaving any green. Cut the melon in half, scoop out the seeds and pulp from the center, and discard. Cut the flesh into small (about 1-inch) chunks.

BANANA BLISS SMOOTHIES

Makes about 1 quart (32 fluid ounces)

Nothing could be simpler than a smoothie with only two or three ingredients, and bananas are one of my favorite ingredients for smoothies because they're inexpensive, easy to find, and so sweet and creamy. Banana and celery are a surprisingly delicious combination, with a natural hit of sodium from the celery. And blackberries and basil taste amazing together!

HERE'S WHAT YOU NEED:

BANANA CELERY SMOOTHIE

7 bananas, peeled and cut in chunks, frozen if desired

3 celery stalks, cut in chunks

BANANA BLACKBERRY BASIL SMOOTHIE

4 bananas, peeled and cut in chunks

1 pint blackberries

6 fresh basil leaves

EQUIPMENT

Sharp chopping knife

Cutting board

High-speed blender, such as Vitamix

32-ounce Mason jar or large glass for drinking, preferably chilled

HERE'S WHAT YOU DO:

Have all of your ingredients well chilled.

Put everything in the blender and blend until smooth, starting on the slowest speed and gradually working up to the fastest. Blend on the highest speed until the mixture is uniformly smooth and the sound of the blender is high pitched and steady.

Reduce the speed of the blender to the lowest setting before turning it off.

Drink immediately, or refrigerate for up to 4 hours in a tightly closed container. Shake before serving.

COCONUT BANANA SMOOTHIE WITH A SPECK OF CINNAMON

Makes about 1 quart (32 fluid ounces)

You can drink this luxurious smoothie every day if you wish. It's simple, sweet, velvety, and satisfying. It's also affordable and can be made year-round. You can make it into an ice cream by using peeled, frozen bananas (instead of room-temperature bananas), and cutting the coconut water by half. Seriously . . . go bananas!

HERE'S WHAT YOU NEED:

5 to 6 ripe bananas, peeled and cut in chunks

Seeds scraped from ½ vanilla bean

¼ teaspoon ground cinnamon

1 cup fresh young coconut water (from 1 young coconut, see page 35), or store-bought raw coconut water

EQUIPMENT

Sharp chopping knife

Cutting board

High-speed blender, such as Vitamix

32-ounce Mason jar or large glass for drinking, preferably chilled

HERE'S WHAT YOU DO:

Put everything in the blender and blend until smooth, starting on the slowest speed and gradually working up to the fastest. Blend on the highest speed until the mixture is uniformly smooth and the sound of the blender is moderately high pitched and steady.

Reduce the speed of the blender to the lowest setting before turning it off.

Drink immediately, or refrigerate for up to 4 hours in a tightly closed container. Shake before serving.

How to Remove the Seeds from a Vanilla Bean

Split the vanilla bean lengthwise and run the blade of a paring knife down the interior of each side of the bean, scraping out the tiny black seeds.

HONEY DEW BE MINE

Makes about 1 quart (32 fluid ounces)

Sometimes, there is no greater pleasure than cutting your ripe melon in half, sitting outside in the sun, and scooping it up with a spoon with a smile on your face. Next to that experience, this smoothie is the next best thing! There is an art to identifying a ripe melon, and the key is allowing your melon to ripen until it smells sweet on the outside and feels ever-so-slightly soft to the touch. You can tell if a melon is ripe by holding it in both hands and pushing your thumbs against the blossom end (the one with the flat beige scab). If the melon gives and smells sweet, it's ready to go!

HERE'S WHAT YOU NEED:

1 honeydew melon (3 to 4 pounds), peeled, seeds and pulp removed, and cut in chunks

EQUIPMENT

Sharp chopping knife

Cutting board

High-speed blender, such as Vitamix

32-ounce Mason jar or large glass for drinking, preferably chilled

HERE'S WHAT YOU DO:

Have the honeydew well chilled.

Put the melon (and other ingredients, if using) in the blender and blend until smooth, starting on the slowest speed and gradually working up to the fastest. Blend on the highest speed until the mixture is uniformly smooth and the sound of the blender is moderately high pitched and steady.

Reduce the speed of the blender to the lowest setting before turning it off.

Drink immediately, or refrigerate for up to 4 hours in a tightly closed container. Shake before serving.

Got Juice?

Any melon smoothie can be turned into juice by running the same ingredients through a juicer instead of a blender.

VARIATIONS

CUCUMBER MELON

½ honeydew melon, peeled, seeds and pulp removed,
   and cut in chunks

1 unwaxed cucumber (about 10 ounces),
   cut in chunks

HONEYDEW GRAPE

½ honeydew melon, peeled, seeds and pulp removed,
   and cut in chunks

2 cups seedless green grapes

PINEAPPLE HONEYDEW

½ honeydew melon, peeled, seeds and pulp removed,
   and cut in chunks

½ large pineapple, leaves and rind removed, cored
   and cut in chunks (see page 136)

HONEYDEW NECTARINE

½ honeydew melon, peeled, seeds and pulp removed,
   and cut in chunks

3 nectarines, pitted, cut in chunks

CANTALOUPE HONEYDEW

½ honeydew melon, peeled, seeds and pulp removed,
   and cut in chunks

½ cantaloupe, peeled, seeds and pulp removed,
   and cut in chunks

TOTALLY TROPICAL SMOOTHIE

Makes about 1 quart (32 fluid ounces)

Whether you are out in cold weather, in the office, or driving in your car, sometimes you'd rather feel like you were in a tropical paradise. This smoothie takes me back to the beach, under the sun with a big smile on my face. The combination is hydrating and sweet, with a tropical taste that will leave you wanting more!

HERE'S WHAT YOU NEED:

2 large mangoes (about 2 pounds), peeled and pitted (see page 181), cut in chunks

3 bananas, peeled and cut in chunks

¼ ripe pineapple, leaves and rind removed, cored, and cut in chunks (1 ½ to 2 cups)

2 to 3 leaves lacinato (dinosaur) or curly kale, tough stems removed

1 cup fresh young coconut water (from 1 young coconut, see page 35), or store-bought raw coconut water

EQUIPMENT

Vegetable peeler

Sharp chopping knife

Cutting board

High-speed blender, such as Vitamix

32-ounce Mason jar or large glass for drinking, preferably chilled

HERE'S WHAT YOU DO:

Put all ingredients in the blender and blend until smooth, starting on the slowest speed and gradually working up to the fastest. Blend on the highest speed until the mixture is uniformly smooth and the sound of the blender is moderately high pitched and steady.

Reduce the speed of the blender to the lowest setting before turning it off.

Drink immediately, or refrigerate for up to 4 hours in a tightly closed container. Shake before serving.

Peeling Pineapple

To peel a pineapple, cut off the top and bottom, stand it upright, and then use a knife to slice off the rind in strips from top to bottom. To remove the core, cut off the sides of the pineapple, working around the core.

CHERRY NECTARINE DELIGHT

Makes about 1 quart (32 fluid ounces)

It is an old culinary adage that when fruits are in season together they tend to taste good together. I can't speak for every possible combo, but nectarines and cherries seemed destined to mate. They blend into this blushingly beautiful sunset-hued smoothie, and their floral fragrance and slight natural tartness are exquisite. I've added a few grapes for extra sweetness and moisture to help the smoothie flow.

HERE'S WHAT YOU NEED:

1 cup seedless grapes

¾ pound (about 60) ripe sweet cherries, stems and pits removed

4 ripe nectarines (about 1 pound), pitted and coarsely chopped

EQUIPMENT

Cherry pitter (optional)

Sharp chopping knife

Cutting board

High-speed blender, such as Vitamix

32-ounce Mason jar or large glass for drinking, preferably chilled

HERE'S WHAT YOU DO:

Have all of your ingredients well chilled.

Put all ingredients in the blender and blend until smooth, starting on the slowest speed and gradually working up to the fastest. Blend on the highest speed until the mixture is uniformly smooth and the sound of the blender is moderately high pitched and steady. Reduce the speed of the blender to the lowest setting before turning it off.

Drink immediately, or refrigerate for up to 4 hours in a tightly closed container. Shake before serving.

VARIATIONS

ANTIOXIDANT POWER

¾ pound (about 60) sweet cherries, stems and pits removed

4 ripe nectarines (about 1 pound), pitted and coarsely chopped

1 pint blueberries

TROPICAL CHERRY

½ pound (about 40) sweet cherries, stems and pits removed

½ large pineapple (about 1 pound), leaves and rind removed, cored and cut in chunks (see page 136)

SOUPS, DIPS & DRESSINGS

I never eat anything but pure whole fresh fruits, vegetables, and sometimes nuts and seeds. That means no oil, no salt, no sugar, no vinegar, not ever, not at all, not in anything—*nada!* Not even in salad dressings. I have found through years of creating delicious raw salad dressings and dips that oil and salt aren't necessary. There is enough natural sodium in vegetables that adding salt is redundant, and as for oil, I can get more flavor from a pureed ripe fruit than I would from any oil.

My dressing recipes are made with fruits, vegetables, and sometimes nuts and seeds, combined in a way that makes them healthy and delicious. You can make as much or as little as you wish, and it's really easy to add in a few (more) nuts or seeds if you want your dressing to be creamier or thicker, or to eliminate them (where applicable) if you want your version to be lighter and lower in fat. Most taste best when eaten immediately, but they will last in your refrigerator for approximately 24 hours. If you add more citrus juice, it can help to extend the shelf life by one or two days. The big advantage to working this way is that almost every one of my recipes for salad dressing is equally good eaten as a soup or used as a dip.

You will find that most of the soup recipes make about 1 quart. I find this amount to be the perfect size for a large soup meal for one, or for two if you are serving the soup along with a salad or other main dish. It's also a good amount for dressing a big bowl of salad. If you are unused to working with raw food dressings, I know a quart of dressing can seem like a lot, but trust me, it's perfect. When your dressing is nothing more than pureed fruit and vegetables, it becomes just one more produce ingredient in your salad.

The nutritional benefits of salad dressing made completely from fresh fruits, vegetables, nuts, and seeds are obvious. But you may not be aware of one huge culinary benefit—no wilting! I'm sure you've seen how greens dressed with oil-and-vinegar dressings get wilted and soggy after a few hours. While most leaves naturally repel water, which is why raindrops bead up on leaves and roll off, oil permeates the leaf surface easily, breaking leaves down, releasing their moisture, and making them wilt. My dressings can sit on a salad for hours and never make it soggy. Can your bottled dressing do that?

WATERMELON GAZPACHO

Makes about 1 quart (32 fluid ounces), 1 large serving

Like most fruit, watermelon is high in water and low in calories, so you can indulge as much as you want without worrying about gaining weight. Even though watermelon is incredibly sweet tasting, it is relatively low in sugar (15 to 20 percent less than cantaloupe or honeydew). The reason it tastes so sweet is that it is very low in sodium: A good size wedge has less than 3 milligrams! So feel free to indulge. The more you eat, the healthier you get! Did you know that watermelon and cucumber are from the same botanical family, Cucurbitaceae? No wonder they taste so awesome together! I know you usually cut the rind off, but watermelon rind is delicious. You can leave it on for this soup, and in salads, too!

HERE'S WHAT YOU NEED:

3 pounds watermelon, rind removed or left on
    (or as much as you want)

1 unwaxed cucumber (about 10 ounces),
    cut in chunks

1 yellow or red tomato, stem removed, cut in chunks

1 red or yellow bell pepper, stem and seeds removed,
    cut in chunks

1 to 2 cups fresh orange juice (from 3 to 6 oranges)

1 tablespoon fresh lemon juice (optional)

Small handful of chopped fresh basil or cilantro

EQUIPMENT

Sharp chopping knife

Cutting board

Large soup bowl and spoon

Citrus juicer

Food processor

HERE'S WHAT YOU DO:

Chop up the watermelon into pretty small pieces, somewhere in between chunky and soupy; you'll want about 3 cups. Transfer the watermelon to a large bowl, along with any juices that splash out onto the cutting board. I know you want to use the food processor to chop the watermelon, but please don't! You will end up with sweet pink water, which would be great if you were making juice, but not cool when you want a bowl of soup.

Finely chop the cucumber, tomato, and bell pepper in a food processor. Add to the bowl with the watermelon. Stir in the orange juice and the lemon juice, if using. Top with the chopped herbs.

Serve immediately, or refrigerate for up to 24 hours in a tightly closed container.

CHERRY TOMATO AND BASIL SOUP

Makes about 1 quart (32 fluid ounces), 1 large serving

You thought you didn't like tomato soup, but just wait until you try this one! It's incredibly simple. You don't even need to chop anything, and the soup bursts with herbalicious goodness! The recipe is amazingly versatile: In addition to enjoying it as a soup, I frequently use it as a salad dressing, as a dip for veggies, or as a marinara sauce over zucchini noodles. You can replace the cherry tomatoes with any chopped-up ripe tomato.

HERE'S WHAT YOU NEED:

3 pints cherry tomatoes (about 2 pounds), stems removed

6 sprigs fresh basil

¼ garlic clove

1 tablespoon lemon or lime juice (optional)

Additional herbs from your garden, such as thyme, oregano, or mint (optional)

EQUIPMENT

High-speed blender, such as Vitamix

Large soup bowl and spoon

HERE'S WHAT YOU DO:

Put all ingredients in the blender and blend until smooth, starting on the slowest speed and gradually working up to the fastest. Blend on the highest speed until the mixture is uniformly smooth and the sound of the blender is moderately high pitched and steady. Reduce the speed of the blender to the lowest setting before turning it off.

Pour the soup into a large soup bowl. Serve immediately, or refrigerate for up to 24 hours in a tightly closed container.

MANGO GAZPACHO

Makes about 1 quart (32 fluid ounces), 1 large serving

This chunky, sweet-and-savory soup is a perfect way to start a big salad meal, or it can be used as a sauce for kale tacos, a dip for veggies, a dressing, or a sauce for veggie noodles. Come to think of it, there isn't much it *can't* do.

HERE'S WHAT YOU NEED:

2 large mangoes (about 2 pounds), peeled and pitted (see page 181), cut in chunks

1 red bell pepper, stem and seeds removed

2 green onions (white and green parts), roots trimmed, coarsely chopped

⅓ cup cilantro leaves, chopped

12 cherry tomatoes, stems removed, halved and thinly sliced

EQUIPMENT

Sharp chopping knife

Cutting board

Food processor

Large soup bowl and spoon

HERE'S WHAT YOU DO:

Pulse the mango, bell pepper, and green onions in the food processor until everything is finely chopped (not pureed).

Pour into a large soup bowl. Stir in the cilantro and sliced cherry tomatoes. Serve immediately, or chill for up to 2 hours before serving.

Acid Adds Sparkle!

The complex taste of tomatoes and other fruit comes from a delicate balance of tart and sweet. We love sweetness in our fruit, but fruit that is just sweet tastes flat. It needs a little tartness to give it "sparkle." Although I love cherry tomatoes for their beautiful pulpy texture—which makes raw tomato sauces effortlessly thick and rich— they can often lack acidity. I find adding a drop of lemon or lime juice to a tomato (or other sweet fruit) recipe enlivens every- thing. Make your life sparkle!

PINEAPPLE CUCUMBER GAZPACHO

Makes about 1 quart (32 fluid ounces), 1 large serving

When confronted with a brimming bowl of fresh gazpacho—oozing juice, popping with colorful bits of herb and red onion, radiating aromas of tropical pineapple, ripe tomato, and crispy cucumber—don't you just want to eat it for your whole meal? Who says it has to be a side dish? Make a huge batch and eat it up! What is "cool" about this gazpacho is that it is cooling—fabulously sweet, savory, light, and hydrating. If you are sensitive to pineapple, you can always use mango or papaya instead. Remember that each of my gazpachos can be used as a side dish, a dip, a dressing, a full meal, or a snack. Enjoy!

HERE'S WHAT YOU NEED:

½ large pineapple (about 1 pound), leaves and rind removed, cored (see page 136)

1 large unwaxed cucumber (about 12 ounces)

1 beefsteak tomato (about 12 ounces) or 1 pint cherry tomatoes, stems removed

1 small red bell pepper (about 6 ounces), stem and seeds removed

Leaves from ½ small bunch cilantro (about ½ ounce)

¼ jalapeño chile, stem and seeds removed (optional)

Juice of 1 lemon (about ¼ cup)

½ small red onion (about 2 ounces), minced

1 green onion (white and green parts), trimmed, very finely chopped

EQUIPMENT

Sharp chopping knife

Cutting board

Citrus juicer

Food processor

Large soup bowl and spoon

HERE'S WHAT YOU DO:

Cut the pineapple, cucumber, tomato, bell pepper, cilantro, and jalapeño, if using, into chunks that will blend easily. If you'd like, reserve some chopped veggies and use them to garnish the soup at the end. Pulse in the food processor, in two or three batches, until everything is finely chopped (not pureed).

Pour the soup into a large bowl and stir in the lemon juice, red onion, and green onion. Serve immediately, or chill for up to 2 hours before serving.

SPINACH SOUP

Makes about 1 quart (32 fluid ounces), 1 large serving

I usually crave something savory in the evenings, and this is why I love to eat large salads. If I am not eating a large salad, I will typically make a savory soup or gazpacho. This spinach soup is a miracle—creamy, savory, and filling. It is delicious eaten by the bowlful and also makes an elegant salad dressing or dip. For a casual meal, I frequently just assemble a bunch of greens (kale, romaine, spinach, chard, arugula, escarole, you name it) and start dipping them into the dressing and munching. "Rip and dip"—my favorite meal plan!

HERE'S WHAT YOU NEED:

2 large beefsteak tomatoes or 2 pints cherry tomatoes (about 2 pounds), stems removed, cut in chunks

3 cups packed spinach leaves (about 6 ounces)

3 celery stalks, cut in chunks

1 tablespoon lemon juice

½ red bell pepper, stem and seeds removed, cut in chunks

1 small garlic clove, halved

¼ cup packed fresh herb leaves, such as basil, oregano, thyme, or cilantro

EQUIPMENT

Sharp chopping knife

Cutting board

High-speed blender, such as Vitamix

Large soup bowl and spoon

HERE'S WHAT YOU DO:

Put all ingredients in the blender and blend on the highest speed until the mixture is uniformly smooth and the sound of the blender is high pitched and steady. Reduce the speed of the blender to the lowest setting before turning it off.

Pour the soup into a large bowl. Serve immediately, or refrigerate for up to 24 hours in a tightly closed container.

PAPAYA TOMATO SOUP

Makes about 1 quart (32 fluid ounces), 1 large serving

This soup is wonderfully creamy, slightly sweet, and very satisfying. The flavor is reminiscent of cream of tomato soup—without the cream, or the calories. It has a pleasantly salty nuance from the tomatoes, accentuated by the contrast of the sweetness of the papaya. You can easily adjust the volume to make larger or smaller portions.

HERE'S WHAT YOU NEED:

1 papaya (about 1 pound), peel and seeds removed

3 tomatoes (about 1 ½ pounds), preferably heirloom, stems removed

Juice of ½ juice orange

EQUIPMENT

Sharp chopping knife

Cutting board

Citrus juicer

High-speed blender, such as Vitamix

Large soup bowl and spoon

HERE'S WHAT YOU DO:

Cut the papaya and tomato into chunks that will blend easily. Put in the blender with the orange juice, and blend on the highest speed until the mixture is uniformly smooth and the sound of the blender is high pitched and steady. Reduce the blender speed to the lowest setting before turning it off.

Pour the soup into a large bowl. Serve immediately, or refrigerate for up to 24 hours in a tightly closed container.

Beware of Papaya Seeds

The seeds of the papaya are slightly bitter and quite spicy, sort of a cross between mustard seeds and peppercorns. Most of the time I remove them, but they are said to have a few potent health benefits, like ridding the intestines of parasites and reversing cirrhosis of the liver. If you have recently returned from rain forest exploration or are a reformed alcoholic, you might want to give them a try. They definitely won't hurt you and could have a general medicinal effect.

NECTARINE AND CHERRY TOMATO SOUP

Makes about 1 quart (32 fluid ounces), 1 large serving

Some soups are savory, some are sweet, some are tangy, and some are all of the above! In the summer, when both nectarines and tomatoes overflow farm stands, this soup is a standout. But I have made it with frozen peaches in the winter, and substituted papaya or mango when nectarines or peaches aren't available. As always, if you can get all local ingredients, the soup will be incredible. Your taste buds will thank you!

HERE'S WHAT YOU NEED:

8 nectarines or peaches (about 2 pounds), pitted

1 pint cherry tomatoes (about 12 ounces), stems removed

4 large sprigs fresh herbs (basil or mint taste spectacular)

EQUIPMENT

Sharp chopping knife

Cutting board

Food processor

Large soup bowl and spoon

HERE'S WHAT YOU DO:

Cut the nectarines into chunks that will blend easily. Put all ingredients in the food processor and pulse until finely chopped (not pureed).

Pour the soup into a large bowl. Serve immediately, or chill for up to 2 hours before serving.

VARIATION

TOMATO NECTARINE SALAD DRESSING

Blend in a high-speed blender, like a Vitamix, until smooth and creamy. Pour over salad and enjoy!

SWEET PERSIMMON SOUP

Makes about 1 quart (32 fluid ounces), 1 large serving

During persimmon season it is not unusual for me to eat five or six large persimmons as an evening appetizer before I start my salad. Sometimes, though, I blend those persimmons to make a soup that is sweet, savory, and delicious. It helps to satisfy my cravings before I start eating my salad, and sometimes it's *so* good that I just pour it onto my salad and eat it that way! Ha! The soup is filling, so if you don't have room for a salad after, that is perfectly fine. You may even want to simply grab some kale or romaine and dip your greens right into the soup. Why not? Persimmons are very high in pectin, a substance in fruits that makes jellies gel. The pectin makes pureed persimmon very rich and creamy. It also causes the puree to thicken as it sits, so if you refrigerate this soup you may want to thin it with more coconut water to adjust its consistency. You could also eat the thickened soup as a pudding for dessert!

HERE'S WHAT YOU NEED:

5 ripe Fuyu persimmons or 3 large ripe Hachiya persimmons (about 1 ⅓ pounds), stems and leaves removed

½ large ripe papaya, seeds scooped out

1 teaspoon ground cinnamon

¼ to ½ cup fresh young coconut water (from 1 young coconut; see page 35) or store-bought raw coconut water

EQUIPMENT

Sharp chopping knife

Cutting board

High-speed blender, such as Vitamix

Large soup bowl and spoon

HERE'S WHAT YOU DO:

Cut the persimmons and papaya into large chunks that will blend easily. Put the fruit in a blender along with the cinnamon and ¼ cup of the coconut water. Blend until smooth, starting on the slowest speed and gradually working up to the fastest.

Blend on the highest speed until the mixture is uniformly smooth and the sound of the blender is moderately high pitched and steady.

Reduce the speed of the blender to the lowest setting before turning it off. Adjust the consistency with more coconut water, if desired.

Pour the soup into a large bowl and serve immediately, or refrigerate for up to 24 hours in a tightly closed container. Enjoy cold as a pudding, if desired, or thin with a little more coconut water as needed.

How to Tell when a Persimmon Is Ripe

There are two commonly available types of persimmons. Fuyu persimmons look like tiny pumpkins or lanterns, with flat, slightly rounded bottoms. They can be eaten when firm, but they get sweeter as they soften, an indication that the starchy carbohydrates in the under-ripe fruit have converted into sugars. Hachiya persimmons are larger and have pointed tips. They *must* be eaten when extremely soft—so soft that when you hold one in your hand it feels like a water balloon. Ripe Hachiya are extremely sweet, but underripe (firm) ones are so astringent (mouth puckering) as to be inedible.

Persimmon Skin

Some people have a hard time digesting persimmon skins. If you tend to have delicate digestion, feel free to peel your persimmons before blending.

ORANGE AVOCADO CILANTRO PICANTE

Makes about 1 quart (32 fluid ounces), 1 large serving

Avocado is the only fruit (other than olives) that stores the great majority of its energy in the form of fat. In a world of sweet fruit, not only is it *not* sweet but it is also innately rich, so a little goes a long way. Serve this gazpacho-cum-guacamole as a soup or as an amazing salad dressing.

HERE'S WHAT YOU NEED:

3 large navel oranges, peeled

1 avocado, pitted and peeled, cut into chunks

Leaves from ½ small bunch cilantro (about ½ ounce), coarsely chopped

1 large beefsteak tomato (about 1 pound), stem removed, coarsely chopped

3 green onions (white and green parts), trimmed, chopped

¼ small red onion, finely chopped

1 small garlic clove, quartered

¼ jalapeño chile, stem and seeds removed, finely chopped

EQUIPMENT

Sharp chopping knife

Cutting board

Food processor

Large soup bowl and spoon

HERE'S WHAT YOU DO:

Remove any large sections of pith (the white membrane) from the oranges. Cut the flesh of each orange into 8 chunks.

Toss all ingredients and pulse in the food processor, in two or three batches, until everything is finely chopped (not pureed).

Pour the soup into a large bowl and serve immediately, or chill for up to 2 hours before serving.

Avocado Prep

A Hass avocado has dark green-black-brown skin that yields to light pressure when ripe. To remove the skin and pit, halve the avocado lengthwise with a paring knife, guiding it around the pit in the center. Then twist the two halves in opposite directions to separate them. Insert the tip of your knife into the pit and twist to release it. Cut each half of the avocado in half again, lengthwise. Peel the skin from each quarter away from the flesh, starting at the narrow ends.

DAZZLING DATE DIP

Makes about 2 cups, 2 to 4 servings

Wanna date? And by date, perhaps I should clarify that I mean something sweet. This sweet dipping sauce is almost like caramel. It has the consistency of a nut butter, but it is free of fat and tastes like candy. You can use it as a dip for apples, celery, carrots, and more—or just eat it with a spoon for a sweet treat. It will stay fresh for days at room temperature, so it is great to take with you to work, school, or any other on-the-go destination. It is also great for athletes who need an easy, energy-rich snack. It is high in carbohydrates to keep you well fueled throughout the day.

HERE'S WHAT YOU NEED:

24 fresh Medjool dates (about 1 pound),
    pitted and halved

1 cup water

Juice of ½ lemon (about 2 tablespoons)

¼ teaspoon ground cinnamon (optional)

EQUIPMENT

Paring knife

Citrus juicer

Small mixing bowl

Food processor

Rubber spatula

Dip bowl

HERE'S WHAT YOU DO:

Soak the dates in the water in a small bowl until very soft, about 1 hour.

Lift the soaked dates from the water (reserve the water), put them in the food processor, and pulse until the dates are finely chopped (not pureed). Add the reserved soaking liquid, lemon juice, and cinnamon, if using, and process until the mixture is pureed, scraping the sides with a rubber spatula as needed to keep the mixture smooth.

Transfer to a bowl for dipping. The dip can be stored in the refrigerator in a tightly closed container for up to 1 week.

AMAZING LOW-FAT GUACAMOLE

Makes about 2 cups, 2 to 4 servings

You can have your *guac* and eat it too! Low fat, nutrient rich, and unbelievably delicious, this guacamole is mostly zucchini, which cuts the fat and the calories from traditional guac. You can serve it as a dip, but it is also amazing as a salad dressing, and especially luxurious coating a brilliantly colored rainbow salad.

HERE'S WHAT YOU NEED:

2 cups diced zucchini (from 1 large zucchini, about 12 ounces)

1 avocado, pitted and peeled (see page 154)

¼ red bell pepper, stem and seeds removed, cut in chunks

¼ small red onion, finely chopped

1 cup packed cilantro leaves (from a large, 4-ounce bunch)

½ jalapeño chile, stem and seeds removed, finely chopped

1 small garlic clove, halved

Juice of 1 lime or ½ lemon (about 2 tablespoons)

EQUIPMENT

Sharp chopping knife

Cutting board

Citrus juicer

Food processor

Rubber spatula

Dip bowl

HERE'S WHAT YOU DO:

Put all ingredients in the food processor and pulse until finely chopped, about 30 seconds. Scrape the sides of the bowl with a rubber spatula. Process until the mixture is thick and interspersed with lots of finely chopped veggies.

Transfer to a bowl for dipping or use as a creamy salad dressing. Use immediately, or refrigerate in a tightly closed container for up to 24 hours.

LOW-TECH METHOD

If you don't have a food processor, you can still make this dish. Simply chop up all the ingredients as finely as you can and then use a fork to mash them into the avocado.

FULLY RAW HUMMUS

Makes about 3 cups, about 3 servings

I am half Lebanese and half Ecuadorian, and my family loves to celebrate our cultures and *loves* to eat! Sharing food is an integral part of our family bonding experience. Sharing food is sharing love. When I first went Fully Raw, one of the most difficult things to overcome was denying my mother's Lebanese food. It wasn't that I craved the food, but I missed the cultural aspect of sharing a dish and that bond with my family and friends. And I also wanted to share my new passion for health and raw foods with them. Therefore, I came up with this Fully Raw hummus. Eating ethnic dishes doesn't have to be unhealthy; they can be delicious, colorful, and savory. Hummus, the all-time Arabic favorite, can be used as a dip for veggies or a salad dressing. Raw food is beautiful food!

HERE'S WHAT YOU NEED:

1 large or 2 medium zucchini, stems removed

1 cup raw unhulled sesame seeds

½ cup fresh lemon juice (from about 2 lemons)

1 garlic clove, halved

EQUIPMENT

Sharp chopping knife

Cutting board

Citrus juicer

High-speed blender, such as Vitamix

Dip bowl

HERE'S WHAT YOU DO:

Cut the zucchini into chunks that will blend easily. Put in the blender with the remaining ingredients and blend on the highest speed until the mixture is uniformly smooth and the sound of the blender is high pitched and steady. Reduce the speed of the blender to the lowest setting before turning it off.

Pour the hummus into a bowl for dipping and serve, or refrigerate for up to 24 hours in a tightly closed container.

CHERRY TOMATO-BEET TOP DRESSING

Makes about 1 quart (32 fluid ounces), enough for 1 large salad

Beet greens and their gorgeous crimson stems have a pungent flavor, similar to kale, and lots of nutrition, including tons of vitamin A and a significant jolt of protein. So when juicing beets, I usually throw in the tops. This dressing is another way to get their goodness. You can either save your beet greens, or use the same amount of beet microgreens or red Swiss chard. Did you know that chard is the cultivated stems and leaves of beets? A long time ago farmers found that they could cultivate some beets for their roots, and others for their leaves. The root beet plants developed bulbous roots and relatively spindly stems and greens, while the leaf beets became chard, with skinny carrot-shaped roots, meaty colorful stems, and wide velvety leaves.

HERE'S WHAT YOU NEED:

2 pints cherry tomatoes (about 1 ½ pounds), stems removed

4 ounces beet greens, beet microgreens, or Swiss chard leaves, cut in chunks

4 celery stalks, cut in chunks

1 tablespoon fresh lemon juice

¼ cup packed cilantro leaves

EQUIPMENT

Sharp chopping knife

Cutting board

High-speed blender, such as Vitamix

HERE'S WHAT YOU DO:

Put all ingredients in the blender and blend on the highest speed until the mixture is uniformly smooth and the sound of the blender is high pitched and steady. Reduce the speed of the blender to the lowest setting before turning it off.

Use immediately, or refrigerate for up to 24 hours in a tightly closed container.

YELLOW BELL PEPPER AND MANGO DRESSING

Makes about 2 cups (16 fluid ounces), enough for 1 or 2 large salads

Silky smooth, creamy, tangy, sweet, and the color of a brilliant summer day, this dressing is perfect whenever mangoes are plentiful and yellow peppers are on sale. Even before you put it on your salad, there is a ton of your day's vitamin A and vitamin C in this dressing alone.

HERE'S WHAT YOU NEED:

2 large mangoes (about 2 pounds), peeled and pitted (see page 181), cut in chunks

1 yellow bell pepper, stem and seeds removed, cut in chunks

3 tablespoons raw unhulled sesame seeds or raw hemp seeds

1 tablespoon fresh rosemary leaves

EQUIPMENT

Chopping knife

Cutting board

High-speed blender, such as Vitamix

HERE'S WHAT YOU DO:

Put all ingredients in the blender and blend on the highest speed until the mixture is uniformly smooth and the sound of the blender is high pitched and steady.

Reduce the speed of the blender to the lowest setting before turning it off.

Use immediately, or refrigerate for up to 48 hours in a tightly closed container.

LEMON GINGER DRESSING

Makes about 1 cup (8 fluid ounces), enough for 1 or 2 large salads

Bottled salad dressings are usually processed, contain additives and preservatives, and depend on fatty oils and/or starches for their mouthfeel and texture. My lemon ginger dressing is low in fat and soaring with flavor. Its lemony kick is intense, so a little goes a long way.

HERE'S WHAT YOU NEED:

Juice of 4 lemons (about 1 cup)

2 tablespoons raw unhulled sesame seeds

1 large thumb (about 2 inches) fresh ginger, coarsely chopped

EQUIPMENT

Citrus juicer

Sharp chopping knife

Cutting board

High-speed blender, such as Vitamix

HERE'S WHAT YOU DO:

Put all ingredients in the blender and blend on the highest speed until the mixture is uniformly smooth and the sound of the blender is high pitched and steady. Reduce the speed of the blender to the lowest setting before turning it off.

Use immediately, or refrigerate for up to 48 hours in a tightly closed container.

Getting the Most Juice from a Lemon

To extract the maximum amount of juice from a citrus fruit, roll it under your palm on the counter, bearing down a bit. This will bruise the fibers inside that hold the juice, getting them ready to release everything they hold once you cut the fruit open and put on a major squeeze. Be sure to cut the fruit along its equator: Think of the lemon as a globe with an axis running from its stem to its blossom end (the dimple with the little scar). The imaginary perpendicular line around the widest part of the lemon is its equator.

ORANGE GINGER SESAME DRESSING

Makes about 2 cups (16 fluid ounces), enough for 1 or 2 large salads

If you love Asian salad dressings, then this recipe is for you. My inspiration is the Asian-style dressing served in Japanese restaurants, but mine is free of salt and oil. It's sweet, it's sour, and it's creamy! When I have friends over for dinner, I typically make this dressing because I know that everyone will love it. It tastes wonderfully fresh and has a creamy richness. I predict it will become a classic in your home.

HERE'S WHAT YOU NEED:

1 cup fresh orange juice (from about 3 oranges)

Juice of 1 lime (about 2 tablespoons)

¼ cup raw unhulled sesame seeds

¼ cup raw shelled pistachios

¼ cup packed cilantro leaves

1 medium thumb (about 1 inch) fresh ginger, cut in chunks

1 green onion (white and green parts), trimmed, coarsely chopped

EQUIPMENT

Citrus juicer

Sharp chopping knife

Cutting board

High-speed blender, such as Vitamix

HERE'S WHAT YOU DO:

Put all ingredients in the blender and blend on the highest speed until the mixture is uniformly smooth and the sound of the blender is high pitched and steady. Reduce the speed of the blender to the lowest setting before turning it off.

Use immediately, or refrigerate for up to 4 days in a tightly closed container.

CILANTRO TAHINI DRESSING

Makes about 2 cups (16 fluid ounces), enough for 2 large salads

The dressing is what makes or breaks a salad. Without a good dressing, the salad just isn't as yummy. This recipe has savor and spice, it's creamy and green, and it's delicious! Cilantro is a powerful herb that is said to cleanse heavy metals from the body. Sesame seeds are high in calcium, magnesium, manganese, phosphorous, copper, and zinc. The dressing is gorgeous and flavorful when paired with a salad of tomatoes, cucumber, bell pepper, corn, red cabbage, and greens.

HERE'S WHAT YOU NEED:

2 large zucchini (about 1 ½ pounds), stem removed, cut in chunks

¼ cup raw unhulled sesame seeds, or 1 tablespoon sesame tahini

1 ½ large bunches cilantro (about 4 ounces), leaves and stems, coarsely chopped

Juice of 1 lemon (about ¼ cup)

HERE'S WHAT YOU DO:

Put all ingredients in the blender and blend on the highest speed until the mixture is uniformly smooth and the sound of the blender is high pitched and steady. Reduce the speed of the blender to the lowest setting before turning it off.

Use immediately, or refrigerate for up to 48 hours in a tightly closed container.

EQUIPMENT

Sharp chopping knife

Cutting board

Citrus juicer

High-speed blender, such as Vitamix

CUCUMBER DILL DRESSING

Makes about 2 cups (16 fluid ounces), enough for 1 or 2 large salads

Sometimes, you want something that is light, sweet, and creamy for your salad. When I was little, my mother used to make a traditional Lebanese salad dressing with *lebne* (yogurt), cucumber, dill, and herbs. It was basically like eating seasoned yogurt and cucumbers in a gazpacho form. I missed the light and creamy flavors of her dressing, so I created my own vegan version that is delicious enough to eat as a gazpacho-style soup or use as a salad dressing. It tastes like it's fresh from the garden. The dressing tastes best when you use all freshly picked ingredients.

HERE'S WHAT YOU NEED:

1 large unwaxed cucumber (about 12 ounces), cut in chunks

Handful of fresh dill (about ½ ounce)

1 celery stalk, cut in chunks

Juice of 1 lemon (about ¼ cup)

1 tablespoon raw pine nuts (optional)

EQUIPMENT

Sharp chopping knife

Cutting board

Citrus juicer

High-speed blender, such as Vitamix

HERE'S WHAT YOU DO:

Put all ingredients in the blender and blend on the highest speed until the mixture is uniformly smooth and the sound of the blender is high pitched and steady. Reduce the speed of the blender to the lowest setting before turning it off.

Use immediately, or refrigerate for up to 48 hours in a tightly closed container.

BLACKBERRY AND BLUE-SPICE-BASIL DRESSING

Makes about 2 cups (16 fluid ounces), enough for 1 or 2 large salads

I love to grow herbs in my garden. One of my favorites (and easiest to grow) is basil. I grow four varieties: holy basil, cinnamon basil, lemon basil, and blue spice basil. My absolute favorite is the blue spice because it smells sweet and has a unique taste—minty and slightly aerating across the tongue, like eucalyptus. When you add it to a dressing, it creates something truly savory and different.

HERE'S WHAT YOU NEED:

2 cups blackberries or blueberries

10 fresh Medjool dates, pitted and coarsely chopped

Small handful of fresh blue spice basil (about ½ ounce), or other sweet basil

⅓ to ¾ cup fresh orange juice (from 1 to 3 juice oranges)

EQUIPMENT

Sharp chopping knife

Cutting board

Citrus juicer

High-speed blender, such as Vitamix

HERE'S WHAT YOU DO:

Put the berries, dates, basil, and ⅓ cup orange juice in the blender and blend on the highest speed until the mixture is uniformly smooth and the sound of the blender is high pitched and steady. Reduce the speed of the blender to the lowest setting before turning it off. Adjust the consistency with more orange juice if needed.

Use immediately, or refrigerate for up to 48 hours in a tightly closed container.

LEMON CRÈME DRESSING

Makes about 2 cups (16 fluid ounces), enough for 1 or 2 large salads

I go through phases where I fall in love with one dressing, and I will eat it every day for at least a month. I have done this several times, and for even more than a month-long streak, with this lemon dressing. The citrus of the lemon balances perfectly with the fat of the hemp seeds and pine nuts. In my mind, it almost tastes like a fettuccine sauce but with a hint of lemon flavor. My friends, this dressing is perfection—the crème de la crème.

HERE'S WHAT YOU NEED:

Juice of 4 lemons (about 1 cup)

2 tablespoons raw hemp seeds

1 small thumb (about ½ inch) fresh ginger, cut in chunks

Leaves from 6 herb sprigs, such as mint, basil, oregano, or thyme

1 tablespoon pine nuts (optional)

EQUIPMENT

Citrus juicer

Sharp chopping knife

Cutting board

High-speed blender, such as Vitamix

HERE'S WHAT YOU DO:

Put all ingredients in the blender and blend on the highest speed until the mixture is uniformly smooth and the sound of the blender is high pitched and steady. Reduce the speed of the blender to the lowest setting before turning it off.

Use immediately, or refrigerate for up to 48 hours in a tightly closed container.

RED PEPPER-HEMP SEED ORANGE DRESSING

Makes about 2 cups (16 fluid ounces), enough for 1 or 2 large salads

Feeling hot? Or not? Either way, this dressing will bring some pepper to your salad! You can make it sweet or spicy. It's easy enough to make every night, and you should make a big batch . . . because I promise you will want more! In addition, it is really best to let your salad marinate in the dressing for about 30 minutes to help the ingredients soak up the flavor even more. It's simply irresistible.

HERE'S WHAT YOU NEED:

1 cup fresh orange juice (from about 3 juice oranges)

1 large red bell pepper, stem and seeds removed, cut in chunks

2 tablespoons raw hemp seeds

Leaves from 6 herb sprigs, such as basil, mint, or cilantro

Small slice jalapeño chile (optional)

EQUIPMENT

Citrus juicer

Sharp chopping knife

Cutting board

High-speed blender, such as Vitamix

HERE'S WHAT YOU DO:

Put all ingredients in the blender and blend on the highest speed until the mixture is uniformly smooth and the sound of the blender is high pitched and steady. Reduce the speed of the blender to the lowest setting before turning it off.

Use immediately, or refrigerate for up to 48 hours in a tightly closed container.

EPIC MEALS

While juices, smoothies, and basic salads are delicious, simple, and fun, let's face it: Sometimes you want something that is hearty and filling. It's nice to feel like you are sitting down to a real meal, one that you can share with family and friends in a social setting. As I mentioned before, eating Fully Raw can be as simple or as complicated as you wish it to be. The previous chapters have been filled with simple recipes that are time efficient, cost effective, and fun to make. This chapter is filled with (brace yourself!) the most delicious, scrumptious, and filling meals you will ever enjoy.

An essential part of getting people to eat more raw foods is helping them understand that they don't have to give up anything to eat healthy. Almost any cooked dish can be replicated raw, and that's what I've done in this chapter: re-created many popular dishes to be Fully Raw, especially some of my favorites growing up. They are far healthier and, in my opinion, far tastier.

The chapter starts with large, filling main-dish salads that are very easy and fast to make and use many of the dressings you have already become familiar with. Then I move on to some of my raw replicas of your favorite cooked foods—think chili, lasagna, burritos, tacos, pasta with marinara sauce, fettuccine Alfredo, even pad thai. These dishes are a little more elaborate, but so impressive that I don't think you will mind the extra effort.

I hope that you have fun making these Fully Raw entrees and that they become classics in your kitchen, as they have in mine. They are made with love just for you!

RAINBOW SALAD: BASIC RECIPE

Makes 2 large or 4 regular salads

I call most of my large dinner salads Rainbow Salads because they are all about *color!* The base is always a good amount of dark leafy greens—romaine, kale, red-leaf lettuce, arugula, spinach, frisée, and/or escarole—the freshest and brightest greens you can find. I top those greens with more beautiful colors—red and yellow bell peppers, cherry tomatoes, chives, avocado, beets, purple cabbage, and/or fruit. The colorful pigments in fruits and vegetables are all antioxidant vitamins and minerals that help your body fight disease. The simplest way of making sure you are getting a full array of these nutrients is to make sure that every salad you prepare *pops* with color! The key to making any salad truly delicious is a vibrant dressing. Store-bought salad dressings are typically loaded with oils, salts, and preservatives. I make my own dressings by blending up a few fresh ingredients that leave my salad saturated with extra flavor and great nutrition. I typically use about a quart of dressing for each salad. When your dressing is made from fresh produce, you can't use too much—the dressing is really just another salad ingredient.

HERE'S WHAT YOU NEED:

2 large heads or bunches greens of your choice, about 3 pounds or 3 ½ quarts (see chart, page 176)

1 quart dressing of your choice (see chart, page 176)

1 ½ quarts (6 cups) chopped fruits and vegetables of your choice (see chart, page 176)

¼ to 1 cup toppings of your choice, such as nuts, seeds, and herbs (see chart, page 176), optional

EQUIPMENT

Sharp chopping knife

Cutting board

High-speed blender, such as Vitamix

Large salad bowl for tossing

Large bowls for serving

HERE'S WHAT YOU DO:

Wash the greens thoroughly and shake off as much water as you can. Don't worry if they are not bone dry. Chop the greens into small pieces. The shape of the cut is up to you (strips, squares, dice, minced, or random chop), but you want the pieces to be fine enough so that an ample amount of dressing will cling to them. The more exposed cut surfaces, the better!

Put the greens in the salad bowl and toss with half the dressing.

Scatter or arrange the chopped fruits and vegetables over the greens, depending on how composed or casual you prefer the presentation.

Pour the remaining dressing over the top, and set the salad aside for 10 to 15 minutes to allow the dressing to soak into the ingredients. This will help to soften tough greens like curly kale and escarole.

Add any toppings, if desired, and toss everything before serving. I like to serve my Rainbow Salads in large wooden bowls.

MAKE YOUR OWN RAINBOW SALADS

Use the suggestions in this chart and the Basic Recipe on page 172 to create my favorite Rainbow Salads. Or, get creative and make up other salads using any beautiful in-season vegetables and fruits!

RECIPE NAME	GREENS	FRUITS AND VEGGIES	DRESSING	TOPPING
	3 ½ quarts trimmed and finely sliced, chopped, or shredded	1 ½ quarts trimmed and cut in dice, choppped, shredded, in strips, etc.	1 quart	1 cup (unless noted)
	2 large heads or bunches (1 to 2 pounds each)	Number and weight vary by type/variety		
Rainbow Salad with Orange Avocado Dressing	Romaine Kale	Red bell pepper Yellow bell pepper Red cabbage Cherry tomatoes Pineapple Raspberries Avocado Cucumber	For Orange Avocado Dressing, blend 3 cups orange juice, 1 avocado, and a handful of chopped herbs	Avocado slices (from 1 medium)
Rainbow Salad with Cilantro Tahini Dressing	Romaine Swiss chard or Kale Baby greens	Mango Oranges Cherry tomatoes Red bell pepper	Cilantro Tahini Dressing (page 163)	More cherry tomatoes or ¼ cup hemp seeds
Spring Alive Salad with Strawberry Vinaigrette	Romaine Arugula Bibb lettuce	Strawberries Carambola Navel orange Kiwis Heirloom tomatoes Red raspberries Radishes Alfalfa Sprouts	Strawberry Vinaigrette (page 193)	Raw pecans (¼ cup)
Abundant Asian Salad with Orange Ginger Sesame Dressing	Baby bok choy Romaine Kale Spinach Arugula	Purple cabbage Broccoli Snap peas Red, yellow, orange, and green bell pepper	Orange Ginger Sesame Dressing (Page 162)	Cherry tomatoes Lemon zest
Tropical Fruit Salad with Lemon Crème Dressing	Romaine Cilantro	Mango Blackberries Cucumber Cherry tomatoes Kiwis Other berries of choice	Lemon Crème Dressing (page 167)	Hemp Seeds (¼ cup)

RECIPE NAME	GREENS	FRUITS AND VEGGIES	DRESSING	TOPPING
	3 ½ quarts trimmed and finely sliced, chopped, or shredded	1 ½ quarts trimmed and cut in dice, choppped, shredded, in strips, etc.	1 quart	1 cup (unless noted)
	2 large heads or bunches (1 to 2 pounds each)	Number and weight vary by type/variety		
Beautiful Beet Salad with Cherry Tomato Vinaigrette	Green curly kale Lacinato kale Beet greens	Beets (shredded) Tangerines/oranges Optional: Carrots (shredded)	Use Cherry Tomato and Basil Soup (page 144) as the vinaigrette	Fresh basil (¼ cup)
Rainbow Salad with Cherry Tomato–Beet Top Dressing	Baby greens Arugula Romaine Kale	Cucumber Purple cabbage Swiss chard stems Cherry tomatoes Orange bell peppers Carrots (shredded)	Cherry Tomato–Beet Top Dressing (page 144)	Optional: Cilantro (½ cup)
Rainbow Salad with Blackberry and Blue-Spice-Basil Dressing	Kale Rainbow Swiss chard	Celery Red, yellow, and orange bell peppers Strawberries Carrots Mango	Blackberry and Blue-Spice-Basil Dressing (page 166)	None
Light & Delicious	Romaine	Cucumbers Cherry tomatoes Mango Plum or cherry tomatoes Yellow bell peppers	Yellow Bell Pepper and Mango Dressing (page 160)	Carrots (shredded) Cherry tomatoes Purple cabbage bits
Rainbow Salad with Red Pepper–Hemp Seed Orange Dressing	Arugula Kale Baby greens Spinach	Yellow, red, and orange bell pepper Carrots (shredded) Celery Okra Zucchini (shredded or spiralized) Heirloom tomatoes Any other desired fruit	Red Pepper–Hemp Seed Orange Dressing (page 168)	Hemp seeds (¼ cup) or 1 medium avocado

KALE SALAD WITH CILANTRO TAHINI DRESSING

Makes 2 large or 4 regular salads

One of the well-known "secrets" for enjoying tough, assertive greens like kale is to massage a creamy dressing into the greens. Most recipes, even "healthy" vegan recipes, call for oil, but I never use extracted oils because of their high fat content and their lack of flavor. Using seeds in your dressings instead achieves the same luxurious consistency but with much richer flavor.

HERE'S WHAT YOU NEED:

2 bunches lacinato (dinosaur) or curly kale, tough stems removed, finely sliced (see page 90)

1 cup diced red, orange, or yellow bell peppers (about 1 ½ peppers)

2 green onions (white and green parts), trimmed, thinly chopped

1 pint cherry or grape tomatoes (about 12 ounces), stems removed, halved

2 cups Cilantro Tahini Dressing (page 163)

EQUIPMENT

Sharp chopping knife

Cutting board

Large salad bowl for tossing

Large bowls for serving

HERE'S WHAT YOU DO:

Combine the kale and the remaining vegetables in a large salad bowl.

Pour the dressing over the salad ingredients and toss with your hands, massaging the greens lightly to help coat them with dressing. Set the salad aside to allow the dressing to soak into the ingredients for 10 to 15 minutes. This will help to soften the tough fibers in the kale.

Serve in large bowls.

Know Your Kale

Green curly kale is the most commonly available variety. You will also find lacinato (aka dinosaur) kale, which is darker green. You can always substitute one for the other, but lacinato will be slightly tougher and have a more bitter taste.

FULLY RAW SWEET CORN SALAD

Makes 2 large or 4 regular salads

This dish celebrates my Ecuadorean roots. When you have fresh local corn, there is no better salad to make than this one! It tastes like summer and rocks like a party in your mouth. It's as easy as chopping up all of your ingredients, mixing them in a bowl, and sharing the beauty with those you love. This salad is a classic in my house and loved by all, especially my father. Be sure to chop all the vegetables about the same size as the corn kernels.

HERE'S WHAT YOU NEED:

For the salad

Kernels from 3 ears sweet corn (about 2 ¼ cups)

3 ripe tomatoes (about 1 ½ pounds), stems removed, cut in small dice

1 unwaxed cucumber, cut in small dice

1 celery stalk, cut in small dice

1 red bell pepper, stem and seeds removed, cut in small dice

3 leaves lacinato (dinosaur) or curly kale, tough stems removed, finely sliced (see page 90)

¼ cup finely diced red onion

Leaves from 1 bunch cilantro (about 1 cup), finely chopped

½ small avocado, pitted and peeled (see page 154), diced (optional)

1 peach or mango, peeled and pitted (see opposite), cut in small dice (optional)

Juice of 1 lemon or 2 limes (about ¼ cup)

For the dressing

3 ripe tomatoes (about 1 ½ pounds), stems removed, cut in chunks

½ small avocado, pitted and peeled (see page 154), diced

3 celery stalks, cut in chunks

1 slice of yellow onion

EQUIPMENT

Sharp chopping knife

Cutting board

Citrus juicer

High-speed blender, such as Vitamix

Large salad bowl for tossing

Large bowls for serving

HERE'S WHAT YOU DO:

To make the salad, collect the corn kernels and any juice that was released when cutting and put them in the salad bowl.

Add the remaining salad ingredients, and toss briefly.

To make the dressing, combine all ingredients in the blender and blend until smooth, starting on the slowest speed and gradually working up to the fastest. Blend on the highest speed until the mixture is uniformly smooth and the sound of the blender is high pitched and steady. Use the tamper to help everything blend smoothly. Reduce the speed of the blender to the lowest setting before turning it off.

Pour the dressing over the salad ingredients and toss with your hands, massaging lightly to help coat all of the vegetables with dressing. Set the salad aside to allow the dressing to soak into the ingredients for 10 to 15 minutes. Serve in large bowls.

Cutting Corn Kernels

To cut kernels off the cob, remove the husks and silks from the corn. Stand a corncob upright on the cutting board and cut straight down the sides, slicing the kernels off the cobs.

Prepping Mango

A cool way to cut your mango is to stand the mango on its thick end and cut the sides off the center pit, curving the knife around the pit. Working with one side at a time, cut the flesh of the mango in a grid pattern without slicing through the peel. Now bend the cut half of the mango and flip it inside out. The cubes of mango will splay out from the skin; slice off the cubes or simply eat the mango just like that!

POMEGRANATE SALAD WITH ORANGE BASIL DRESSING

Makes 1 large salad

The best way to seed a pomegranate is to cut off the pointy end, fill a big bowl with water, and put the pomegranate in the water. With your hands, break the fruit into four or five large chunks. Working piece by piece, gently rub the red seeds to separate them from the white pithy areas. Leave the seeds in the water, and discard the rind, the pith, and any bits of white membrane. The seeds will float to the top, then you can simply drain. In the recipe below, everything is tossed together, but you could also arrange the ingredients decoratively in the bowl and even add a few berries for a garnish—an edible work of art!

HERE'S WHAT YOU NEED:

2 quarts (about 5 ounces) spring mix lettuce

2 red radishes, spindly roots trimmed, quartered or halved if large, and thinly sliced

Seeds from 1 pomegranate (see above for how to extract seeds)

5 navel oranges or tangelos, peeled, white membrane cut away

Leaves from 1 bunch fresh basil (about ¾ ounce)

EQUIPMENT

Sharp chopping knife

Cutting board

Large salad bowl for tossing and serving

High-speed blender, such as Vitamix

HERE'S WHAT YOU DO:

Wash the lettuce thoroughly and shake off as much water as you can. Don't worry if it is not bone dry. Toss the lettuce, radishes, and a handful of pomegranate seeds in the salad bowl. Separate the oranges into sections; cut half of the sections in half and add to the bowl.

To make the dressing, put the remaining orange sections and the basil in the blender. Blend until smooth, starting on the slowest speed and gradually working up to the fastest. Blend on the highest speed until the mixture is uniformly smooth and the sound of the blender is high pitched and steady. Use the tamper to help everything blend smoothly. Reduce the speed of the blender to the lowest setting before turning it off.

Pour the dressing over the salad ingredients and toss with your hands. Add the remaining pomegranate seeds and toss again. Dig in and enjoy!

HEAVENLY PEACH AVOCADO SALAD

Makes 2 large salads

I know what you're thinking . . . salads are *boring*! They are made of tasteless, chewy, green rabbit food that gets stuck in your teeth, and are a pain to eat. Right?! Wrong! Salads are the way to get your minerals and a ton of other nutrients, especially if you are in the midst of adapting to a raw lifestyle or trying to get healthy. I like to mix fruit in with my salads for beauty and interest. Many fruits have a creamy consistency (I'm thinkin' peach and avocado, like in this salad, but also mango and apricot) that complements the crisp quality of most vegetables.

HERE'S WHAT YOU NEED:

5 peaches, pitted

2 red or yellow bell peppers, stems and seeds
    removed

2 bunches (about 1 ½ pounds) hearty greens like
    lacinato (dinosaur) or curly kale, romaine,
    or spinach, tough stems removed,
    finely sliced (see page 90)

1 to 2 pints cherry tomatoes (as many as you want),
    stems removed

½ avocado, pitted and peeled (see page 154)

1 bunch fresh basil or mint (about ¾ ounce)

EQUIPMENT

Sharp chopping knife

Cutting board

Large salad bowl for tossing and serving

High-speed blender, such as Vitamix

HERE'S WHAT YOU DO:

Cut three of the peaches into small dice. Cut one of the peppers into small dice. Toss all of the cut greens, peaches, and peppers in your salad bowl. Halve or quarter the cherry tomatoes if large and scatter them over the top.

To make the dressing, cut the remaining 2 peaches and 1 pepper into chunks and put in the blender. Coarsely chop the avocado and add to the blender. Add the herbs, and blend until smooth, starting on the slowest speed and gradually working up to the fastest. Blend on the highest speed until the mixture is uniformly smooth and the sound of the blender is high pitched and steady. Use the tamper to help everything blend smoothly. Reduce the speed of the blender to the lowest setting before turning it off.

Pour the dressing over the salad ingredients and toss with your hands, massaging the greens lightly to coat them with dressing. Set the salad aside to allow the dressing to soak into the ingredients for 10 to 15 minutes and give the flavors time to mingle. Dig in and enjoy!

SPICY MANGO BASIL SALAD

Makes 1 large salad

Let the sweet heat of this exotic Thai salad enliven your taste buds. The textures are smooth and creamy, the fruit is soothing and relaxing, and the hit of cayenne is just what your palate needs to hop to attention.

HERE'S WHAT YOU NEED:

For the salad

4 mangoes, peeled and pitted (see page 181), diced

2 sprigs fresh basil, finely chopped

¼ small red onion, finely diced

For the dressing

1 ripe mango, peeled and pitted (see page 181), cut in chunks

Juice of 1 juice orange (about ⅓ cup)

¼ teaspoon ground cayenne pepper

½ teaspoon ground aniseed

EQUIPMENT

Sharp chopping knife

Cutting board

Citrus juicer

Large salad bowl for tossing and serving

High-speed blender, such as Vitamix

HERE'S WHAT YOU DO:

To make the salad, mix all ingredients in a large salad bowl.

To make the dressing, put all ingredients into the blender and blend until smooth, starting on the slowest speed and gradually working up to the fastest. Blend on the highest speed until the mixture is uniformly smooth and the sound of the blender is high pitched and steady. Use the tamper to help everything blend smoothly. Reduce the speed of the blender to the lowest setting before turning it off.

Pour the dressing over the salad ingredients and toss with your hands, massaging the mango lightly to help coat it with dressing. Set the salad aside for 10 to 15 minutes to allow the dressing to soak into the ingredients and give the flavors time to mingle.

RAW VEGAN CHILI, BABY!

Makes 2 super-large or 3 regular servings

Hearty, satisfying, rich, and fun, this bowl of epic deliciousness is a special treat to share with all your family and friends! Or share my chili with your own happy tummy in front of a movie or on game day! It's low in fat and *so* rich and satisfying that it is sure to leave you hungry for more! Are you ready to spice it up!?!

HERE'S WHAT YOU NEED:

3 to 4 cups no-salt, no-oil sun-dried tomatoes

3 to 4 cups coarsely chopped ripe tomatoes (from 3 to 4 medium tomatoes, stems removed)

1 cup sliced cherry or grape tomatoes, stems removed

1 tablespoon chili powder

2 teaspoons sweet or hot paprika

½ teaspoon rubbed sage

1 teaspoon ground cumin

1 to 2 garlic cloves, minced

1 jalapeño chile (if you like it hot!), stem and seeds removed, minced

Dash of ground cayenne pepper (if you like it really hot!)

2 ¼ cups corn kernels (from about 3 ears, see page 181)

1 cup diced zucchini (from 1 medium zucchini)

½ cup diced celery (1 large stalk)

1 cup diced red bell pepper (1 large pepper)

½ cup chopped carrot (1 medium carrot)

½ cup chopped green onions (white and green parts) (from about 4 green onions)

½ cup finely chopped red onion (about ½ medium onion)

½ cup chopped cilantro leaves (from about ½ bunch)

4 basil leaves, chopped

Leaves from 1 sprig fresh thyme

1 cup sliced mushrooms

1 avocado, pitted and peeled (see page 154), sliced

EQUIPMENT

Sharp chopping knife

Cutting board

High-speed blender, such as Vitamix, or food processor

Rubber spatula

Mixing bowl

Bowls for serving

HERE'S WHAT YOU DO:

Put the sun-dried tomatoes in a mixing bowl and cover with water. Set aside for 30 to 60 minutes, until the tomatoes are plumped and tender. Drain the tomatoes.

Combine the sun-dried tomatoes, chopped tomatoes, cherry tomatoes, chili powder, paprika, sage, and cumin in the blender or food processor and process into a thick paste. With a spatula, scrape the spiced tomato base into a mixing bowl. Mix in the garlic, jalapeño, and cayenne, if using. These are powerhouse ingredients, so use as little or as much as you want, depending on how shy your mouth is feeling.

Pile on the corn, zucchini, celery, bell pepper, carrot, green onion, and red onion and mix into the tomato base.

Scatter the herbs, mushrooms, and avocado on top. Fold in so that the pieces are still bright and visible. Dig in and get spicy!

FULLY RAW LASAGNA

Makes 6 large servings

Lasagna is an all-time favorite of mine, and this is a Fully Raw masterpiece. It's delicious! It's nutritious! It's super rich! And it's even low in fat, so you can enjoy a big slice all by yourself! Your family will *love* this recipe. It's like a big slice of heaven! My Herbaceous Spread packs a seriously nutrient-rich punch. So not only is my lasagna rich and delicious, it's also super nutritious for you and your family.

HERE'S WHAT YOU NEED:

For the zucchini "noodles"
5 large zucchini (about 4 ½ pounds), stems removed

For the Herbaceous Spread
1 to 2 cups fresh flat-leaf (Italian) parsley, leaves and
    stems
3 cups arugula
½ bunch cilantro (about 1 ½ ounces), leaves and
    stems, coarsely chopped
1 small bunch spinach (about 6 ounces)
3 to 4 Swiss chard leaves, stems removed and saved
1 to 2 green onions (white and green parts), trimmed,
    cut in chunks

For the Epic Marinara Sauce
4 cups cherry tomatoes, or other chopped tomatoes,
    stems removed (or use sun-dried tomatoes;
    see Fully Raw Lasagna tips, page 192)
Reserved stems from Swiss chard leaves
Small handful of fresh oregano
A few sprigs fresh basil

For the Pine Nut Crème
1 small zucchini, stem removed, cut in chunks
¾ cup raw pine nuts
1 small garlic clove (optional)

For garnish
A few cherry tomatoes, stems removed, halved

EQUIPMENT

Sharp chopping knife
Cutting board
Mandoline, very sharp knife, or vegetable peeler
Food processor
Rubber spatula
High-speed blender, such as Vitamix
3 bowls
Deep-dish lasagna pan or platter

HERE'S WHAT YOU DO:

To make the zucchini "noodles," you will need a mandoline, a very sharp knife, or a vegetable peeler. First, cut the zucchini in half lengthwise. Then cut long, thin lengthwise slices (noodles) by running the zucchini down your mandoline, slicing by hand with a knife, or peeling with a vegetable peeler.

To make the Herbaceous Spread, puree all of the ingredients into a rich green paste in a food processor. Scrape into a bowl with a spatula and set aside.

To make the Epic Marinara Sauce, put all of the ingredients into the blender and blend until smooth. Pour into a bowl and set aside.

To make the Pine Nut Crème, put all ingredients into a blender and blend into a beautiful thick creamy filling. Pour into a bowl and set aside.

You now should have a lot of sliced zucchini "noodles," a bowl of herbaceous spread, a bowl of marinara sauce, a bowl of nut crème, and a couple pints halved cherry tomatoes. All you have left to do is assemble the lasagna:

Line the bottom of your deep-dish pan, if using, with a double layer of zucchini slices. The bottom layer needs to support a lot of food, so make sure this layer is thick and sturdy. You could also assemble everything on a platter, without the pan, for a more freestanding lasagna.

Top the zucchini layer with ingredients in the following order:

herbaceous spread (about a third)

marinara (about a third)

zucchini (8 or 10 slices)

more herbaceous spread (half of the remaining amount)

nut crème (about half)

more zucchini

the remaining herbaceous spread

more marinara (half of the remaining amount)

Place the lasagna in the freezer for about 30 minutes to help firm the layers. Remove from the freezer and add:

more zucchini

the remaining nut crème

the remaining marinara

final layer of zucchini

Freeze for another 2 hours (but no longer; see note on page 192) to help everything firm up and make the lasagna easier to slice.

If you want to sprinkle more marinara sauce on top, go for it! Cut the lasagna into squares and serve garnished with cherry tomato halves.

Fully Raw Lasagna Tips

Straining your marinara sauce after it has been blended will prevent the lasagna from getting watered down or runny. If you really want the dish to be firm, you can use 1 cup sun-dried tomatoes instead of fresh tomatoes. Look for the oil-free, salt-free variety, usually sold in bulk bins or online. You can use either the moist type (similar to the texture of raisins) or the hard, crispy type. You can use dried herbs in this dish, but I highly recommend fresh herbs for maximum flavor and intensity.

The Science of Freezing Vegetables

Although frozen fruit and vegetables are still raw, the process of freezing them can change their texture. Plant cells are loaded with water, up to 96 percent (see Water Content of Fruits and Vegetables, page 29), and their cell walls are rigid, unlike animal cells, which contain less water and have flexible, permeable walls. When you freeze anything containing water the water expands slightly. Freeze a plastic bag of water and the bag will expand with its contents, but freeze a glass jar and the glass will likely break because it is too brittle to expand along with its contents. Raw plant cells are like that glass jar. If they freeze solid they will rupture, leach out their water, and become soft and mushy. In the lasagna recipe most of the vegetables have been pureed before you put the lasagna in the freezer, so their cell walls are already broken, but the halved cherry tomatoes and the zucchini need to remain in their current form; if they should freeze completely they will break down. That is why you want to freeze the lasagna just long enough to firm everything up, but not so long that it freezes solid.

STRAWBERRY SPINACH SALAD

Makes 1 large salad or 2 regular salads

This is a beautiful salad—ruby red slices of ripe strawberries burst against a field of dark green spinach leaves. And the flavor combo is just as glorious! You can lighten the fat content by using fewer nuts, or if you don't like pecans, you can replace them with walnuts or leave the nuts out altogether. The longer you allow the salad to sit, the more the flavors meld, and the more delicious the salad becomes.

HERE'S WHAT YOU NEED:

For the salad

12 ounces ripe strawberries, greens removed

⅓ cup raw pecan halves

2 bunches spinach leaves, thinly sliced
    (see page 90)

¼ red bell pepper, stem and seeds removed, finely
    diced (optional)

For the Strawberry Vinaigrette

4 ounces ripe strawberries

2 tangerines, peeled

Juice of 1 lemon (about ¼ cup)

EQUIPMENT

Sharp chopping knife

Cutting board

Citrus juicer

Large salad bowl for tossing

High-speed blender, such as Vitamix

Large bowls for serving

HERE'S WHAT YOU DO:

To make the salad, thinly slice the strawberries. Smash the pecan pieces with the flat side of a broad-bladed knife. Combine the spinach, sliced berries, pecans, and bell pepper, if using, in a large salad bowl.

To make the Strawberry Vinaigrette, put the strawberries, tangerines, and lemon juice in the blender and blend until smooth, starting on the slowest speed and gradually working up to the fastest. Blend on the highest speed until the mixture is uniformly smooth and the sound of the blender is high pitched and steady. Use the tamper to help everything blend smoothly. Reduce the speed of the blender to the lowest setting before turning it off.

Pour the dressing over the salad ingredients and toss with your hands, massaging the greens lightly to coat them with dressing. Set the salad aside for 10 to 15 minutes for the dressing to soak into the ingredients before serving.

AWESOMESAUCE BURRITOS

Makes 8 burritos, 2 large servings

These bee-YOU-tee-ful burritos contain every color of the rainbow. They're satisfying. They're low in fat. And the spicy sesame-lemon Awesomesauce ROCKS! Devour with gusto!

HERE'S WHAT YOU NEED:

For the burritos

8 large collards leaves, tough stems shaved flat with a knife

2 red, yellow, or orange bell peppers, stems and seeds removed, cut in strips

1 unwaxed cucumber (about 10 ounces), julienned

2 carrots, peeled and coarsely shredded

1 pint cherry tomatoes (about 12 ounces), halved

Leaves from 1 small bunch cilantro (about 1 ounce), roughly chopped

1 green onion (green parts), trimmed, finely chopped

1 cup alfalfa sprouts

¼ avocado, pitted and peeled (see page 154)

¼ red onion, thinly sliced

For the Awesomesauce

1 zucchini (about 8 ounces), cut in chunks

3 ½ tablespoons raw unhulled sesame seeds

Juice of 2 lemons or 4 limes (about ½ cup)

1 green onion (green and white parts), trimmed, cut in chunks

1 red bell pepper, stem and seeds removed, cut in chunks

1 jalapeño chile, stem and seeds removed, cut in chunks

EQUIPMENT

Sharp chopping knife

Cutting board

Citrus juicer

High-speed blender, such as Vitamix

Large platter for serving

Serving bowl for sauce

HERE'S WHAT YOU DO:

Arrange all of the burrito ingredients for easy assembly.

To make the Awesomesauce, put all ingredients in the blender and blend until smooth, starting on the slowest speed and gradually working up to the fastest. Blend on the highest speed until the mixture is uniformly smooth and the sound of the blender is high pitched and steady. Use the tamper to help everything blend smoothly. Reduce the speed of the blender to the lowest setting before turning it off.

To assemble the burritos: Lay a collard leaf out flat. Coat with a tablespoon or two of Awesomesauce.

Arrange some of each burrito ingredient on one side of the collard, leaving a border on both ends. Fold in the side borders and roll up like a burrito. Flip it over, seam side down, and cut in half.

Repeat with the remaining ingredients. You can either build all of the burritos before serving or serve the fixings and let everyone make their own.

MACHO TACOS

Makes 8 tacos, 2 large servings

Sometimes, you just gotta have a little *umph* in your life to make you feel macho! These romaine-wrapped tacos take just ten minutes to prepare, and they're rockin' awesome! Enjoy!

HERE'S WHAT YOU NEED:

For the filling

Kernels from 3 ears sweet corn (about 2 ¼ cups; see page 181)

1 large mango (about 1 pound), peeled and pitted (see page 181), diced

1 pint cherry tomatoes (about 12 ounces), stems removed, halved and sliced

⅛ red onion, finely chopped

Leaves from 1 small bunch cilantro (about 1 ounce), chopped

½ avocado, pitted and peeled (see page 154), diced

3 romaine leaves, cut in thin strips (see page 90)

2 celery stalks, thinly sliced

For the sauce

1 large tomato (about 12 ounces), coarsely chopped

1 small bunch basil (about ¾ ounce), coarsely chopped

Juice of ½ lemon (about 2 tablespoons)

½ jalapeño chile, stem and seeds removed, chopped

For assembly

8 large romaine leaves, washed and dried

EQUIPMENT

Sharp chopping knife

Cutting board

Citrus juicer

High-speed blender, such as Vitamix

Large bowl, for serving

Platter

HERE'S WHAT YOU DO:

To make the filling, collect the corn kernels and any juice that was released when cutting and put in a large bowl. Add the remaining filling ingredients and toss.

To make the sauce, put all ingredients into the blender and blend until smooth, starting on the slowest speed and gradually working up to the fastest. Blend on the highest speed until the mixture is uniformly smooth and the sound of the blender is high pitched and steady. Use the tamper to help everything blend smoothly. Reduce the speed of the blender to the lowest setting before turning it off.

Pour the sauce over the filling and toss with your hands, massaging lightly to coat. Set aside for 10 to 15 minutes to give the flavors time to mingle.

To serve, scoop the filling into the romaine leaves or transfer to a bowl and surround with romaine for scooping. Eat up!

JICAMA RICE WITH ORANGE SPICE

Makes 1 large or 2 regular servings

Need an alternative to conventional rice? Or perhaps you just need more spice in your life? Yup! This is the recipe for you! Dance in your kitchen along with me as we make this "rice" together!

HERE'S WHAT YOU NEED:

1 bunch lacinato (dinosaur) or curly kale, tough stems removed, finely sliced (see page 90)

1 large jicama or 3 kohlrabi (about 1 pound), roots and stem trimmed, peeled

Leaves from 1 small bunch cilantro (about 1 ounce), coarsely chopped

½ red or green bell pepper, stem and seeds removed, coarsely chopped

¼ small red onion, coarsely chopped

Juice of 5 oranges (about 2 ¼ cups)

Juice of 1 lemon (about ¼ cup)

Pinch of ground cayenne pepper

2 green onions (white and green parts), trimmed, thinly chopped

EQUIPMENT

Sharp chopping knife

Cutting board

Citrus juicer

Food processor

Large platter for serving

HERE'S WHAT YOU DO:

Pile the kale on the platter as a bed for the jicama rice.

Cut the jicama in chunks sized to fit through the feed tube of your food processor. Use the fine shredding disk to process the jicama into tiny bits that resemble grains of rice. Pile on the bed of kale.

Wipe out the food processor and use the blade attachment to make the sauce: Pulse the cilantro, bell pepper, and red onion until finely chopped. Add the orange juice, lemon juice, and cayenne and process briefly to combine.

Pour the sauce over the jicama rice and kale and scatter the green onions over the top. Serve immediately and enjoy!

STUFFED RED PEPPERS WITH AVOCADO SALSA

Makes 3 large servings

Are you ready to get *hot?* Because they're made with sweet bell peppers rather than chiles, my stuffed peppers may not be *spicy* hot, but they look so alluring—they're *sexy* hot, which is so much better than just spicy! The stuffing tastes best when made with a variety of greens, but feel free to use 4 or 5 leaves of a single type. You can also substitute spinach leaves, but you will need a big bunch to get enough filling.

HERE'S WHAT YOU NEED:

2 lacinato (dinosaur) or curly kale leaves, tough stems removed, finely sliced (see page 90)

1 Swiss chard leaf, finely chopped

1 collard leaf, tough stem removed, finely chopped

2 tomatoes (about 1 pound), stems removed, coarsely chopped

2 celery stalks, coarsely chopped

Leaves from 1 small bunch cilantro (about 1 ounce), coarsely chopped

1 green onion (white and green parts), trimmed, coarsely chopped

1 small avocado, pitted and peeled (see page 154), diced

1 cup packed spinach leaves

3 large red bell peppers, tops cut off and reserved, seeds removed

1 pint cherry tomatoes (about 12 ounces), stems removed, halved

12 chives, cut in ½-inch lengths

EQUIPMENT

Sharp chopping knife

Cutting board

Food processor

2 mixing bowls

Serving plate

HERE'S WHAT YOU DO:

Combine the kale, chard, and collards in a bowl. Toss and set aside.

Combine the tomatoes, celery, cilantro, green onion, avocado, and spinach in the food processor and pulse until all of the vegetables are finely chopped and the avocado is creamy.

Pour two-thirds of the salsa over the greens and mix until well combined.

Stuff the peppers with the greens mixture. Scatter the cherry tomatoes and chives over all and dollop with the remaining salsa. Replace the pepper tops.

RAW ZUCCHINI PASTA WITH FRESH TOMATO MARINARA

Makes 1 large or 2 regular servings

I get notes from people all the time asking me what is my favorite salad dressing. Well, this marinara has got to be it. Not only is it great as a salad dressing, but it's also a wonderful, simple cold soup, as well as a go-to marinara that I put on pretty much everything, like zucchini noodles. Which brings us to this recipe, right here! The finished dish is hearty and filling and the zucchini noodles are naturally al dente. You will want to slurp up every bit. Yum!

HERE'S WHAT YOU NEED:

4 large zucchini (about 3 pounds), stems removed

4 medium tomatoes (about 2 pounds), stems removed, cut in chunks

3 celery stalks, cut in chunks

Juice of ½ lemon (about 2 tablespoons)

1 cup packed fresh basil leaves (about 1 ½ ounces)

¼ cup fresh oregano or thyme leaves, plus more for garnish

¼ cup raw pine nuts; or ½ avocado, pitted and peeled (see page 154), optional

EQUIPMENT

Sharp chopping knife

Cutting board

Citrus juicer

Spiral slicer, julienne peeler, mandoline, or vegetable peeler

Food processor

Large bowl for serving

HERE'S WHAT YOU DO:

Use a spiral slicer, julienne peeler, mandoline, or vegetable peeler to make noodles (see opposite page) from the zucchini. Transfer to a large bowl and set aside.

Put the remaining ingredients, except the pine nuts or avocado, in a food processor and pulse until saucy but still chunky—definitely not pureed. If you would like the sauce to have a creamier texture, add the pine nuts or avocado.

Pour the sauce over the zucchini pasta and garnish with extra oregano or thyme leaves. Toss and enjoy!

How to Make Zucchini Noodles

Two of my best weight-loss foods are cucumbers and zucchinis. One of my favorite, and most addictive, ways to enjoy them is by making them into long, thin slices that look and feel a lot like perfectly cooked noodles . . . or what I like to call noodley doodley "zoodles." They are filling and delicious and low in sugar and calories too. You can eat as *much* of these zoodles as you wish and be in the negative calorie zone for the day.

There are many ways to make veggie noodles: You can use a sharp knife and considerable knife skills, or you can use a julienne peeler or a serrated vegetable peeler (hold the peeler in one hand and the vegetable in the other, and run the peeler down the length of the vegetable). My favorite method is to use a spiral slicer for perfect zucchini linguine. I like the Spiralizer, but other popular brands include Spirelli and Veggetti. The Spiralizer consists of a frame that holds a vertical blade, and a spindle that holds a cylindrical vegetable, like a zucchini or cucumber, by its end. You insert the vegetable on the spindle and turn the handle attached to it. The vegetable will move forward, spinning into the blade. It emerges on the other side cut into perfect spiraled ribbons—zoodles!

FULLY RAW FETTUCCINE ALFREDO

Makes 1 large or 2 regular servings

When I first went Fully Raw, I sat down and thought of all of the recipes that I loved to make but were making me sick (see My Story, page 44). One of these was fettuccine Alfredo. Everybody *loves* fettuccine Alfredo. But with its high fat content, we have to admit a bowl weighs us down with a big "gut lump." Well, my version has hardly any fat and leaves you feeling light and lively. The secret is cauliflower. By mincing up cauliflower florets in a food processor, you get a soft snowy avalanche that looks and feels like fluffy Parmesan cheese. It's amazing. Finally, a low-fat raw vegan recipe for fettuccine Alfredo! Are you dreaming?

HERE'S WHAT YOU NEED:

5 large zucchini (about 4½ pounds), stems removed, peeled if desired

1 celery stalk, cut in chunks

¼ cup raw pine nuts

1 garlic clove, halved

Juice of ½ lemon (about 2 tablespoons)

Leaves from 3 fresh basil sprigs

4 fresh sage leaves

Florets from ½ head cauliflower, coarsely chopped

EQUIPMENT

Sharp chopping knife

Cutting board

Citrus juicer

Spiral slicer, julienne peeler, mandoline, or vegetable peeler

High-speed blender, such as Vitamix

Food processor

Rubber spatula

Large bowl for serving

HERE'S WHAT YOU DO:

Use a spiral slicer, julienne peeler, mandoline, or vegetable peeler to make zucchini noodles (see page 201) with 4 of the zucchini. Transfer to a large bowl and set aside.

Cut the remaining zucchini into chunks and put in the blender along with the celery, pine nuts, garlic, lemon juice, basil, and sage. Blend until smooth, starting on the slowest speed and gradually working up to the fastest. Blend on the highest speed until the mixture is uniformly smooth and the sound of the blender is high pitched and steady. Use the tamper to help everything blend smoothly. Reduce the speed of the blender to the lowest setting before turning it off. Pour the sauce over the noodles.

Pulse the cauliflower in the food processor until it becomes like soft flakes of snow. This finely chopped cauliflower is going to be the "cheese" for our noodles.

Scrape half of the cauliflower into the sauced noodles with a spatula and toss to coat all of the noodles. Transfer to a serving bowl and scatter the remaining cauliflower "cheese" over the top.

MEDITERRANEAN TABOULI

Makes 3 large servings

One of the first recipe videos that I put up on YouTube was for Mediterranean Tabouli. Tabouli (or tabbouleh) was a staple in my Lebanese household. The salad is generally made with all raw ingredients and grains, usually bulgur. I've replaced the bulgur with finely processed cauliflower. Cauliflower gives the same texture, but a much deeper flavor, because it absorbs the lemon and tomato juice and truly brings out all of the flavors in the dish.

HERE'S WHAT YOU NEED:

Florets from ½ head of cauliflower

Leaves from 3 large bunches (6 ounces) flat-leaf (Italian) or curly parsley, coarsely chopped

1 bunch mint (about ½ ounce), coarsely chopped

3 beefsteak tomatoes (about 2 pounds), stems removed, cut in small dice

1 unwaxed cucumber (about 10 ounces), cut in small dice

2 celery stalks, cut in small dice

3 green onions (white and green parts), trimmed, thinly chopped

Juice of 2 lemons (about ½ cup)

EQUIPMENT

Sharp chopping knife

Cutting board

Citrus juicer

Food processor

Large salad bowl for tossing

Large bowls for serving

HERE'S WHAT YOU DO:

Pulse the cauliflower in the food processor until finely chopped. It will be soft and fluffy, like snow. Transfer to the salad bowl.

Process the parsley and mint in the food processor until finely chopped. Add to the bowl with the cauliflower and toss.

Add the tomato, cucumber, celery, and green onions and toss well. Add the lemon juice and toss again. Set aside for 15 minutes to allow the flavors to mingle. Toss before serving.

The Fully Raw Household

When I first went Fully Raw, it was difficult for my family to accept my new way of eating. Going from an Ecuadorean-Lebanese diet that is heavy in meat and dairy to one that is rich in fruits and vegetables and devoid of animal products was challenging. Creating Fully Raw versions of the dishes my family enjoys enabled me to continue to share food with them.

FULLY RAW PAD THAI

Makes 2 large servings

Fully Raw vegan pad thai! Bright, vibrant, rich, delicious, creamy! My mother and I developed this healthy Asian feast as we were experimenting with creative dishes to enjoy together. I am so proud of my mother for going vegan and eating healthier, and I hope that she inspires you to greater health as well! Get your chopsticks; ready—go!

HERE'S WHAT YOU NEED:

For the pad thai

2 large zucchini (about 1 ½ pounds), stems removed, coarsely shredded

2 to 3 carrots (about 1 pound), coarsely shredded

¼ small red cabbage (about 6 ounces), coarsely shredded

1 red bell pepper, stem and seeds removed, cut in thin strips

8 ounces small white mushrooms (about 2 cups), thinly sliced

4 ounces (about 1 cup) mung bean sprouts

1 jalapeño chile, stem and seeds removed, minced

For the sauce

¾ cup raw unhulled sesame seeds

¼ cup raw shelled pistachios

½ cup fresh apple juice (from about 1 apple)

⅓ cup fresh orange juice (from about 1 orange)

1 lime, peeled and cut in chunks

¼ lemon, peeled and cut in chunks

1 medium thumb (about 1 inch) fresh ginger, cut in chunks

For the garnish

½ cup chopped cilantro leaves

¼ cup packed fresh mint leaves, coarsely chopped

1 bunch green onions (white and green parts), trimmed, thinly chopped

¼ cup raw shelled pistachios, finely chopped

EQUIPMENT

Sharp chopping knife

Cutting board

Citrus juicer

Large mixing bowl

High-speed blender, such as Vitamix

Rubber spatula

Large serving platter

HERE'S WHAT YOU DO:

To make the pad thai, toss all ingredients in a large mixing bowl.

To make the sauce, put all ingredients in the blender and blend until smooth, starting on the slowest speed and gradually working up to the fastest. Blend on the highest speed until the mixture is uniformly smooth and the sound of the blender is high pitched and steady. Use the tamper to help everything blend smoothly. Reduce the speed of the blender to the lowest setting before turning it off.

With a spatula, scrape the sauce from the blender into the bowl of pad thai and toss. Mound onto a serving platter and garnish with the cilantro, mint, green onions, and pistachios.

DESSERTS

Sweets are the way to anyone's heart. Over the past few years, I have become a master at creating Fully Raw desserts. I have learned to turn raw fruits and veggies into art forms that resemble ice cream, pies, cakes, and more. Fruit in and of itself is a dessert and can even be eaten as a whole meal. If you think about it, a mono-meal of fruit could be a whole meal of dessert! And that's okay! Eating Fully Raw is about indulging in abundance that's good for you! In fact, when your every meal consists of fresh fruits and vegetables, there is very little difference between a main meal and a dessert. They are all just different ways of pleasing your palate while eating the healthiest ingredients you can.

I have made most of these dessert recipes low in fat so that you can enjoy large portions without feeling any guilt. I want you to be able to eat with freedom. Enjoy these desserts in balance with the rest of the recipes in this book, and you will be in good shape.

This chapter contains recipes for a few cakes and pies that, while they can be consumed as soon as they are assembled, benefit from some time in the freezer to help them firm up enough to slice cleanly. Normally this takes about 4 hours. When this is the case, be sure to plan ahead. I have found it easiest to make the dessert the night before, and remove it from the freezer about an hour before I plan to serve it, to give it time to lose its chill.

Let these treats take you to heaven! They are amazing, and I hope that you enjoy them as much as I do!

BANANA BERRY "NICE" CREAM

Makes 2 servings, about 1 ½ cups each

Low-fat raw vegan soft-serve-style ice cream is one of the easiest and most delicious desserts to make at home. Although any fruit can be used with this simple method, bananas give the creamiest result. I like to peel overripe bananas and freeze them in a resealable bag, to keep on hand for a "nice" treat anytime!

HERE'S WHAT YOU NEED:

8 very ripe bananas, peeled and frozen solid, cut in 2-inch pieces

Pinch of ground cinnamon

Seeds scraped from ½ vanilla bean (see page 133)

1 cup fresh raspberries

1 cup fresh strawberries, greens removed

More berries for garnish (optional)

EQUIPMENT

Sharp chopping knife

Cutting board

High-speed blender, such as Vitamix

Rubber spatula

Medium mixing bowl

2 bowls, for serving

HERE'S WHAT YOU DO:

Put the bananas, cinnamon, and vanilla seeds in the blender and blend until smooth, starting on the slowest speed and gradually working up to the fastest. Blend on the highest speed until the mixture is uniformly smooth and the sound of the blender is high pitched and steady. Use the tamper to help everything blend smoothly. If you are using a Vitamix, turn the switch on the right from variable speed to high halfway through blending to get the smoothest mixture. Reduce the speed of the blender to the lowest setting before turning it off.

Scrape the banana mixture into the mixing bowl with a spatula. Rinse the blender, then add the raspberries and strawberries and blend until smooth.

Pour the berry puree into the banana mixture. Using a spatula, swirl the berries into the frozen banana mixture, making streaks of color—do not blend too well. Serve the ice cream and top with more berries, if desired. This dessert can be kept in the freezer for about 2 hours, but after that it will start to freeze solid and will need to be chopped up and blended again to come back to a creamy consistency.

HAPPY BIRTHDAY! CARROT CAKE

Makes 1 large cake, about 8 servings

I created this cake for my 27th birthday (more than a quarter century—makes a girl think!). It's fragrant and rich and multilayered and creamy and rich (did I say that already?) ... extraordinary in every way. When I was little I loved carrot cake, so I created this recipe to relive that childhood memory, only this time with great nutrition so that I can enjoy a huge piece and share it with all of my family and friends. Life is worth celebrating! Happy birthday to me! Happy living to you!

HERE'S WHAT YOU NEED:

For the cake

4 to 6 cups pulp from about 3 pounds carrots (enjoy the juice too!)

2 cups dried mulberries (about 8 ounces)

1 cup raisins (see page 214)

2 cups fresh Medjool dates (about 1 pound), pitted

1 teaspoon ground ginger

1 tablespoon ground cinnamon

Seeds scraped from ½ vanilla bean (see page 133)

For the frosting

3 ½ cups raw cashews, soaked in water for about 30 minutes and drained

3 ½ cups fresh young coconut water (from 3 to 4 young coconuts; see page 35), or store-bought raw coconut water

10 fresh Medjool dates, pitted and coarsely chopped

1 tablespoon fresh lemon juice

1 teaspoon ground cinnamon

Seeds scraped from ½ vanilla bean

1 teaspoon rose water (as a special birthday treat, because it is sweet and floral and magical)

For the topping

½ cup raw pistachios, coarsely chopped

½ cup shredded coconut

2 tablespoons finely grated orange zest

EQUIPMENT

Sharp chopping knife

Cutting board

9-inch parchment paper circle

9-inch springform pan

Citrus juicer

Citrus zester or Microplane

Food processor

High-speed blender, such as Vitamix

Rubber spatula

Serving platter

HERE'S WHAT YOU DO:

Line the springform pan with the parchment paper and set aside.

To make the cake, process all ingredients in the food processor until everything is very finely chopped and the mixture clings to itself in a ball.

To make the frosting, put all ingredients in the blender and blend until smooth, starting on the slowest speed and gradually working up to the fastest. Blend on the highest speed until the mixture is uniformly smooth and the sound of the blender is high pitched and steady. Use the tamper to help everything blend smoothly. Reduce the speed of the blender to the lowest setting before turning it off. The frosting should be thick, like whipped cream.

To assemble the cake, spread about one-third of the cake mixture in a layer in the bottom of the pan using a spatula. Top with one-quarter of the frosting. Repeat with another one-third of the cake mixture,

another one-quarter of the frosting, the remaining cake, and another one-quarter of the frosting (you will still have one-quarter of the frosting left). Put the cake, still in its pan, in the freezer for about 2 hours, until set.

Remove the side from the pan and transfer the cake to a serving platter. Spread the remaining frosting around the side of the cake with the spatula and then top with a sprinkling of the topping ingredients. Cut in slices, serve, and don't forget to sing "Happy Birthday."

Raw Dried Fruit

Fruit that is dried at low temperature (118°F or below) is considered raw and will be labeled as such.

FULLY RAW STRAWBERRY SHORTCAKE

Makes 10 to 12 servings

Raw vegan strawberry shortcake? No way! Yes, WAY!!! This is a miraculous, mind-blowing extravaganza of a dessert. The results are pretty massive, so I usually save this for when I have to feed and impress a crowd. The preparation is intensive, but I promise that I will never make you spend time with food preparation unless I believe the results will be spectacular.

HERE'S WHAT YOU NEED:

For the crust

1 pound (about 24) fresh Medjool dates, pitted and quartered

2 ounces dried mulberries (about ½ cup)

3 ounces (4 to 6) raw dried white or black figs, stems removed, quartered

Seeds scraped from ½ vanilla bean (see page 133)

2 teaspoons ground cinnamon

For the filling

2 ¾ pounds strawberries (about 2 ½ pints), greens on

1 cup raw almond milk, preferably freshly made (see page 222)

1 banana, peeled and frozen, coarsely chopped

½ pound raw cashews (about 2 cups)

For the glaze

¼ pound strawberries, greens removed

4 fresh Medjool dates, pitted and coarsely chopped

EQUIPMENT

Sharp chopping knife

Cutting board

9-inch springform pan

9-inch parchment paper circle

Mixing bowl

Food processor

High-speed blender, such as Vitamix

Rubber spatula

Thin-bladed knife

Cake platter

HERE'S WHAT YOU DO:

Line the springform pan with the parchment and set aside.

To make the crust, toss all ingredients in a mixing bowl. Put half in the food processor and pulse until the mixture is smooth enough to cling to itself in a ball. Transfer to the springform pan and repeat with the rest of the crust ingredients. Wet your hands with cold water and press all the crust mixture evenly across the bottom of the pan. If the crust should start to stick to your hands, wet them again. Set the pan aside.

To make the filling, set aside 10 perfect strawberries for the garnish. Remove the greens from the rest and slice in ¼-inch slices. Set aside.

Put the almond milk, frozen banana, and cashews in the blender. Blend until smooth, starting on the slowest speed and gradually working up to the fastest. Blend on the highest speed until the mixture is uniformly smooth and the sound of the blender is high pitched and steady. Use the tamper to help everything blend smoothly. Reduce the speed of the blender to the lowest setting before turning it off. The filling should be thick like whipped cream.

To assemble the dessert, arrange about one-third of the sliced strawberries in a single layer on the crust. Top with a coating of about one-third of the filling. Repeat with another layer of strawberries, another layer of filling, a final layer of strawberries, and a final layer of filling.

To finish the dessert, make the glaze. Wash out the blender. Put the strawberries and dates in the blender and puree following the same method you used for blending the filling. Pour onto the top of the cake and spread evenly with a spatula.

Cut the reserved strawberries in half lengthwise, leaving their greens on for decoration, and arrange on the top of the cake around the edge.

Put the cake in the freezer to firm for about 4 hours.

To serve, run a knife around the edges and then remove the side of the springform pan. Put a sheet of parchment paper over the cake and cover with a cutting board. Invert the cake with the cutting board so that the base of the springform is now on top. Remove the pan base, using the parchment paper between the crust and pan base to help you lift it. Invert the cake again on to the cake platter and remove the parchment paper from the top. Cut the cake into serving pieces, and allow them to rest at room temperature for about 10 minutes or in the refrigerator for up to 2 hours to allow the harder frozen section to soften.

This cake can be frozen solid and stored in the freezer for up to 2 weeks, although the texture of the berries will suffer a little. If you do this, thaw in the refrigerator for at least 4 hours before slicing.

FULLY RAW CHOCOLATE PECAN PIE

Makes 12 servings

It's not quite the holidays without a slice of pecan pie, so here is my Fully Raw-ified version of that all-time holiday classic. I have made it even more indulgent by adding a chocolate twist, so it's decadent, it's rich, it's sweet, and it's probably the most insane pie that I have *ever* made. Now, I know what you may be thinking . . . this pie must be incredibly high in fat. Well, it kinda is, because it has both pecans and cashews in it. But you gotta indulge a little during the holidays, right? Why not do it with a Fully Raw pie that is way healthier than pies made with sugar, corn syrup, butter, white flour, and eggs?

HERE'S WHAT YOU NEED:

For the crust

8 ounces dried mulberries (about 2 cups)

9 fresh Medjool dates, pitted and coarsely chopped

For the cashew crème

¼ pound raw cashews, soaked in water for about 30 minutes and drained

¾ cup fresh young coconut water (from 1 young coconut; see page 35), or store-bought raw coconut water

8 fresh Medjool dates, pitted and coarsely chopped

For the pecan layer

4 apples (about 2 pounds), cored and cut in chunks

14 fresh Medjool dates, pitted and coarsely chopped

3 ounces raw pecan pieces (about ¾ cup)

Seeds scraped from ½ vanilla bean (see page 133)

1 teaspoon ground cinnamon

For the chocolate icing

14 fresh Medjool dates, pitted and coarsely chopped

1 cup raw organic carob powder

1 cup fresh young coconut water (from 1 young coconut), or store-bought raw coconut water

1 teaspoon ground cinnamon

For decoration

4 ounces raw pecan halves (about 1 cup)

EQUIPMENT

Sharp chopping knife

Cutting board

Food processor

9-inch springform pan

High-speed blender, such as Vitamix

Rubber spatula

Thin-bladed knife

HERE'S WHAT YOU DO:

To make the crust, put the mulberries and dates in the food processor and pulse until the mixture is sticky enough to climb the sides of the work bowl. Transfer to the springform pan. Wet your hands with cold water and press the crust mixture evenly across the bottom of the pan. If the crust should start to stick to your hands, wet them again.

To make the cashew crème, put all ingredients in the blender and blend until smooth, starting on the slowest speed and gradually working up to the fastest. Blend on the highest speed until the mixture is uniformly smooth and the sound of the blender is high pitched and steady. Use the tamper to help everything blend smoothly. Reduce the speed of the blender to the lowest setting before turning it off. Pour the crème over the crust layer in the pan and spread evenly with a rubber spatula. Wash out the blender.

To make the pecan layer, put all ingredients in the blender and blend using the same method, until the mixture becomes smooth and the consistency of thick creamy applesauce. Pour over the cashew crème layer in the pan and spread evenly with a rubber spatula. Wash out the blender.

To make the chocolate icing, put all ingredients in the blender and blend using the same method. Pour over the pecan layer in the pan and spread evenly with a rubber spatula.

Decorate the top of the pie with concentric circles of raw pecan halves.

Although you can serve the pecan pie at this point, it will be too soft to slice into neat pieces, so I recommend delaying gratification and freezing it for at least 6 hours to help it set up. Even if it should stay in the freezer for 24 hours or more, the pie will not freeze solid; it will retain a creamy consistency. To serve, run a thin-bladed knife around the edge of the pie, separating it from the side of the pan. Remove the side of the pan. Cut your pie into serving pieces and indulge!

HOLIDAY RAW NOGS

Each variation makes 2 large or 4 small servings

Get cozy with a Fully Raw nog. It hits the spot and reignites the comforting nostalgia of sitting by a fire at holiday time. Because it involves no heating and only simple ingredients, it's fast and easy to prepare. Share the love by the glass with your friends and family. Let others know that there is no reason to feel like you can't be healthy *and* social. They will *love* this drink as much as you and I do! Make any one or all of the following three holiday nogs. All are suitable for guests who cannot tolerate lactose.

HERE'S WHAT YOU NEED:

Classic Holiday Raw Nog

1 cup fresh young coconut water (from 1 young coconut; see page 35), or store-bought raw coconut water

1 cup homemade cashew crème or milk or almond crème or milk (see page 222) or store-bought raw nut milk

6 fresh Medjool dates (about 4 ounces), pitted and coarsely chopped

1 banana, peeled and cut in chunks

1 teaspoon pumpkin pie spice

Fat- and Nut-Free Holiday Nog

2 bananas, peeled and cut in chunks

1 pear, stemmed, cored, and cut in chunks

½ teaspoon ground cinnamon

1 cup ice cubes

My Special Super-Sweet Holiday Nog

6 bananas, peeled and cut in chunks

6 fresh Medjool dates (about 4 ounces), pitted and coarsely chopped

¼ teaspoon ground cinnamon

Pinch of ground nutmeg

1 or 2 ice cubes, enough to provide the desired chill

EQUIPMENT

Sharp chopping knife

Cutting board

High-speed blender, such as Vitamix

8- to 32-ounce glasses, for serving

HERE'S WHAT YOU DO:

For all three versions, put the ingredients in the blender and blend until smooth, starting on the slowest speed and gradually working up to the fastest. Blend on the highest speed until the mixture is uniformly smooth and the sound of the blender is high pitched and steady. Use the tamper to help everything blend smoothly. Reduce the speed of the blender to the lowest setting before turning it off.

Pour into glasses and enjoy with those you love!

Nut Crèmes and Milks

You can use nuts to make smooth, delicious crèmes and milks with no dairy whatsoever. Cashews and almonds are especially good for this. Using a blender yields a rich, creamy liquid—I call that one crème. Using a juicer makes the finished milk thinner and lower in fat—I call that one milk. This recipe makes about 1 quart of either. Both the crème and milk can be refrigerated for up to 1 week in a tightly closed container.

Cashew or Almond Crème and Milk

If you are using cashews: Soak 2 cups (8 ounces) raw cashews in 2 cups fresh young coconut water (see page 35) or store-bought raw coconut water for about 2 hours. If using almonds: Soak 2 cups raw almonds overnight in enough water to cover. Drain. Cover the almonds with 2 cups fresh young coconut water or store-bought raw coconut water. Pour the cashew or almond mixture into a high-speed blender to make crème or a slow juicer to make milk.

    If you are using a blender, blend the nuts and their soaking liquid until smooth, starting on the slowest speed and gradually working up to the fastest. Blend on the highest speed until the mixture is uniformly smooth and the sound of the blender is high-pitched and steady. Reduce the speed of the blender to the lowest setting before turning it off. Pour through a fine strainer or a nut-milk bag, and use in recipes.

    If using a slow juicer, run the soaked nuts and their liquid through the juicer. Strain.

FULLY RAW APPLE PIE

Makes 8 to 10 servings

Yummy yummy yummy, I got *pie* in my tummy! And not just any pie, it's a Fully Raw apple pie with a scrumptious dried fruit crust, and a crunchy creamy cinnamon-spiced filling made from alternating layers of a silky apple-date puree and thinly sliced apples. There's no better pie to bring to a holiday feast! You want the apple slices to be thin enough to almost see through. If you are skilled with a knife you can certainly slice them with your favorite blade, but if you are feeling less confident, a mandoline works great.

HERE'S WHAT YOU NEED:

For the crust

1 pound (about 24) fresh Medjool dates, pitted and quartered

8 ounces (about 10) raw dried white or black figs, stems removed, quartered

1 teaspoon ground cinnamon

For the filling

2 apples (about 1 pound), preferably Fuji or Honeycrisp, cored and coarsely chopped

1 pound (about 24) fresh Medjool dates, pitted and quartered

1 teaspoon ground cinnamon

⅛ teaspoon freshly grated nutmeg

For assembling

4 apples (about 2 pounds), preferably Fuji or Honeycrisp, cored and thinly sliced

EQUIPMENT

Sharp chopping knife

Cutting board

Mandoline (optional)

Mixing bowl

Food processor

High-speed blender, such as Vitamix

9-inch springform pan

Rubber spatula

Serving platter (optional)

HERE'S WHAT YOU DO:

To make the crust, toss all ingredients in a mixing bowl. Put half the mixture in the food processor and pulse until it is smooth enough to cling to itself in a ball. Transfer to the springform pan and repeat with the rest of the crust ingredients. Wet your hands with cold water and press the crust mixture evenly across the bottom of the pan. If the crust should start to stick to your hands, wet them again. Set the pan aside.

To make the filling, put all ingredients in the blender and blend until smooth, starting on the slowest speed and gradually working up to the fastest. Blend on the highest speed until the mixture is uniformly smooth and the sound of the blender is high pitched and steady. Use the tamper to help everything blend smoothly. Reduce the speed of the blender to the lowest setting before turning it off. The filling should be thick like whipped cream.

To assemble the dessert, arrange about one-quarter of the sliced apples in a single layer on the crust.

Top with about one-quarter of the pureed apple filling, using a rubber spatula to spread it thinly and evenly. Repeat with three more alternating layers of apples and filling, ending with filling. Refrigerate for at least 1 hour or up to 4 hours to help the filling set.

To serve, remove the side of the springform pan and, if desired, transfer the pie to a serving platter. Cut the pie into pieces, and serve immediately.

HOLIDATES

Makes 2 dozen

This is the easiest and most delicious recipe you can make during the holiday season! Almonds or pecan halves are embedded in fresh Medjool dates in place of their pits. The effect is at once simple and extravagant, as if nature had decided that the already-opulent date required even more lushness to be properly dressed for the holiday. When you bite through the sweet plump flesh into the crackling bit of fatty nut inside, it almost feels like you're having a secret romance or a "holi-date," just by sitting down to indulge! These are perfect to serve at a party or just to have ready as a special treat.

HERE'S WHAT YOU NEED:

1 pound (about 24) fresh Medjool dates

24 raw pecan halves or whole raw almonds

EQUIPMENT

2 hands

Serving platter

HERE'S WHAT YOU DO:

Carefully pry the dates open with your fingertips along one side to reveal the pit. Remove each pit, but be sure to not rip the dates in half. Wash your hands; they will have gotten sticky.

Insert a nut into the hollow in the center of each date. Set on a platter and serve. Store well wrapped at room temperature for up to 1 week.

BERRYLICIOUS FRUIT SORBET

Makes 1 quart, 2 to 3 servings

Want something sweet to eat? This mouth-watering frozen treat can be eaten anytime and enjoyed by all! It's so much fun to make, and it is *so* good for you! Plus, it's fat free! Feel free to adjust any of the ingredients to make your portions bigger or smaller. There is no going wrong on this one!

HERE'S WHAT YOU NEED:

1 pound berries, a combination of strawberries (greens removed, coarsely chopped), blueberries, and/or raspberries

5 fresh Medjool dates, pitted and chopped

1 pear, stemmed, cored, and coarsely chopped

Juice of 1 tangelo or juice orange (about ⅓ cup)

EQUIPMENT

Sharp chopping knife

Cutting board

Citrus juicer

High-speed blender, such as Vitamix

8-inch square glass dish

Food processor

Bowls

HERE'S WHAT YOU DO:

Put all ingredients in the blender and blend until smooth, starting on the slowest speed and gradually working up to the fastest. Blend on the highest speed until the mixture is uniformly smooth and the sound of the blender is high pitched and steady. Use the tamper to help everything blend smoothly. Reduce the speed of the blender to the lowest setting before turning it off.

Pour the mixture into the dish, cover tightly, and freeze until solid, at least 4 hours, or up to 5 days.

Remove the dish from the freezer and set out at room temperature for 10 minutes to thaw slightly. Cut the frozen mixture into cubes. Scrape the cubes into the food processor and pulse until the mixture becomes smooth and creamy.

Scoop into bowls and serve immediately.

TRIPLE-LAYER NEAPOLITAN TORTE

Makes 10 servings

In the last quarter of the 19th century, ice cream artisans from Naples, Italy, started an ice cream rage in New York. Their creations became known as Neapolitan-style, and the ones that sandwiched three colors of ice cream next to one another in the image of the Italian flag became the most popular form of Neapolitan ice creams. The juxtaposition of vanilla, chocolate, and strawberry became the most common, probably because those three flavors were the most popular ice creams at the time. I've used the classic Neapolitan as the inspiration for my triple layer frozen decadence. The bottom layer is a nut and date crust, topped with a layer of frozen "chocolate" crème and then a layer of red berries and frozen bananas. This gorgeous recipe will have you raving for hours about how delicious it tastes!

HERE'S WHAT YOU NEED:

For the crust

2 cups raw nut pieces, such as almonds, walnuts, or pecans, or dried mulberries

15 fresh Medjool dates, pitted and coarsely chopped

For the blackberry (blue) layer

1 pound blackberries

3 to 4 fresh Medjool dates, pitted and coarsely chopped

3 to 4 bananas, peeled and frozen, cut in small chunks

For the crème layer

4 bananas, peeled and frozen, cut in small chunks

10 fresh Medjool dates, pitted and coarsely chopped

2 tablespoons nut milk (see page 222), fresh young coconut water (see page 35), or store-bought raw coconut water

1 tablespoon raw organic carob powder

Seeds scraped from 1 vanilla bean (see page 133)

For the strawberry (red) layer

1 pound strawberries, greens removed, plus more for garnish

3 ounces red raspberries (about ½ cup)

5 fresh Medjool dates, pitted and coarsely chopped

2 bananas, peeled and frozen, cut in small chunks

EQUIPMENT

Sharp chopping knife

Cutting board

9-inch springform pan

9-inch parchment paper circle

Food processor

Rubber spatula

Thin-bladed knife

Serving platter

HERE'S WHAT YOU DO:

Line the springform pan with the parchment paper.

To make the crust, put the nuts and dates in the food processor and pulse until the mixture is sticky enough to climb the sides of the work bowl. Transfer to the springform pan. Wet your hands with cold water and press the crust mixture evenly across the bottom of the pan. If the crust should start to stick to your hands, wet them again. Set the pan in the freezer while you make the blackberry layer.

To make the blackberry layer, put all ingredients in the food processor and pulse until smooth. Pour over the frozen crust in the pan and spread evenly with a rubber spatula. Freeze until firm, about 1 hour.

To make the crème layer, put all ingredients in the food processor and pulse until smooth. Pour over the frozen blackberry layer in the pan and spread evenly with a rubber spatula. Freeze until firm, about 30 minutes.

To make the strawberry layer, put all ingredients in the food processor and pulse until smooth. Pour over the crème layer in the pan and spread evenly with a rubber spatula. Cut the strawberries for garnish lengthwise, and arrange on top of the torte. Freeze until all the layers are firm, at least 1 hour, or overnight if you are serving the next day.

To serve, run a thin-bladed knife around the sides of the torte, separating it from the side of the pan.

Remove the side of the springform pan. Put a sheet of parchment paper over the torte and cover with a cutting board. Invert the torte with the cutting board so that the base of the springform is now on top. Remove the pan base, using the parchment paper between the crust and pan base to help you lift it. Invert again on to a serving platter and remove the parchment paper from the top. Cut the torte into pieces and serve.

FRUIT PARFAIT WITH ORANGE NUT CRÈME

Makes 4 servings

Indulgence isn't always a bad thing. When it's Fully Raw, it can be decadently sweet and unbelievably rich, and still completely healthy! You can treat yourself to something special without fear of backsliding on the diet. The occasional dessert helps to keep you true to your new lifestyle long term, giving you dietary options that will help you succeed! Serve these in tall glasses to show off the layers.

HERE'S WHAT YOU NEED:

3 navel oranges

4 ounces unsalted raw macadamia nuts or cashews (about ¾ cup)

5 fresh Medjool dates, pitted and coarsely chopped

12 raspberries

24 blueberries

12 strawberries, greens removed, sliced

EQUIPMENT

Sharp paring knife

Cutting board

Citrus zester or Microplane

High-speed blender, such as Vitamix

4 parfait glasses or champagne flutes

HERE'S WHAT YOU DO:

Remove the zest from 2 of the oranges using a Microplane or zester, and put the zest in the blender. Peel all of the oranges, removing as much of the white pith as possible. Discard the peels and coarsely chop the flesh of the oranges.

Add the orange flesh to the blender along with the nuts and dates. Blend until smooth, starting on the slowest speed and gradually working up to the fastest. Blend on the highest speed until the mixture is uniformly smooth and the sound of the blender is high pitched and steady. Use the tamper to help everything blend smoothly. Reduce the speed of the blender to the lowest setting before turning it off. The orange crème mixture will be smooth and thick, like whipped cream.

Alternate layers of the orange crème and the berries in the parfait glasses, starting and ending with layers of crème. You will have four layers of crème and three berry layers per glass, and you will need 2 to 3 tablespoons of crème in each layer. Serve immediately, or cover and refrigerate for up to 3 hours.

WALNUT "FUDGE"

Makes 2 pounds, about 10 servings

Traditional fudge is sugar, and nothing but sugar! It's decadent but not good for you. Here's a fudge replacement that is deliciously sweet, with lots of fuel but no empty calories. Every serving has 27 percent of the daily value for dietary fiber, a significant amount of B vitamins, 18 percent of magnesium, 30 percent of iron, 50 percent of manganese, and 10 percent of your daily protein. It's guiltless candy that you can feel good about eating on occasion and serving to those you care about. It also makes a unique gift and an easy treat to serve at a party. Indulge and be healthy!

HERE'S WHAT YOU NEED:

1 ½ pounds (about 36) fresh Medjool dates, pitted and coarsely chopped

2 tablespoons raw organic carob powder

1 teaspoon ground cinnamon

½ pound raw walnut pieces (about 2 cups), coarsely chopped, plus more for optional garnish

EQUIPMENT

Sharp chopping knife

Cutting board

Mixing bowl

Food processor

8-inch square glass dish

8-inch square piece of parchment paper

Thin-bladed knife

HERE'S WHAT YOU DO:

Toss all ingredients in a mixing bowl. Working in two batches, pulse the mixture in the food processor until it is uniformly fine and mushy.

Line the interior of the glass dish with the parchment paper. Transfer the date and walnut mixture to the dish and pack evenly, wetting your hands to keep them from sticking to the dates.

To serve, run a thin-bladed knife around the edge of the dish. Cover the dish with a cutting board and invert. Remove the dish and the parchment paper. Cut into squares and serve as a sweet treat! If you want, you can decorate each square with a walnut piece.

FULLY RAW BANANA COCONUT CRÈME PIE

Makes 10 to 12 servings

This pie is a one-way ticket to a tropical paradise. You may never want to come back. The recipe is not complicated, but the results are memorable. Similar to a bakery cream pie, the pie is a chewy sweet crust of ground dates and mulberries topped with a rich and creamy banana coconut layer. The coconut meat is from young coconuts, which are available at high-end groceries like Whole Foods—but also at Asian groceries, usually for a fraction of the cost. When eating raw, you tend to use a lot of young coconut water, so having a recipe for coconut meat is helpful.

HERE'S WHAT YOU NEED:

For the crust

1 pound (about 24) fresh Medjool dates, pitted and coarsely chopped

6 ounces dried mulberries (about 1 ½ cups)

For the filling

4 bananas, peeled, broken in small pieces

Meat from 2 young coconuts (about 8 ounces, or 2 cups; see page 35)

5 fresh Medjool dates, pitted and coarsely chopped

Pinch of ground nutmeg

½ teaspoon ground cinnamon, plus more for serving

For the topping

Meat from 2 young coconuts (about 8 ounces, or 2 cups)

1 ½ cups fresh young coconut water (from about 1 to 2 young coconuts), or store-bought raw coconut water

3 fresh Medjool dates, pitted and coarsely chopped

Seeds scraped from 1 vanilla bean (see page 133)

EQUIPMENT

Sharp chopping knife

Cutting board

Butcher's cleaver or coconut tool, like Coco Jack (see opposite page)

9-inch parchment paper circle

9-inch springform pan

High-speed blender, such as Vitamix

Rubber spatula

HERE'S WHAT YOU DO:

Line the springform pan with the parchment paper and set aside.

To make the crust, toss the dates and mulberries in a mixing bowl. Put half the mixture in the food processor and pulse until it is smooth enough to cling to itself in a ball. Transfer to the pan and repeat with the rest of the crust ingredients. Wet your hands with cold water and press the crust mixture into an even layer across the bottom of the pan. If the crust should start to stick to your hands, wet them again.

To make the filling, put all ingredients in the blender and blend until smooth, starting on the slowest speed and gradually working up to the fastest. Blend on the highest speed until the mixture is uniformly smooth and the sound of the blender is high pitched and steady. Use the tamper to help everything blend smoothly. Reduce the speed of the blender to the lowest setting before turning it off. The filling should be thick like whipped cream. Pour the filling over the crust and smooth the top with a rubber spatula. Freeze until firm, about 30 minutes. Wash out the blender.

To make the topping, put all of the ingredients in the blender and blend as described above. Pour the topping over the firmed filling and smooth the top. Return to the freezer and freeze until firm, about 4 hours.

To serve, remove the sides of the springform pan, top the pie with a sprinkling of cinnamon, then cut into slices and enjoy!

Opening a Young Coconut

There are a few ways to cut open a young coconut without the fear of losing any appendages. If you have a butcher's cleaver or machete (don't use a good kitchen knife!), whack the coconut around its pointed end with the corner of the base of the blade five times, creating a pentagon-shaped opening around the top. You can then pull off the top part of the coconut and pour out the water. Mastering this method will take some practice. A much easier, faster, and completely cleaver-less method is to use a simple handheld tool specially made for opening young coconuts, such as the Coco Jack. You can find instructional videos at coco-jack.com.

To harvest the coconut meat, drain out the water, then scrape out the meat with the back of a spoon. If you used a Coco Jack, or if the opening you cut isn't large enough for a spoon, you'll need to cut the coconut in half again using a heavy-duty knife. You may want to do this outside on cement—you'll have better leverage than in the kitchen, and you won't have to worry about shrapnel flying!

FULLY RAW PUMPKIN PIE BROWNIES

Makes 16 brownies

These brownies are the perfect Thanksgiving treat! They are low in fat, nutritious, and so absolutely delectable that you can feel awesome about serving them at your holiday table. Thanksgiving is a time to express our gratitude for all of the gifts we have. These brownies are the perfect treat to show your family and friends how grateful you are for their love. And they are so delicious, everyone will be thanking you in return.

HERE'S WHAT YOU NEED:

For the bottom layer

½ pound (about 12) fresh Medjool dates, pitted and coarsely chopped

4 ounces pecan pieces (about 1 cup)

¼ teaspoon ground cinnamon

For the middle layer

½ pound (about 12) fresh Medjool dates, pitted and coarsely chopped

8 fresh black figs, stemmed and quartered

½ cup raw organic carob powder

1 teaspoon ground cinnamon

Water, as needed

For the top layer

1 pie pumpkin (about 2 pounds), peeled, seeded, and coarsely chopped

1 pound (about 24) fresh Medjool dates, pitted and coarsely chopped

5 large super-ripe Fuyu or 3 super-ripe Hachiya persimmons (about 1 ⅓ pounds), stems removed

2 teaspoons pumpkin pie spice

1 small thumb (about ½ inch) fresh ginger, chopped

Seeds scraped from 1 vanilla bean (see page 133)

EQUIPMENT

Sharp chopping knife

Cutting board

Food processor

8-inch square glass dish

High-speed blender, such as Vitamix

Rubber spatula

HERE'S WHAT YOU DO:

To make the bottom layer, put the ingredients in the food processor and pulse until the mixture is sticky enough to climb the sides of the work bowl. Scrape into the baking dish. Wet your hands with cold water and press the mixture evenly across the bottom of the dish. If the mixture should start to stick to your hands, wet them again.

To make the middle layer, put all ingredients in the blender. Blend until smooth, starting on the slowest speed and gradually working up to the fastest. Blend on the highest speed until the mixture is uniformly smooth and the sound of the blender is high pitched and steady. Use the tamper to help everything blend smoothly. Reduce the speed of the blender to the lowest setting before turning it off. The filling should be thick like whipped cream.

Pour the filling into the baking dish and smooth the top with a rubber spatula. Wash out the blender. Freeze the middle layer while you make the top layer.

To make the top layer, put all ingredients in the blender and blend using the same method you used for the previous layer. Spread over the firmed middle layer, smooth the top, and freeze until completely firm, about 2 hours or up to 2 days.

Cut in squares, share, and enjoy!

Pie Pumpkins

Pie pumpkins are small, meaty, and sweet. Unlike jack-o'-lantern pumpkins, which are designed for carving, these little babies are grown to eat. They look like carving pumpkins, but are much smaller, usually about 2 pounds. Their flesh is dark orange and aromatic. They usually appear in markets in September and continue through November. The most popular variety is Sugar Pie, but you may also find Winter Luxury and Golden Cushaw.

FRESH FRUIT ICE POPS

Each variation makes 6 ice pops

These frozen pops are easy to make and fun for all family members, especially kids! All you need are ice pop molds and a high-speed blender. Then it's as easy as blending the ingredients, pouring the mixture into your molds, and freezing them. Adding slices of fresh fruit or small berries to the molds is optional but gives them cool colors and added texture. Make any one or all of the following variations. Are you ready to pop pop POP!?

HERE'S WHAT YOU NEED:

Razzle Dazzle

2 cups watermelon chunks (no rind, from about 3 pounds melon)

1 cup raspberries

2 teaspoons fresh lime juice

Tropical Twist

2 cups mango chunks (from 1 large mango, peeled and pitted; see page 181)

1 cup peeled and cored (see page 136) pineapple chunks

Sweetie

3 cups peeled honeydew melon chunks

Dreamsicle

5 to 8 tangelos, depending on size, peeled

2 cups fresh young coconut water (see page 35), or store-bought raw coconut water

5 apples, preferably Fuji or Gala, stems removed

Juice of 5 large carrots

Seeds scraped from ½ vanilla bean (see page 133)

EQUIPMENT

Sharp chopping knife

Cutting board

High-speed blender, such as Vitamix

6 (4-ounce) ice pop molds

HERE'S WHAT YOU DO:

For all four variations, put the ingredients in the blender and blend until smooth, starting on the slowest speed and gradually working up to the fastest. Blend on the highest speed until the mixture is uniformly smooth and the sound of the blender is high pitched and steady. Use the tamper to help everything blend smoothly. Reduce the speed of the blender to the lowest setting before turning it off.

Pour the mixture into the molds, then insert the sticks. Freeze until solid, 4 to 5 hours. Once the pops are frozen, peel off the mold covers and enjoy!

FULLY RAW CHERRY COBBLER

Makes 6 servings

Get excited . . . because I have perfected my recipe for Fully Raw Cherry Cobbler. And who doesn't *love* cherry cobbler? The good news: Whether you eat your fruit picked off a tree or stacked up into a super spectacular dessert, you are still getting all of its natural goodness!

HERE'S WHAT YOU NEED:

¾ pound (about 18) fresh Medjool dates, pitted and coarsely chopped

¼ cup raw almonds

2 pounds fresh sweet cherries, stems and pits removed, halved (about 5 cups)

6 fresh black figs, stemmed, cut in eighths

Meat from 1 young coconut (about 1 cup; see page 35)

¼ teaspoon ground cinnamon

EQUIPMENT

Sharp chopping knife

Cutting board

Food processor

6 parfait glasses

High-speed blender, like Vitamix

Rubber spatula

HERE'S WHAT YOU DO:

Put half of the dates and all the almonds in a food processor and pulse until the mixture is sticky enough to form a ball. Remove from the processor and crumble three-quarters of the mixture into the parfait glasses, a few tablespoons in each.

Put a small handful of cherries (about 12 halves), and a few pieces of fig in each glass.

Put 2 cups of the halved cherries and one-third of the remaining dates in the blender and blend until smooth, starting on the slowest speed and gradually working up to the fastest. Blend on the highest speed until the mixture is uniformly smooth and the sound of the blender is high pitched and steady. Use the tamper to help everything blend smoothly. Reduce the speed of the blender to the lowest setting before turning it off.

Pour the mixture into the 6 glasses. Top with another handful of the date-nut crumble, more cherries, and the rest of the figs.

Rinse out the blender, but don't worry if it is not completely clean. Put 1 cup of the remaining cherries (you should still have some cherry pieces left over), the remaining dates, the coconut meat, and the cinnamon in the blender. Blend using the same method as above.

Pour into each parfait glass, filling just below the brim. Top with a portion of the remaining date-nut crumble mixture and crown each parfait with one of the remaining cherry halves, if desired. If you love cherries, say yum!

FULLY RAW PEACH COBBLER

Makes 8 servings

I absolutely love fresh peaches when they are in season—when they are ripe, juicy, and at their most delectable. This cobbler is an extravagant layering of peaches and a sticky, gooey date and pecan crumble. Don't worry if the crumble sticks to your fingers as you work. That just means it's gonna taste really good. Also, don't let its extravagance fool you. This is an easy recipe, and takes less than 20 minutes to put together.

HERE'S WHAT YOU NEED:

2 pounds (about 48) fresh Medjool dates, pitted
    and coarsely chopped

12 ounces pecan pieces (about 3 cups)

1 teaspoon ground cinnamon

12 peaches, halved, pitted, and thinly sliced

EQUIPMENT

Sharp chopping knife

Cutting board

Food processor

9-inch springform pan

High-speed blender, such as Vitamix

HERE'S WHAT YOU DO:

Place 1 ½ pounds (about 36) of the dates, the pecans, and ½ teaspoon of the cinnamon in a mixing bowl. Transfer half of the mixture to the food processor and pulse until the mixture is crumbly and just moist enough to stick together when pinched. Scrape into the springform pan. Wet your hands with cold water and press the mixture evenly across the bottom of the pan. If the mixture should start to stick to your hands, wet them again.

Layer one-third of the peach slices over the bottom layer.

Process the remaining nut-date mixture in the food processor until finely ground. Sprinkle evenly over the peaches, and then top with another one-third of the peaches.

Put the remaining ½ pound (about 12) dates and the remaining peach slices in the blender and blend until smooth, starting on the slowest speed and gradually working up to the fastest. Blend on the highest speed until the mixture is uniformly smooth and the sound of the blender is high pitched and steady. Use the tamper to help everything blend smoothly. Reduce the speed of the blender to the lowest setting before turning it off. Drizzle over the peaches in the pan.

To serve, remove the side of the springform pan, and sprinkle the cobbler with the remaining ½ teaspoon cinnamon. Cut into wedges and serve.

FULLY RAW PUMPKIN PIE

Makes 8 servings

You haven't tried pumpkin pie until you have tried my magical Fully Raw Pumpkin Pie! It's all raw, low fat, and *super* sweet! And it's so easy to make. Just crush the crust ingredients and pack them into your pie plate. Then whip up the filling, fill the shell, and freeze for a few hours (this makes it easier to slice).

HERE'S WHAT YOU NEED:

For the crust

1 pound (about 24) fresh Medjool dates, pitted and coarsely chopped

6 ounces raw pecan pieces (about 1 ½ cups)

Pinch of ground cinnamon (optional)

For the filling

1 pie pumpkin (about 2 pounds; see page 237) peeled, seeded, and coarsely chopped

1 ½ pounds (about 36) fresh Medjool dates, pitted and coarsely chopped

1 super-ripe Hachiya persimmon, stem removed

2 teaspoons ground cinnamon

1 small thumb (about ½ inch) fresh ginger, chopped

Seeds scraped from 1 vanilla bean (see page 133)

EQUIPMENT

Sharp chopping knife

Cutting board

Food processor

9-inch pie plate

High-speed blender, such as Vitamix

Rubber spatula

HERE'S WHAT YOU DO:

To make the crust, put the crust ingredients in the food processor and pulse until the mixture is sticky enough to climb the sides of the work bowl. Scrape into the pie plate. Wet your hands with cold water and press the crust mixture evenly across the bottom and up the sides of the plate. If the crust should start to stick to your hands, wet them again.

To make the filling, put the filling ingredients in a blender. Blend until smooth, starting on the slowest speed and gradually working up to the fastest. Blend on the highest speed until the mixture is uniformly smooth and the sound of the blender is high pitched and steady. Use the tamper to help everything blend smoothly. Reduce the speed of the blender to the lowest setting before turning it off. The filling should be thick like whipped cream.

Pour the filling into the crust and smooth the top with a rubber spatula. Freeze until firm, about 2 hours or up to 2 days.

To serve, cut into wedges and enjoy!

PART THREE

FITNESS AND EXERCISE

Stretches, Cardio, and Strength Training

GET ACTIVE!

Being fit and exercising consistently is one of the best things that you can do for your body. Exercising keeps you not only in shape, but also mentally strong and balanced. A part of feeling confident is knowing that your body is strong and agile. Working out is a great way to build your confidence. Personally, I try to work out for at least an hour every day. At a minimum, you should aim for 20 to 30 minutes of intense exercise each day.

My workouts are broken down into three types of exercise: stretches for flexibility, cardiovascular activity to burn calories and increase blood flow, and strength training to build muscle. In my opinion, cardio is by far the most important, and if you can do only one form of exercise on any given day, make it cardio. Strength training puts stress on your muscles and therefore should not be done every day. Your muscles need a day to recover, so only work with weights or other forms of resistance exercise every other day. I usually stretch before and after a workout, regardless of what kind of cardio or strength training I am doing that day.

Everyone has their favorite exercises, and I describe mine in these pages. They are organized by intensity and difficulty: *Easy Does It, Push a Little Harder,* and *Go for It.* If you are new to exercising, I suggest that you stick with the Easy Does It exercises for the first week (and consult your doctor before you begin a new exercise regimen). Going too far too fast can only lead to injury, and when you are injured you need to lay off exercise until you heal. It's difficult to feel good about your body when it's hurt. That said, you also want to push yourself a little every day. If you are overly gentle with your body it will not change, and positive change is why we're doing this, right? I suggest mixing it up. When you are feeling comfortable about your level of exercise, throw in one or two more rigorous ones. If you do that on a regular basis, you will be pleased at how quickly your body builds strength and agility.

STRETCHES

Easy Does It

Toe Touches

1) Stand straight. Fold yourself in half and start to wiggle your fingers, reaching towards your toes. Don't bounce. The goal isn't to touch the floor for a second and bounce back up. It's to stretch your back and leg muscles.

2) Reach as far as you can and when you are at your limit, hold it there for about 20 seconds.

3) Come back up slowly and repeat at least five times. This stretch will release stress and help to relax the muscles.

Child's Pose

1) Start by kneeling. Lower your butt towards your heels and bend forward with your arms stretched out in front of you, your knees tucked into your chest, your stomach resting comfortably on your thighs, and your forehead

touching the floor. Breathe. You will feel the stretch in your buttocks, down your spine, and into your arms.

2) Keep your shoulders and neck relaxed. Don't force your butt to move any closer to your heels than is comfortable. When you have stretched for about a minute, raise your upper body, slowly starting from the base of your spine, allowing your arms to drop gently to your sides. Repeat as many times as you like.

The Twist

1) Sit on the floor with your legs straight before you. Bend your knees, keeping your feet on the floor.

2) Now slide your left foot under your right leg until it is resting next to your right hip. The outside of your left leg should be resting on the floor. Now step the right foot over your left leg, placing it flat on the floor outside your left thigh. Your right knee should be pointing directly towards the ceiling.

3) Exhale and twist your torso to the right. Press your right hand to the floor just behind your right buttock, and set your left upper arm on the outside of your right knee. Concentrate on lengthening your torso as you breathe, twisting a little more with each exhalation. Stay for about a minute. If you want to increase the twist, turn your head to the right. Return to the starting position.

4) Repeat, switching sides.

Push a Little Harder

Ankle Touch

1) Stand up and spread your feet slightly farther than shoulder width apart. Bend over to one side and touch your fingers to one ankle.

2) Move over to the other side and touch the other ankle.

3) Last, move to the middle and touch the center of the floor with both hands. Hold each position for about 20 seconds. This will stretch your back, butt, and legs.

Quad Stretch

1) Stand tall. For balance you can face a wall and put your right hand on it.

2) Bend your left knee, lifting up your foot.

3) Reach back with your free hand, grab your foot and hold it behind you, then pull it as close to your bottom as possible. Feel the stretch in your quad.

4) Do the other side.

Side Stretch

1) Stand tall like a tree, and then step out with one foot just far enough so that you feel well balanced and your weight is centered.

2) Raise your right arm and bring it next to your ear. Keep your shoulders relaxed and slowly bend to your left, stretching the sides of your torso. Hold for 20 seconds.

3) Repeat with the opposite side. Do at least five repetitions.

Go for It

Warrior 1

1) Stand tall, with your feet together and arms at your sides. Exhale and step or lightly jump your feet 4 to 5 apart, right forward, left back, keeping your legs parallel. Inhale and lift your arms overhead, shoulder width apart, palms facing each other.

2) Exhale and turn your back foot outward 90 degrees. Turn your front foot inward about

a minute, taking deep, slow breaths. To come out of the pose, lower your arms, straighten your right leg, and return your feet to their starting position.

4) Repeat, switching legs. Warrior works all of the major muscle groups, particularly your shoulders, back, hip, and legs.

Warrior 2

1) Stand tall, with your feet together and arms at your sides. Exhale and step or lightly jump your feet 4 to 5 feet apart, right forward, left back, keeping your legs parallel. Inhale and lift your arms out to the sides at shoulder height, with palms facing down.

2) Exhale and turn your back foot outward 90 degrees. Turn your front foot inward about 45 degrees. Shift your hips so that they square with your right foot. This takes practice; be patient; when you are doing it right you will greatly increase your flexibility.

3) Inhale deeply. As you exhale, bend your right knee and center it over your foot. Get as close to a 90-degree angle as you can while keeping your back foot flat on the floor. To align your spine, concentrate on drawing your ribs into your body and your tailbone towards the floor, elongating your spine and neck.

4) Turn your face to the right and look towards your right hand. Hold for about a minute, taking deep, slow breaths. To come out of the pose, lower your arms, straighten your right leg, and return your feet to their starting position.

5) Repeat, switching legs and turning in the other direction. Warrior works all of the major muscle groups, particularly your shoulders, back, hip, and legs.

45 degrees. Shift your hips so that they square with your right foot. This takes practice; be patient; when you are doing it right you will greatly increase your flexibility.

3) Inhale deeply. As you exhale, bend your right knee and center it over your foot. Get as close to a 90-degree angle as you can while keeping your back foot flat on the floor. To align your spine, concentrate on drawing your ribs into your body and your tailbone towards the floor, elongating your spine and neck. Hold for about

Lunge Stretch

1) Stand with legs together. Step your right foot forward and lower into a lunge, stretching your back leg out behind you so that you really feel the stretch in your left hamstring and quad muscle.
2) Come back to center and then switch sides.

Cobra Stretch

1) Lie belly down on the floor. Place your palms flat on the floor next to either side of your chest with your elbows bent and your fingers pointing straight ahead.
2) Pressing into your palms, curl your shoulders and chest off the floor. Do not use your arms to lift you. Test by raising your hands off the floor without losing your position.
3) Press farther into your palms and lift your torso and hips off the floor into a mini backbend. Hold for 10 seconds.
4) Lower your hips, belly, and shoulders to the floor. Touch the floor with your forehead. Release your arms and put them at your sides, palms up. This strengthens your back muscles and opens up your chest.

CARDIOVASCULAR EXERCISES
Easy Does It

Jumping Rope

1) If you are new to jumping rope, start with a heavier rope, which will make you jump more slowly. As you get better, move to a lighter rope so you can move faster.
2) Stand with your knees slightly bent. Hold the rope at hip height with your palms facing your body.

3) Swing the rope over your head and jump as it passes your feet. Jump just enough to clear the rope. Push evenly off the balls of your feet, keeping your knees soft and your torso upright. Land evenly on both feet and resist the urge to bounce between jumps.
4) Continue for 1 minute, then rest for 1 minute. Repeat as often as you like.

CARDIOVASCULAR EXERCISES

Anything that gets your heart pumping builds your cardiovascular system and burns calories. This includes running, jogging, sprinting, walking, and almost any sport that involves these activities—tennis, basketball, football, soccer, handball, squash—you know what I mean. You also get cardio exercise from cycling, boxing, wrestling, gymnastics, and numerous types of cardio exercise classes. I am not going to tell you how to do any of these activities. I assume you already know how to walk, and you can learn the others by participating in them. Here I give some calisthenics that help exercise your cardio chops.

Jumping Jacks

1) Stand straight with your feet together and your arms at your sides.
2) Bend your knees slightly and jump a bit into the air. While in the air, bring your legs out to the sides, about shoulder width or a little wider.
3) As your legs move outward, raise your arms over your head, keeping them slightly bent.

Your feet should hit the ground at the same time your hands meet above your head.

4) Jump back to the starting position and repeat as many times as you want.

Push a Little Harder

Horses—Back and Forth Sprints

1) Stand in a spot (point A). Pick another spot about 12 feet away (point B). Now pick 2 more spots, one about 4 feet away from you (point C) and the other about 6 feet away (point D).

2) Sprint from point A to point B (the longest distance).

3) Then from point B to Point C (two-thirds of the way back).

4) Then from point C to point D (just 2 feet).

5) Then from point D to point A (back to the start).

6) Keep going. The regular bursts of energy each time you start a sprint, quickly followed by the contraction of energy to stop yourself, is a real workout.

Go for It

Jumps to the Sky

1) Stand straight with your feet spread shoulder width apart and pointed straight ahead. Look forward.

2) Bend your knees and squat down, and bring your arms down between your legs so that your hands touch the ground. Keep your back straight and your torso upright. Your knees should not extend past your toes and your shins should stay at a 90-degree angle to the floor.

3) Swing your arms forward and upward as you propel yourself upward as hard and as fast as

you can. Reach up as high as you can as you ascend. When you land, return to the squatting position. Repeat.

STRENGTH TRAINING

Easy Does It

Squats

1) Stand straight with your hands on your hips and your feet set about shoulder width apart, pointing straight forward.

2) Bend your knees and squat about halfway down. Keep your back straight and your torso upright. Your knees should not extend past your toes and your shins should stay at a 90-degree angle to the floor.

3) Straighten your knees and stand back up straight. Repeat.

Sit-Ups

1) Lie on your back with your arms at your sides, your knees bent, and your feet flat on the floor. You may want to pin your feet underneath a sturdy object.

2) Put your hands on opposing shoulders so that your arms are crossed over your chest.

3) Tighten your abs by drawing your belly button towards your spine.

4) Keeping your feet flat on the ground, contract your abdominal muscles as you slowly lift your head, followed by your shoulder blades and back until your elbows touch your knees. Hold for a second.

5) Slowly lower your torso back down to the floor, keeping your abs tight, until your shoulder blades touch the floor. Do not lie flat; rather keep your abs engaged and sit up again.

Planks

1) Start in a push-up position (see below).
2) Lower both of your forearms to the ground so that both your elbows and your hands are touching the ground. Your hands should be balled up in loose fists and your elbows should be directly under your shoulders.
3) Engage your abs by tucking in your pelvis and pulling your belly button toward your spine.
4) Straighten your body, keeping your neck and spine relaxed. Imagine your body as straight as a plank of wood. Avoid raising your behind.
5) Tighten your abs and squeeze your glutes. Keep your eyes on the floor in front of you and hold the position for 30 seconds to 1 minute.
6) Lower your body and relax for a minute. Repeat.

Push a Little Harder

Push-Ups

1) Lie down on your stomach. Bend your elbows so your palms are flat on the floor and your hands are placed directly under your shoulders or slightly wider than your shoulders.
2) Lift your body by straightening your arms. Your weight should be resting on the balls of your feet, which will stabilize the bottom half of your body. Tighten your abs and glutes so that your body is straight. Resist the tendency to raise your butt or sway your lower back. Keep your eyes focused towards the floor about 3 feet in front of you to keep your neck and shoulders from straining.
3) Keeping your back flat and your body straight, bend your elbows as you inhale and lower your body slowly until your chest just grazes the floor. Keep your shoulder blades drawn back and down and keep your elbows tucked close to

your body so that your upper arms are parallel to the floor at the bottom of the push-up.
4) Keep your abs tight and exhale as you straighten your arms, raising your upper body explosively. No sagging back or raised-up butt. Keep that body straight and do another one.

Variation for beginners: Place your hands on the back of a park bench with your arms and feet shoulder-width apart. Look forward and not down. Bend your elbows and lower your body toward the bench, then lift your body by straightening your arms.

Jumping Squats

1) Stand straight with your hands on your hips and your feet set about shoulder width apart, pointing straight forward.
2) Bend your knees and squat about halfway down. Keep your back straight and your torso upright. Your knees should not extend past your toes and your shins should stay at a 90-degree angle to the floor.
3) Propel yourself upward as hard and as fast as you can. When you land, return to the squatting position. Repeat.

Go for It

Burpees!

1) Stand with your feet shoulder width apart. Bend your knees so that your body is in a full squatting position with your arms outside your knees and your palms flat on the ground. Your arms should be straight.
2) Kick your feet back so that you are in the top position of a push-up with your arms supporting your body.

3) Bend your arms until your chest just grazes the ground, just like doing a push-up.

4) Straighten your arms as if you were continuing the push-up, and as your upper body rises, kick your feet forward back into their original position. Stand up and jump into the air while clapping your hands overhead. Repeat.

Knee Touches

1) Stand with your feet shoulder width apart. Turn your left foot and leg 45 degrees outward and raise your left arm overhead.

2) Bend your left knee and raise it up as high as you can towards the left side of your chest. At the same time, bend your left elbow to meet your knee. Repeat with your right side.

3) Try to build up speed until you can do 20 in about a minute.

APPENDIX: RAW SCIENCE

AS FAR AS I KNOW, no animals, other than humans, cook their food. I've heard that birds eat fermented berries, and bees turn flower nectar into honey, but has anyone ever observed any animal, other than humans, apply fire to food before they eat it? This should lead logically to the conclusion that raw foods are innately healthy. Unfortunately the science establishment that studies nutrition looks at the world through a cooked-food perspective, so most of the nutritional advice we receive doesn't even consider a Fully Raw food diet as a legitimate lifestyle choice.

In this appendix I am going to cover the basics of human nutrition and what the latest research says about our nutritional needs, and then explain how to meet them every day by eating Fully Raw.

FUEL VS. ENERGY

IN ORDER TO FUNCTION your body needs to move. I'm not just talking about running and jumping, and hugging and dancing. Everything your body does, including taking a breath and thinking a thought, requires your cells to kick into gear and *move!* All of that movement takes energy, and your cells need an ongoing supply of energy to run at peak efficiency. Two interdependent physiological systems provide your cells with energy:

The digestive system processes food into fuel that powers your cells.

The nervous system triggers cellular reactions that burn the fuel, releasing its vital nerve energy to our muscles and organs (including our brains), allowing them to function as nature intended.

The systems work similarly to the ones that power the engine of your car: Our food is the fuel, the same as gasoline in a car, and our nervous system corresponds to a car's battery. The engine needs gas to run, but it can't use that gas to move the car until a spark from the battery starts a chain reaction that combusts the fuel and releases its energy.

Vigorous health requires both enough food to meet your activity needs and enough rest to charge your nervous system so that it can use the food you eat efficiently. Especially if you wish to lose weight, I can't emphasize enough the importance of sleep for effective dieting and weight maintenance. Lack of sleep makes you feel unfocused and lethargic, so getting yourself motivated to exercise requires a super-power level of discipline. But lack of sleep also disturbs your metabolism, increasing insulin resistance and decreasing glucose tolerance, which are precursors to type 2 diabetes and factors that cause you to burn your fuel reserves far less efficiently. When you are well rested, activity is fun, not a chore, and your body uses every calorie you take in for its optimal potential.

You can easily recognize the difference between lack of energy due to sleep deficiency and lack of energy from food deprivation. When you are exhausted at the end of a long day, eating a large meal is not going to revive you (in truth it can make you feel sleepier), but a good night's sleep naturally recharges your battery and gets you ready for more activity.

CALORIES

CALORIES ARE THE WAY we measure energy. A gram of carbohydrate or protein contains about 4 calories; a gram of fat contains about 9 calories, more than double. Although we talk about calories in terms of food, the measurement can be applied to anything that holds energy or uses it up. For instance, a gallon of gasoline contains about 31,000 calories, 1 pound of seedless grapes has about 313 calories, and a pound of kale contains 222 calories. So, if you could power your Prius (assuming it gets 35 mpg) with grapes (or greens) it would take about 2.8 pounds of grapes (or a little less than 4 pounds of kale) to drive 1 mile.

The number-one reason diets fail is that calorie deprivation is unsustainable. If you want to live with vitality you need to eat enough calories every day. Our perspective on how much food we should eat has been skewed over time due to the concentration of calories in cooked foods (especially animal-based food). Cooking plants softens their fiber and depletes them of water. Raw fruits and vegetables, with all of their fiber and water, have far fewer calories per bite than cooked foods and fatty animal foods. When you switch over to a raw diet, you have to eat a lot more bites to get the calories you need. Animals in the wild, who exist totally on raw foods, eat constantly. Most birds eat up to half their body weight daily; otters eat about 30 percent of their body weight; and lions can consume 80 pounds of raw meat in one meal.

When starting to eat raw you will probably have to get your stomach muscles back in shape. To do this, you want to eat until you feel full and then eat a few more bites. Because the food is raw, this won't give you many more calories, but it will help stretch your stomach muscles, which will gradually increase their flexibility. It's important to recognize that this doesn't make your stomach bigger, just stretchier and more elastic. As soon as it empties, your stomach will snap back to its smallest dimension.

NUTRIENTS

NUTRIENTS ARE THE COMPONENTS in food that your body digests and metabolizes to meet its basic fuel needs for producing energy, for growth, and for cell maintenance. The three nutrients that we use the most—carbohydrates, proteins, and fats—are called "macronutrients," because we have to consume them in relatively large amounts (by the pound) to meet our physical needs. "Micronutrients" include vitamins and minerals that we need in relatively small amounts (by the milligram) to keep us healthy. Two other components, water and fiber, are also plentiful in food and essential to maintaining health, but they are not technically nutrients, because they are not digested or metabolized.

MACRONUTRIENTS
Carbohydrate

Carbohydrates are the way plants store energy, so all but a small fraction of the energy we get from plant-based foods (fruits and vegetables) comes from carbohydrates. All carbohydrates are built of sugar molecules, which comprise the only nutrient that we can use directly as fuel. So plants are our most direct source of fuel. Any food you eat must be broken down into sugar or converted into sugar in order for your cells to use it for energy. Simple carbohydrates, like fruits, have only one or two sugar molecules per molecule of carbohydrate, so your body can break down and metabolize simple carbohydrates into energy quickly and easily. Simple carbohydrates taste sweet, and we are highly attracted to that taste, because our bodies innately know they are the best source of energy we have. That is why my Fully Raw eating regimen gets most of its calories, about 80 percent, from simple carbohydrates.

Larger carbohydrate molecules, made up of many sugar molecules strung together, are called complex carbohydrates. These complicated molecules need to be broken down into simple sugars (usually by cooking) for our bodies to use them for energy. Because the energy from complex carbohydrates like rice, pasta, bread, and potatoes is less readily available, we are not as attracted to them and we do not taste these molecules as sweet. Rather we taste complex carbohydrates as starchy, a flavor that we perceive of as caloric but not particularly delicious in its raw form. Your taste buds are pretty smart; let them guide your food choices.

Fat

Fruits also store a small amount of energy as fat, mostly in their seeds (only avocados and olives store a significant amount of fat in their fruit). Fat is an essential nutrient, and we need small amounts to help digest the fat-soluble vitamins (A, D, E, and K) and keep electrical impulses flowing through our nervous systems. Fat is necessary for the production of many hormones and is our primary insulator, protecting us from extreme changes in cold and heat.

Fat is also the main way our bodies store energy. Although we hold a small amount of carbohydrate reserves in many of our cells for quick energy, the bulk of our stored energy reserves is held in our

FRUIT AND BLOOD SUGAR

Eating a diet that contains a large amount of fresh sweet fruit does not contribute to high blood sugar. The glycemic index measures the rate at which the sugar in food is broken down during digestion and enters your blood. Because fruit is easily digested into sugars that are quickly delivered to your cells to provide energy, people often have the mistaken impression that its glycemic index is very high, but that is not the case (see chart, opposite). In addition, the glycemic index is only part of the story when calculating the effect of food on blood sugar. Another metric, called the glycemic load, is the more relevant number to heed.

Glycemic index measures only the amount of sugar in a food. It does not take into consideration that a high percentage of water dilutes the sugar in whole fruits (see Water Content of Fruits and Vegetables, page 29). Glycemic load, on the other hand, is a measure of how the whole food affects blood sugar and therefore is the more important number to look at. When the amount of water and fiber are included into the calculation, the glycemic load of watermelon (which is 92 percent water) drops to 4, which is in the very low range. Dried fruit, which has had more than half its water evaporated off, has a glycemic load that is closer to its glycemic index and therefore should be eaten in moderation. The glycemic load for all fresh fruit is low. And even the glycemic index is low to moderate for most fruits . . . including bananas and grapes!

fat. When we eat more calories than we need, our bodies do not throw them away. Nope. They hang on to those extra calories for a rainy day when we may not be able to eat enough to meet our energy needs, depositing the extra calories in the fat tissue that lines the skin and surrounds our organs, protecting them against jarring and other physical shocks.

Our body fat and the fat of all animals, and most animal products, is dense, so dense that it is solid at room temperature. We call fats that are solid at room temperature "saturated." This saturation allows us, and all animals, to carry around a maximum amount of energy in a minimum amount of space. Pound for pound, fat contains twice the calories of either carbohydrates or proteins. If animals held their bodies' main energy stores in the form of carbohydrates, the way plants do, they would have to be twice their size to carry around the same amount of stored energy.

You know from our previous discussion about carbohydrates that sugar (simple carbs) is the only form that our body can use to meet its cellular fuel needs. This means that fat has to be converted into

GLYCEMIC INDEX VS. GLYCEMIC LOAD OF SIMPLE AND COMPLEX CARBOHYDRATES		
SIMPLE CARBOHYDRATES (FRUIT: 120 GRAMS)	GLYCEMIC INDEX MEDIUM = 56-69	GLYCEMIC LOAD MEDIUM = 11-19
Watermelon	72 (high)	4 (low)
Cantaloupe	65 (medium)	4 (low)
Pineapple	59 (medium)	4 (low)
Banana	52 (low)	12 (medium)
Grapes	46 (low)	8 (low)
Peach	42 (low)	5 (low)
Strawberries	40 (low)	1 (low)
Apple	38 (low)	6 (low)
COMPLEX CARBOHYDRATES (STARCHES: 1 SERVING)	GLYCEMIC INDEX MEDIUM = 56-69	GLYCEMIC LOAD MEDIUM = 11-19
Baked potato	85 (high)	26 (high)
Whole-wheat bread	71 (high)	9 (low)
White rice	64 (medium)	23 (high)
Sweet potato	61 (medium)	27 (high)
Wild rice	57 (medium)	18 (medium)
Corn	54 (low)	9 (low)
Pasta	42 (low)	20 (high)
Bran cereal	42 (low)	8 (low)

sugar in our bodies in order to be used for fuel. This takes more metabolic steps, more time, and more energy, so our bodies prefer carbohydrate for its quick and efficient energy. Our bodies store a limited amount of carbohydrate in the form of glycogen, which we use first for our energy needs. Only after our glycogen is depleted will we start to digest fat for energy.

Because plants don't have to move around the way animals do, they don't usually need to condense their stored energy in the form of fat. The one time that plants do need to rely on a big store of energy is during the growth spurt at the beginning of life, which is why seeds and nuts hold the main fat stores for most plants. Because these fat stores are needed for only a brief period, plant fats are not as dense as animal fats. They tend to be liquid at room temperature. We call liquid fats "oils." Most oils are less saturated than solid animal fats, but different oils have different saturation levels. Denser oils are called monounsaturated or diunsaturated; more fluid oils are polyunsaturated. Although most animal fats are solid and most plant fats are liquid, there are exceptions—for example, fish oils are liquid at room temperature and coconut oil is solid.

How much fat do you need? Most Americans get about 35 percent of their daily calories from fat. This has led to all sorts of chronic disease. In contrast, omnivorous animals in the wild that rely mostly on fruits and vegetables for their calories consume very little fat. Assuming they eat whole fruits and vegetables including the seeds and nuts, they would get about 10 percent of their calories in the form of fat, which is plenty to meet all of the fat-related nutritional needs of your body.

Vegetable oils are extracted from the seeds and fruits of plants like olives, soy, almonds, walnuts, corn, rabe (canola), sunflowers, etc. I don't use any extracted oils in my Fully Raw recipes. By eating a full range of fruit and vegetables, including some avocado every now and then, and augmented with a small amount of seeds and nuts, it is easy to get about 10 percent of my daily calories from fat, on average.

What about cholesterol? Cholesterol is a type of fat, and makes up every cell membrane in our bodies. Cholesterol exists only in animal tissue and animal food products, so a vegan diet contains no dietary cholesterol. Fortunately, our livers manufacture all of the cholesterol we need, so we have no need to eat cholesterol. There is some controversy as to whether diet or genetics contributes most significantly to high cholesterol, but either way, eating a vegan diet would ensure that dietary cholesterol does not affect that reading.

Protein

Our bodies are built out of protein—all of our muscles, organs, blood, and bodily fluids are protein. Because protein is so much a part of who we are, and plants do not contain nearly as much protein as animals, people are naturally concerned about getting enough protein on a Fully Raw vegan diet. The question isn't whether you can get protein from plant-based food. You can. The question is how much protein you need to maintain health.

Although protein requirements are significant when your body is growing (that is, when you are a child), or growing someone (that is, when you are pregnant), most fully grown adults do not need much protein to maintain their bodies. A certain percentage of your cells are wearing out and need to be replaced all of the time, so there is some need for protein there, and if you get injured your protein needs would increase, but for most us, eating 10 percent of our daily calories in the form of protein is more than sufficient.

PERCENTAGE OF CALORIES FROM FAT FOR COMMON FRUITS, VEGETABLES, NUTS, AND SEEDS

ITEM	AMOUNT	CALORIES	CALORIES FROM FAT	% OF CALORIES FROM FAT
FRUITS				
Apple	1 large	130	3	2%
Avocado	¼ medium	80	62	77%
Banana	1 medium	110	4	4%
Cherries	20 cherries	100	3	3%
Melon	¹⁄₁₀	50	2	4%
Nectarine	1	60	5	8%
Strawberries	8 large	50	3	6%
VEGETABLES				
Beet	1 small	35	1	3%
Bell pepper	1 small	25	2	8%
Carrot	1 medium	25	1	4%
Celery	2 stalks	6	0.5	8%
Corn	1 ear	90	13	14%
Cucumber	⅓ medium	12	0	0%
Tomato	1 medium	25	3	12%
NUTS AND SEEDS				
Almonds	1 ounce	163	126	77%
Cashews	1 ounce	156	111	71%
Coconut	1 ounce	100	85	85%
Pecans	1 ounce	196	183	93%
Pine nuts	1 ounce	178	156	88%
Pistachios	1 ounce	159	107	68%
Sesame seeds	1 ounce	162	126	78%
Sunflower seeds	1 ounce	166	123	74%
Walnuts	1 ounce	185	167	90%

PERCENTAGE OF CALORIES FROM PROTEIN FOR COMMON FRUITS, VEGETABLES, NUTS, AND SEEDS

FRUITS	Protein	VEGETABLES	Protein	NUTS AND SEEDS*	Protein
Apricot	10%	Broccoli	20%	Almonds	13%
Banana	4%	Cabbage	15%	Cashews	12%
Cherries	6%	Carrot	6%	Coconut (mature)	3%
Grapes	4%	Corn	10%	Pecans	5%
Orange	7%	Cucumber	11%	Pine nuts	6%
Peach	8%	Kale	16%	Pistachios	13%
Strawberries	7%	Romaine	18%	Sesame seeds	11%
Tomato	16%	Spinach	30%	Sunflower seeds	14%
Watermelon	7%	Sprouts, mungbean	25%	Walnuts	8%

Note: Nuts and seeds are a much better source of protein than they appear to be in this comparison. Because the overwhelming majority of the calories in nuts and seeds are from fat, which is high in calories, the percentage of calories from protein is suppressed. For instance, 100 grams of walnuts (9 percent of calories from protein) delivers 15 grams of protein, while 100 grams of raw spinach (30 percent of calories from protein) has only 3 grams.

All plant foods contain some protein. In fact if you are eating enough calories to meet your daily needs, it would be difficult not to get at least 5 percent of your calories from protein, and if you add nuts, seeds, and/or sprouts to that mix it is not difficult to get at least 8 percent of your calories from protein.

Although this is about half the percentage of calories from protein in the standard American diet (which averages about 17 percent), it is certainly not deficient. Think about what chimpanzees and orangutans eat in the wild—largely fruit and vegetables. These animals, who are massively muscled—pound for pound, nearly five times as strong as a human—get plenty of protein from their plant-based diets.

Dietary protein is not our only source for building the proteins we need. Our bodies recycle several hundred grams of protein every day, breaking it down into its building blocks (amino acids) and reassembling them to meet any current cell regeneration needs.

Body builders have long believed that they need to eat extra protein to build muscle mass, misunderstanding the role of protein in building muscle. But in truth, only weight-bearing exercise builds muscle, and provided they eat enough calories to fuel that exercise, they will not need extra protein in their diets. It's true enough that when you don't eat sufficient carbohydrates to meet your fuel demands, your body will first use its own fat for calories, and then start to digest its own protein. In that scenario, you would certainly lose muscle mass. But only chronic, severe calorie deficiency causes people to digest their own muscle for fuel. On a diet of sufficient calories, regardless of what is eaten, there is virtually no such thing as protein deficiency in fully grown adults.

There is some danger in relying heavily on protein for your calorie needs. Obviously it is inefficient, as your body has to convert the protein into sugar before it can be used as fuel. In addition, the minerals contained in most proteins—chlorine, phosphorus, and sulfur—are primarily acidic. If you eat too much protein, in order to maintain homeostasis (the acid-alkaline balance in your bodily fluids), your body may draw calcium from your bloodstream, which in turn can draw it from your bones and teeth, making you susceptible to osteoporosis and tooth decay.

MICRONUTRIENTS

NOT THAT LONG AGO nutritional science taught us that when it came to thriving, carbohydrates, protein, and fats were the whole shebang. Sure, there existed a collection of micronutrients—vitamins and minerals that we needed in miniscule amounts to help prevent disease—but no one was sure what most of them did or if any of them did much more than prevent problems like rickets or scurvy. In the last thirty years, there has been a revolution in nutrition, and much of it centers on the micro-components of fruits and vegetables. These not only seem to prevent disease, but also are key to our overall health and our ability to stay healthy long into old age.

These micronutrients are numerous, and we are still discovering more every year. Their primary sources are fruits and vegetables, which is why we sometimes call them phytochemicals ("phyto" means plant in Latin). They are divided into two broad categories: vitamins and minerals. Vitamins and minerals work together to boost our immune systems, fight inflammation, regulate our hormones, encourage the growth of beneficial bacteria in our guts, prevent infection, and slow the development of most of the life-threatening diseases that plague us—heart disease, cancer, arthritis, and immune deficiencies.

Although vitamins and minerals perform similar functions, and often work together, they are different from one another. Vitamins can be altered by exposure to heat, air, or acids. Minerals maintain their chemical structure permanently. That means that minerals in the soil stay intact as they find their way into plants and then into your body when you eat those plants. But the integrity of vitamins is more vulnerable. Cooking, storage, or just exposure to air can deteriorate them. Minerals are more stable than vitamins, but the mineral content of soil determines the mineral density of your food. Soil that is depleted in minerals does not produce mineral-rich vegetables. That's a big reason that eating raw and fresh organically grown fruit and vegetables is the best way to ensure you are getting all of the nutrition they have to give.

Vitamins

Vitamins are essential for hundreds of bodily processes, and though we need only trace amounts to sustain life, a deficiency of even one vitamin can endanger the whole body.

There are 13 recognized vitamins, categorized as water soluble or fat soluble. Fat soluble vitamins (A, D, E, and K) are absorbed into the body with the help of fat in the diet or bile from the liver. The vitamins are stored in body fat and so they are generally available as needed even if they are not consumed daily. On the other hand, because they are stored in the body, they can accumulate to toxic levels if too many are consumed over time, which is why it is always preferable to get your vitamins from whole foods, rather than supplements.

Water-soluble vitamins (B complex and C) do not need fat to be absorbed and are generally not stored in body tissue. What the body doesn't need it excretes through urine and perspiration, so there

VITAMINS			
VITAMIN	**SOLUBLE**	**FOOD SOURCES (EXAMPLES)**	**VITAL FUNCTIONS**
A (Carotenoids)	Fat	Apricots, carrots, sweet potato, spinach, kale, broccoli	Eye health, bone growth, skin health, resistance to respiratory infection
B1 (Thiamine)	Water	Nuts, seeds, green peas, acorn squash, asparagus	Maintenance of muscle and nerve tissue, digestion of carbohydrates
B2 (Riboflavin)	Water	Almonds, legumes, dark greens, whole grains	Metabolism of all nutrients, mucous membrane maintenance (skin health), cell respiration
B3 (Niacin, Niacinamide)	Water	Avocado, passion fruit, golden tomato, mushrooms, legumes, nuts, whole grains, tuna, liver, meat, poultry, fish	Health of nervous system and digestion, skin health
B5 (Pantothenic acid)	Water	Widespread in all food, especially nuts, greens, whole grains	Cell building, adrenal hormones, wound healing, metabolism
B6 (Pyridoxine, Pyridoxamine)	Water	Avocado, cantaloupe, bananas, nuts, green vegetables	Sodium-potassium balance, formation of red blood cells, metabolism, health of nervous system
B7 (Biotin)	Water	Dark leafy greens, tomatoes, carrots, nuts, berries	Cell growth, fatty acid production, cell respiration, metabolism
B9 (Folate, Folacin)	Water	Dark leafy greens, broccoli, carrots, asparagus, papaya, oranges, grapefruit, strawberries	Formation of red blood cells, maintenance of nervous system, promotion of mental health, cell reproduction
B12 (Cobalamin)	Water	Reliably found in animal products only, so vegans need supplements	Formation of red blood cells, maintenance of nervous system, energy
C (Ascorbic acid)	Water	Fresh fruit and vegetables, especially citrus, leafy greens, tomatoes, strawberries, melon, bell peppers, cabbage, broccoli, potatoes	Production of collagen and red blood cells; maintenance of blood vessel strength; building bones, teeth, and gums; absorption of iron; healing

VITAMINS			
VITAMIN	SOLUBLE	FOOD SOURCES (EXAMPLES)	VITAL FUNCTIONS
D (Ergocalciferol)	Fat	Sunlight	Formation and maintenance of bones and teeth, absorption of calcium, maintenance of nervous system, blood clotting
E (Tocopherols)	Fat	Almonds, pumpkin seeds, sunflower seeds, Swiss chard, mustard greens, spinach, kale, pine nuts, avocado, broccoli, parsley	Supplying oxygen to cells, formation of red blood cells, maintenance of muscle tissue, antioxidant, healing, softens scar tissue
K (Phylloquinone)	Fat	Dark leafy greens, seaweed, cabbage, broccoli, legumes	Promotion of proper blood clotting, liver function

is no danger of toxicity, but we do need to consume these vitamins every day. Water-soluble vitamins are more prone to damage during cooking and food processing, so raw foods tend to be better sources of water-soluble vitamins than the same ingredients cooked.

Vitamins are so diverse and perform so many functions in the body that it is impossible to say simply how they work. In fact, the exact mechanism by which many vitamins perform their functions is still not well understood. With that caveat, the table on these pages should yield some light on the workings of specific vitamins.

Minerals

Like most vitamins, minerals are essential micronutrients that can't be manufactured by our bodies. We get them only from plant foods or (if you eat meat products) from animals that have eaten plant foods. We need dietary minerals for everything from building bone and regulating metabolism to sending nerve impulses throughout the body.

More than sixteen dietary minerals are important for human health. About six of these are considered major minerals, or macrominerals, because we need them in relatively large amounts of more than 200 mg per day (according to USDA recommendations). About ten others are called trace minerals, or microminerals, because we need less than 200 mg per day. The chart on pages 264 to 265 lists the sixteen important minerals, along with some of the foods highest in the mineral and the mineral's primary functions in human health.

Antioxidants

It seems that just being alive causes a certain amount of wear and tear on our bodies. Breathing in oxygen is essential for the workings of every cell we have. Unfortunately, it turns out that energy generation and other essential bodily processes involving oxygen produce unstable chemical byproducts

MINERALS		
MINERAL	FOOD SOURCES (EXAMPLES)	VITAL FUNCTIONS
MACROMINERALS (RDA >200 MG DAILY)		
Calcium	Almonds, broccoli, collards, dried figs, flax, kale, okra, spinach, turnips, watercress	Strength of bones and teeth, regulation of nerve impulses and muscle contraction, blood clotting
Chloride	Celery, lettuce, mushrooms, parsley, seaweed, tomatoes	Regulation of body fluids along with sodium and potassium, production of hydrochloric acid in stomach for digestion
Magnesium	Apricots, chard, kale, nuts, okra, seeds, spinach	Building bone, helping enzymes produce energy during metabolism, assisting in muscle contraction
Phosphorus	Broccoli, corn, garlic, nuts, peanuts, pumpkin seeds, sunflower seeds	Strength of bones and teeth, using energy during metabolism, formation of DNA
Potassium	Acorn squash, apricots, bananas, beets and beet greens, cantaloupe, chard, citrus, spinach, tomatoes	Regulation of electrolyte and fluid balance, sodium excretion, protein metabolism
Sodium	Celery, lettuce, mushrooms, parsley, seaweed, tomatoes	Regulation of electrolyte and fluid balance, regulation of nerve impulses
MICROMINERALS (RDA <200 MG DAILY)		
Chromium	Broccoli, green beans, nuts, tomatoes, romaine	Regulation of insulin, fat metabolism, maintenance of DNA structure
Copper	Nuts, peanuts, sesame seeds	Component of enzymes that help release food energy, iron absorption
Fluoride	Avocado, lettuce, radishes, seaweed, strawberries	Resisting tooth decay
Iodine	Seaweed	Helping thyroid produce hormones that regulate metabolism
Iron	Dried apricots, green leafy vegetables, nuts, prunes, seaweed, seeds, watermelon	Part of oxygen-carrying hemoglobin in blood, helping enzymes release food energy
Manganese	Avocado, green leafy vegetables, nuts, pineapple, strawberries	Helping release food energy, antioxidant function
Molybdenum	Green leafy vegetables, legumes, strawberries	Helping enzymes use iron and excrete uric acid

MINERAL	FOOD SOURCES (EXAMPLES)	VITAL FUNCTIONS
Selenium	Brazil nuts, sunflower seeds	Antioxidant function
Sulfur	Broccoli, cabbage, garlic, kale, onion	A component of proteins like cysteine, helps enzymes function properly
Zinc	Collards, nuts, peanuts, seeds, spinach	Immune function, wound healing, taste perception, a component of insulin

ANTIOXIDANTS			
ANTIOXIDANT	COLOR	FOOD SOURCES (EXAMPLES)	BENEFITS
Anthocyanins	Blue, purple	Beets, berries, grapes	Slows the development of heart disease
Beta-carotene	Orange	Cantaloupe, carrots, dark leafy greens, ripe bell pepper, sweet potato	Anti-cancer
Chlorophyll	Green	Any green vegetable, the darker the better	Reduces DNA damage
Lutein	Yellow, orange, red	Kale, other greens	Overall eye health
Lycopene	Red	Guava, papaya, tomato, watermelon	Reduces DNA damage
Zeaxanthin	Yellow	Citrus, corn	Slows macular degeneration

called free radicals that can damage the DNA in our cells, causing cells to multiply wildly and grow into a tumor. Oxidative damage can irritate the lining of our arteries and lead to a heart attack or stroke. Ultraviolet rays from the sun create free radicals that can damage our eyes and our skin.

Fresh raw fruits and vegetables are filled with antioxidant molecules that react with free radicals before they have a chance to do any damage. Mostly these antioxidants are pigments, like orange beta-carotene, yellow lutein, and red lycopene. Green chlorophyll is an antioxidant, and the blue-purple anthocyanins have been used to improve vision and treat circulatory disorders. Several antioxidant pigments can be damaged through heating, so eating raw food is the only way to ensure that you are getting the full range of detoxifying effects that fruits and vegetables have to offer.

FIBER

Fiber is the part of plant foods that our digestive enzymes can't break down. There is no fiber in meat or animal-based foods. There are two types of fiber—soluble and insoluble. Insoluble fiber (mostly cellulose and lignin), found mostly in root and stem vegetables, doesn't dissolve in our digestive fluids, and provides bulk to our intestinal contents, causing them to flow more efficiently through our intestines. It is thought that rapid excretion may help to limit exposure to DNA-damaging chemicals and other toxins in our food, and this type of fiber may bond onto these toxins and keep them from being absorbed into our bloodstreams. Soluble fiber (hemicellulose and pectin), found mostly in fruit but also in a few creamier vegetables like cauliflower, can dissolve in the water in our intestines and thereby make our intestinal contents thicker and slower moving. By slowing the movement of food through our intestines, soluble fiber allows more time for absorption of nutrients. Soluble fiber has been shown to reduce blood cholesterol and slow the rise of blood sugar after eating—an explanation for why a large meal of fruit does not spike your blood sugar (providing you keep your fat intake low).

WATER

Your body is about 60 percent water, making up the bulk of your bodily fluids, which makes everything from your digestion to the functioning of individual cells work efficiently. Cooking depletes the amount of water in fresh ingredients, so most diets tell you to drink a lot of water to ensure that you get enough. But in a raw food diet your need for water by the glass is greatly reduced. Fresh fruits and vegetables are loaded with water and, because the water is bound up in the plant fibers, it is released and absorbed into your body gradually and evenly, helping you to maintain the fluid balance in your body without overtaxing your kidneys. I often drink a glass of water before and after strenuous exercise and always in the morning upon waking to start everything flowing, but during the day, for the most part, my diet of raw fruits and vegetables keeps me well hydrated.

ACID-ALKALINE BALANCE

The health of most of our cells requires a neutral to slightly alkaline pH (short for "potential of hydrogen," a measure of acidity or alkalinity). The pH scale ranges from 0 (highly acidic) to 14 (highly alkaline), with 7.0 being neutral (neither acid or alkaline). Your blood pH should be about 7.4, and saliva pH 7. People assume that tangy/acidic fruits, like citrus or pineapple, acidify the body, making it prone to long-term health problems, such as inflammation, acid reflux, arthritis, gout, type 2 diabetes, digestive disorders, malignancies, and chronic fatigue. But the pH of your bodily fluids is influenced by the mineral content of the food you eat, not by the acidity or alkalinity of the food itself. The minerals largely present in fruit and vegetables, such as calcium, potassium, and magnesium, are alkaline forming, so when they are absorbed into the bloodstream they have a net alkalizing effect on your intracellular fluids. In contrast, the minerals present in meats and fried foods, like sulfur, iodine, and phosphorus, are acid forming.

INDEX OF TABLES AND TIPS